DATE			

Critical Essays on
Charles Dickens's
Bleak House

Critical Essays on Charles Dickens's *Bleak House*

Elliot L. Gilbert

G.K. Hall & Co. • Boston

Copyright 1989 by Elliot L. Gilbert
All rights reserved.

825 55 9 42

Library of Congress Cataloging in Publication Data

Critical essays on Charles Dickens's Bleak House / [selected by]
  Elliot L. Gilbert.
      p.   cm.—(Critical essays on British literature)
    Includes index.
    Contents: Introduction / Elliot L. Gilbert—Bleak House / H.M.
  Daleski—Will and society in Bleak House / Joseph I. Fradin—
  "Through a glass darkly" : Esther Summerson and Bleak House /
  Lawrence Frank—The high tower of his mind : psychoanalysis and
  the reader of Bleak House / Albert D. Hutter—The battle of the
  biblical books in Esther's narrative / Janet L. Larson—Bleak
  House, I : suspended animation / Robert Newsom—The ghostly signs
  of Bleak House / Michael Ragussis—Bleak House : iconography of
  darkness / Michael Steig.
    ISBN 0-8161-8771-1 (alk. paper)
    1. Dickens, Charles, 1812–1870. Bleak House.   I. Gilbert, Elliot
  L.   II. Series.
  PR4556.C75   1989
  823'.8—dc20   89-32875
                                                               CIP

The publication is printed on permanent/durable acid-free paper
MANUFACTURED IN THE UNITED STATES OF AMERICA

CRITICAL ESSAYS ON BRITISH LITERATURE

The Critical Essays on British Literature series provides a variety of approaches to both the classical writers of Britain and Ireland and the best contemporary authors. The formats of the volumes in the series vary with the thematic designs of individual editors, and with the amount and nature of existing reviews, criticism, and scholarship. In general, the series represents the best in published criticism, augmented, where appropriate, by original essays by recognized authorities. It is hoped that each volume will be unique in developing a new overall perspective on its particular subject.

Elliot Gilbert's selection of essays, none previously reprinted, covers a wide variety of scholarly approaches to *Bleak House*. Besides being a first-rate contribution, each was chosen as being representative of a school of Dickens criticism, from studies of narrative perspectives, through psychoanalytic, social, and historical aspects, to linguistic analysis. For instance, one study deals with the unique contributions of the illustrations accompanying the texts of Dickens's work, while another deals with sources and textual explication from the standpoint of the knowledge that Dickens's contemporaries brought to their reading of the text. Most treat the novel in ways unique to modern scholarship, such as interpreting the effect that the original serial publication had on the eventual book. Gilbert's own introduction synthesizes and puts into wider perspective the critical approaches these essays illustrate.

ZACK BOWEN, GENERAL EDITOR

University of Miami

For Sandra

CONTENTS

INTRODUCTION

In the Modern Language Association's *Victorian Fiction: A Second Guide to Research,* published in 1978, Philip Collins says of *Bleak House* that it has "lately been the most written about of [Dickens's] novels."[1] Collins does not go on to speculate about the reason for the popularity of this story with literary critics, but a number of explanations suggest themselves. One involves the absolute quality of the book, a book that Geoffrey Tillotson, for example, has designated "the finest literary work the nineteenth century produced in England"[2] and that Harold Bloom reports is "generally regarded now as Charles Dickens's greatest work."[3] Another explanation for the critical interest in *Bleak House* has to do with the novel's representative role in the body of its author's work. Readers of Dickens have long been divided into two groups, those, on the one hand, who prefer the unself-conscious freshness and spontaneity of the early books and those, on the other, who are more drawn to the deliberate structuring and complex thematic development of the later ones. *Bleak House* could be said to mark just the moment in Dickens's artistic career when the early and late manners achieve a perfect balance. Characters like Skimpole, Chadband, Guppy, and the Smallweeds appear to be products of the same improvisational energy that went into the creation of a Jingle or a Fagin or a Pecksniff; at the same time, the controlling symbols of the prison in *Little Dorrit* or the dust heap in *Our Mutual Friend* seem already to have been anticipated, in *Bleak House,* by the elaborate emblematic ramifications of fog and mud and oil. *Bleak House* is, then, the novel for which Dickensians of both camps are most likely to share admiration, and it is such a consensus that may help to account, among other things, for the frequency with which the book is assigned in college courses. And that fact, in turn, no doubt goes far toward explaining the amount of critical attention the work has received.

Already by 1978, the date of Collins's review article, there had been several anthologies of critical essays devoted exclusively to *Bleak House.* Jacob Korg's collection for the Twentieth-Century Views series, published in 1968, brought together a variety of articles and notes among which are J. Hillis Miller's often-cited chapter from *Charles Dickens: The World of His*

1

Novels and a passage from Robert E. Garis's still instructive and controversial *The Dickens Theatre*. Just a year later, in 1969, A. E. Dyson produced a second selection of pieces about the novel, his *Dickens's "Bleak House": A Casebook*, included in which are a number of contemporary reviews, several background pieces, and current essays on such central critical issues in the work as the story's two voices (W. J. Harvey's "*Bleak House*: The Double Narrative") and the Esther Summerson problem (Dyson's own "*Bleak House*: Esther Better Not Born?").

Then, in 1977, the Norton Critical Edition of *Bleak House*, edited by George Ford and Sylvère Monod, offered still a third group of commentaries on the novel, including another selection of contemporary reviews, a portion of the classic study of Dickens by G. K. Chesterton, and several abridgments of modern essays. And most recently, Chelsea House has issued its own selection of *Bleak House* articles, this one edited by Harold Bloom and containing, among its seven reprinted pieces, another J. Hillis Miller contribution, his admirable 1971 introduction to the Penguin edition of the book, as well as a brilliant study of Dickens's "epitaphic chapter titles" by Garrett Stewart, and a useful article by Virginia Blain written from a feminist perspective.

Given the amount of anthologizing of *Bleak House* essays over the last twenty years, it might be assumed that few first-rate articles remain uncollected. But in fact previous compilations have only begun to tap the resources of a field in which even now there are many more critical and scholarly works meriting a second appearance than could be accommodated in several volumes of this size. The availability of so much excellent material has helped determine the principles of selection followed here. First, to provide the greatest service for students of *Bleak House* who already know the earlier collections, it has been decided to reserve these pages for works not previously reprinted. (Only a fragment of the Daleski essay appears in the Norton Critical Edition.) Then, the quantity and range of material to choose from has made it possible to offer a wide variety of approaches to the novel, including, with Michael Steig's essay on the Phiz illustrations, subject matter not represented before in a *Bleak House* anthology, and a number of fresh developments along more traditional lines of inquiry.

The extent and the quality of the material available about the novel, and the difficulty of choosing among competing works, has also made the advice of colleagues especially valuable in this project. With *Bleak House* much on their minds as the focus of the 1988 Santa Cruz Dickens conference, Murray Baumgarten, Edwin Eigner, John O. Jordan, Gerhard Joseph, and Fred Kaplan have been particularly helpful with their comments and recommendations. In addition, Barbara Gottfried provided a useful list of suggestions and Robert Patten proposed that attention be paid to studies of the illustrations. A few works that might have appeared here are, for a number of reasons, unavailable for reprinting, and inevitably there will be readers who miss favorite essays or preferred critical approaches. Certainly, material is even now available for the compilation of still more *Bleak House* anthologies, but for the moment it remains for us to consider the contents of this one.

Whether the tendency in recent years to study Dickens's novels in the classroom in their original weekly or monthly installments has led to a growing critical interest in that form of publication, or whether influence in this matter has in fact run the other way, literary commentators have now started to pay more attention to Dickens as a writer of serial fiction. Inevitably, modern readers experience Dickens's novels as completed books requiring to be judged as whole works, and this is how these novels are usually discussed in the critical literature. Dickens knew, of course, that his works would eventually be read this way, and he conscientiously revised the serial versions of his stories before publishing them in book form. But the revisions could never be thorough enough to alter the fact that the works had first been written and issued in parts, each part conceived and structured to— among other things—assure an audience for the next. And recently, both teachers and scholars have been trying to re-create the experience of that first audience—and perhaps to gain fresh insight into the stories—by reading the books with attention to the original installment breaks. Aiding in this experiment have been such scholarly efforts as Harvey Sucksmith's publication, in 1965, of the *Bleak House* number plans and Archibald Coolidge's 1967 full-length study *Charles Dickens as Serial Novelist*.

Associated with this interest in the parts publication of Dickens's novels, an interest deriving, perhaps, from the more general modern tendency to deal with works of literature as collections of structural and linguistic elements, is what Robert Newsom speaks of as the need to examine *Bleak House* in particular for the way in which it seems "to have its own methods as its subject." The Newsom essay reprinted here, a chapter from the 1977 study *Dickens on the Romantic Side of Familiar Things*, includes among these methods the serial publication of the story, for the piece announces its intention to examine how the whole of the book's first monthly part works, concentrating on "what rules," as Newsom puts it, "the opening number has set up for the novel's narrative." But it also discusses several other formal elements in the story, all of which focus on "the problematic relationship between fiction and reality." Specifically, Newsom writes about such issues as the different levels of reality occupied by the two narrators, the simultaneously real and unreal world created by the book's famous opening passage; in general, about the way in which reality is necessarily "its own satire" in a story that is, to use the well-known Hillis Miller phrase about *Bleak House*, "a document about the interpretation of documents."[4]

Another aspect of the parts publication of *Bleak House* that has recently attracted extended critical attention is the distinguished series of drawings done by Hablôt Knight Browne ["Phiz"] for the original monthly numbers.

Commentaries on the novel have not often treated these drawings as if they had more than a purely decorative function in the book. Instead, readers have been encouraged, especially by modern editions of the work that either dispense with the pictures entirely or substitute newly commissioned ones (liberties of a sort no one would be likely to take with the text), to see the contemporary illustrations as extraneous or even redundant.

The fact is, however, that no writer's career or work during the nineteenth century, not even Thackeray's, was more closely associated with the art of illustration than was Dickens's. *Pickwick*, of course, is the book it is only because the suicide of artist Robert Seymour, the project's prime mover, transferred the principal role in the enterprise to the young author. And from the moment that Hablôt Browne was hired to replace Seymour (after the rejection of Thackeray as a substitute and with the unavailability of Cruikshank), it became clear that Dickens meant to exercise considerable control over the content and even the design of the drawings. At twenty-one, Browne was, as Norman and Jeanne MacKenzie have put it, "a pliable colleague . . . willing to take his brief from the author,"[5] and Dickens early recognized that in plotting the illustrations for his books as carefully as his text, he was developing a significant new form of expression.

By the time of *Bleak House*, some seventeen years after *Pickwick*, Browne had grown considerably in stature and independence as an artist. Still, there is evidence in the drawings for the latter novel that Dickens continued to supply his illustrator with themes and settings and poses to be worked up into pictures. And it is this phenomenon that Michael Steig examines in his 1978 study *Dickens and Phiz*, a selection from which is reprinted here. (Earlier, Thomas W. Hill had discussed Phiz's illustrations for *Bleak House* in an article in the June 1944 *Dickensian;* also in the *Dickensian* [1973], J. R. Tye, considers the novel's illustrations and cover drawing as a guide to the visual imagery in the text; and more recently, in the December 1982 *Dickens Studies Newsletter*, Mary Rosner has combined an interpretation of the wrapper design with a reading of the book's first chapter.)

The premise of Steig's book is that Dickens's open participation in the illustrating of his novel justifies as close and rigorous a reading of the drawings as of the text. (In this connection, one might note how much speculation about the unfinished *Mystery of Edwin Drood*, for example, depends on inferences drawn from the Luke Fildes pictures.) But Steig carries this idea to its dramatic—and entirely logical—conclusion and argues that in some cases the drawings for Dickens's novels do not limit themselves to illustrating scenes and characters in the story. At times, Steig demonstrates, the pictures go as far as to introduce elements that do not appear in the story at all, emphasizing thematic parallels, like the one between Turveydrop and Chadband, that Dickens never puts into words, or communicating, through some emblematic gesture, an idea that has no textual equivalent. In Steig's own words, it is a mistake to assume that the only proper function of illustrations like Browne's is to mirror the import of the text. . . . An illustration may present a point of view and bring out aspects which are not overtly expressed in the text.

A note about the graphics accompanying this essay: even in the original book publication of the chapter, Steig was unable to reprint all the pictures he discusses. We have been still more limited here by considerations of space but have provided a representative sample of those drawings that are analyzed at greatest length.

From its title, Janet Larson's essay seems to belong to a venerable tradition of *Bleak House* commentary, the identification of literary and historical sources. Any book more than a century old is bound to contain a great many references to figures, events, and texts that will have been well known to contemporary audiences but that are wholly obscure to today's readers— sometimes so obscure as to be unidentifiable as references. This is particularly true of the many echoes of biblical language in the story. When, for example, the novel's anonymous narrator, apostrophizing Jo, declares that "from the sole of thy foot to the crown of thy head, there is nothing interesting about thee," Dickens could count on a great many of his first readers recognizing in this passage a sardonic parody of the denunciation in Isaiah, 1:6: "From the sole of the foot even unto the head there is no soundness in it."

Most present-day readers, on the other hand, will not only fail to recognize the phrase as coming from Isaiah, they will very likely be unaware that there is any biblical allusion at all to recognize. Under such circumstances, editorial assistance is required just to keep these works fully intelligible, and the identification of literary and historical sources has long been one of the important duties of Dickens scholarship. Over the years, for example, many commentators have made efforts to find the originals of important characters in *Bleak House* (Hortense, Boythorn, Turveydrop, Skimpole), have pointed to a variety of literary influences on the book (Carlyle, the Brothers Grimm, Bunyan, Bulwer-Lytton, Sydney Smith, and Henry Mayhew), have annotated the novel's religious and scientific imagery, discussed London places in the work, explained procedures of the Court of Chancery, considered the topicality of incidents in the story.

The Janet Larson essay reprinted here is distinctly in this tradition of source identification, with an emphasis on the annotation of biblical allusions. In particular, Larson's work concentrates on the books of Esther and Job as crucial analogues for Dickens's story, though the article's third section discovers a considerably wider range of biblical echoes. Still, the real strength of this piece lies in the fact that its author moves beyond simple *quellenjägerei*, employing the identified references to support a thesis about what she sees as one of the major structural elements in the novel. Specifically, Larson argues that the personality and behavior of Esther Summerson can be understood as having been shaped by a conflict between the values embodied in the biblical stories of Esther and Job, a conflict signaled also by the book's double narrative, which itself reflects nineteenth-century religious anxieties and discords.

In the critic's own words, "because [Esther] so narrowly misses embracing the limited views represented in both biblical subtexts—the easy affirmation and the debilitating despair that are both on trial in *Bleak House*"—her life journey becomes an "uncertain Victorian pilgrimage," and she herself remains, through most of the book, "captive to the unresolved battles of her texts." In the end, however, Larson argues, it is the very instability of the "alternating . . . biblical texts involved in Esther's provisional progress [that] grounds her suffering . . . authenticating her charity and making her more humanly convincing." The essay is itself a convincing one, moving from the traditional identification of sources, through considerations of gender, social status, and spirituality, to a sophisticated modern analysis of several of the novel's principal themes.

In concentrating on the character of Esther Summerson, the Larson essay participates in an even more venerable tradition of *Bleak House* commentary, discussion and analysis of the novel's problematic second narrator. The Lawrence Frank article offered here, and referred to by Larson in her own study, is another in the long line of such essays, works comprising perhaps the most voluminous single body of material on the novel. "The character much the most written about," Philip Collins declares in his MLA research guide essay, "is Esther Summerson,"[6] and he then goes on to list several dozen chapters and articles about the figure, ranging from what he designates "old-fashioned" negative commentaries by Angus Wilson, Sylvère Monod, and himself to favorable analytic studies with such titles as "Esther Summerson: A Plea for Justice," "In Defense of Esther Summerson," and "Esther Summerson Rehabilitated."

The long history of critical response to Esther has indeed been one of ongoing rehabilitation. Early critics of the book, who tended to focus on such matters as the mechanics of plot and the realism of characters, found much to trouble them about Esther, especially the distortions that seemed to them to result from her being called upon to solve some of the technical problems Dickens faced in telling his story. As a mystery novel, *Bleak House* requires both an omniscient voice to supply readers with a variety of facts that no single first-person narrator could possess and a limited first-person storyteller to legitimize Dickens's withholding of certain information from the reader that an omniscient narrator would have no excuse to conceal. In this context, Esther can be seen as a sort of lay figure awkwardly manipulated for plot purposes by the author, forced, for example, to record, as part of her narrative duties, all the flattering remarks people make about her and then to apologize for these reports as a way of preserving her character's humility and self-effacement.

More recent criticism, with its focus on the impossibility of discovering any absolute truth through language, with its interest in the way in which literature raises, as J. Hillis Miller has written of *Bleak House* itself, "questions about its own status as a text,"[7] finds in Esther a figure who brilliantly embodies some of the most complex moral, psychological, and metaphysical issues in the book. For with her dual functions as a narrator promoting the author's reality and an individual seeking her own truth, she becomes the very type of the alienated modern sensibility in quest of an always elusive identity.

Lawrence Frank's essay is principally concerned with describing and commenting on that quest. For Frank, it is, significantly, Jo, the illiterate crossing sweeper who, "knowing nothing," best dramatizes the mystery of identity through his inability to distinguish between Esther and the strangely equivalent figures of Lady Dedlock and Hortense. Frank then goes on to examine the many efforts made by Esther and other characters in the story, efforts involving much mirror gazing, to discover some unequivocal truth about themselves and their world. But, as the critic argues, such truth is, by the very nature of Dicken's *Bleak House* vision, undiscoverable. "We are left," the essay concludes, "with Esther, not seeing face to face, but looking through a glass darkly, seeking the forever elusive self floating within the mirror's depths beyond the reflection on its surface. The veil between the self and self-knowledge is never fully raised."

Perhaps the most venerable critical approach of all to *Bleak House* is to discuss the book as a work of social commentary. Certainly, many of the earliest reviews of the story saw it as offering an analysis of a number of contemporary social problems: the state of the courts, the condition of the poor, the failure of education, the dangers of urban slums. Indeed, some of the first critics of the book took Dickens to task for not being contemporary enough in his attack on social evils, accusing him, for example, of having delayed his satire on the Court of Chancery until many of those evils had already been exposed and corrected. "Had the present work appeared twenty years ago," an anonymous reviewer commented in 1853, "it would have been a revelation. . . . As it is, it only exhibits what has pretty well been made known before through the earnest prose of plainer men."[8] And in the same year an even more acerbic notice, appearing in the *Spectator*, declared that Jarndyce and Jarndyce had been "lugged into [the novel] by the head and shoulders . . . solely to give Mr. Dickens the opportunity of indulging in stale and commonplace satire upon the length and expense of Chancery proceedings."[9]

This tendency to judge the quality of *Bleak House* by the success with which it deals with social problems, or to read the book as in the main a study of the institutions of mid-century British culture, was for some time a characteristic approach of critics to the novel, a number of essays along these lines being published under such titles as "The Crossing Sweeper in *Bleak*

House," "Social Wrongs in *Bleak House* and Today," and "*Bleak House:* The Anatomy of Society." This last idea of the novel as an "anatomy of society," a phrase first popularized by Edmund Wilson in *The Wound and the Bow*, complicates the issue of Dickens's principal concern in *Bleak House*. It suggests that there is an important distinction—discussed by, among others, Jeremy Hawthorn in his *Bleak House* volume for the Critics Debate series— to be made between seeing the author as a reformer, interested in righting specific wrongs with his books, and considering him instead as a student of the structure and character of a whole civilization.

Recent critics have further complicated the matter by seeking to associate the social elements in *Bleak House* with more private spiritual and metaphysical concerns, and Joseph I. Fradin's article "Will and Society in *Bleak House*" is one of the strongest and most persuasive of these attempts. Fradin concedes, as any reader of the novel must, how much the book is preoccupied with social issues, how much, as he puts it, "Dickens's imagination was stimulated by social fact." But he then goes on to argue that while the novel may appear to call for social action in response to the ills it exposes, "it everywhere denies the possibility that any action arising from corporate society will better man's condition." For faith in institutions and "the social will" as a source of change in society, Fradin sees *Bleak House* substituting individual acts of responsibility and love, an insight that may be, he grants, overly familiar (note, for example, G. Armour Craig's 1956 essay "The Unpoetic Compromise") but that is all the more poignant for having, at this late date, to be repeated by both the novel and its commentators.

By suggesting that any resolution of the social issues raised in *Bleak House* must, in Dickens's view, occur at the personal level, Fradin proposes a relocating of the drama of the novel inward; and other commentators, both before Fradin and since, have focused on the several interiorities of the work—moral, metaphysical, and especially psychological. For some readers of Dickens, the psychological—and particularly the psychoanalytic—approach seems inappropriate. In their view, Dickens is the creator of brilliantly memorable but two-dimensional characters, characters lacking the complexity and depth to support a psychological critique, especially where such a critique is defined as the application of psychoanalytic methods to individual figures in a story. Mr. Tulkinghorn, for example, may be a powerful embodiment of the abstract concept of nemesis, these readers would argue, but he lacks the roundedness and motivation to make any examination of his inner life meaningful. (However, see Eugene F. Quirk's 1972 *JEGP* article, "Tulkinghorn's Buried Life.") What other critics have seen, however, is that the nemesis represented by Tulkinghorn is just one of many resonant themes in the general psychodrama of the novel, and that it is this total fictionalized dreamwork, with its ramifications for the author and the reader as well as for the characters, that is the truly promising subject for psychoanalytic investigation.

Among recent examples of such a psychoanalytic approach have been Gordon Hirsch's "The Mysteries in *Bleak House:* A Psychoanalytic Study," published in 1975 in *Dickens Studies Annual,* and the essay reprinted here, Albert D. Hutter's "The High Tower of His Mind: Psychoanalysis and the Reader of *Bleak House.*" The Hutter piece begins by defining the boundaries of contemporary psychoanalytic criticism, one of which, the author points out, is shared with reader-response criticism. The essay then goes on to offer the character of Inspector Bucket as a synthesizing figure who facilitates discussion of the psychologically charged structure of the novel, discussion in which the response of the reader sometimes is and sometimes is not seen to play a definitive role. Specifically, Hutter reminds us that Bucket is presented by Dickens as a protean character: artist, magician, even, in Hutter's phrase, "a very early psychoanalyst," a doctor "ready to cure the ills of society." The detective is also analogous to the novel's omniscient narrator, as, in the pursuit of his investigatory profession, he "mounts a high tower in his mind, and looks out far and wide."

Hutter makes as much as he does of Bucket because he sees the detective as being associated with two polarities that Dickens, too, frequently exploits: "the splitting of figures and objects leading toward mystification and their ultimate reunification through [language]," a splitting and reintegration that has "a universal psychological function transcending any single historical period or social context" and that in *Bleak House* helps to account for the thematic core of the story, the relationship between Esther and Lady Dedlock. The critic then goes on to argue, with Norman Holland, that readers also participate in these polarities, organizing and synthesizing reality out of initial disorder. In the end, however, he sees in the limitations of Bucket's providential authority, revealed during the final encounter with Mlle Hortense, a similar limitation on the reader's own power to shape the text. For, as Hutter puts it, to remain psychologically believable, a "plot cannot be solved in any final sense" and must at some level continue to exist independent of the experience of reading.

Disparate elements requiring integration—the close connection of apparently disconnected things—is also the subject of the H. M. Daleski *Bleak House* essay included here, a chapter from his 1970 book *Dickens and the Art of Analogy.* One of Dickens's major objectives in *Bleak House* is to show how people who think they are strangers to one another are in fact related at every possible level of community. The fog in the novel performs many symbolic functions but none more central to the story than as an emblem of anomie, a condition that obscures relationships and fosters the illusion that human beings can escape the responsibilities of living in the world together. But what the many extraordinary coincidences in the plot say, even to those readers who deplore them, is that there are no two people in the book so separated from one another by class or family or interests that they are not intimately and sometimes fatally connected.

The idea of connectedness being central to a book so full of seemingly irreconcilable elements has been the subject of a number of studies seeking to link the story's theme with its structure, including Leonard W. Deen's 1961 essay "Style and Unity in *Bleak House*," reprinted in the Korg anthology, and, with reservations about the organic wholeness of the novel, W. J. Harvey's "Chance and Design in *Bleak House*," published a year later in *Dickens and the Twentieth Century*. But none deals more fully and explicitly with the idea of inescapable community than does Daleski's. Indeed, Daleski argues that when we first read *Bleak House*, it is "the sense of connections being mysteriously made in a way we cannot comprehend" that is one of our most immediate experiences of the narrative.

Some critics see this experience as deriving from the book's double narrative, which would appear to posit a necessary connection between the exclusive worlds of Esther Summerson and Lady Dedlock. "It seems to me, however," Daleski counters, "that the immediate effect of the double narrative is precisely to deny the existence of a single fixed centre" and thus to augment "our sense of dissociation," But the two narratives soon begin to overlap and even converge, the critic continues, and at the point of ultimate convergence, the moment when the connection between Esther and Lady Dedlock is established, the novel is revealed to have been all along "a unified structure." This unity is achieved, Daleski goes on, by what he calls an analogical process, a process so fully expressed in the double narrative itself that that narrative is revealed to be not a meretricious technical device but a powerful symbolic structure in its own right. And that structure tells the reader, albeit with some lapses and imperfections, "a great deal more what the book is about than the much-praised symbol of the fog."

When Daleski says that the immediate effect of the double narrative in *Bleak House* is to promote our sense of dissociation, he is reminding us of what, in connection with the Lawrence Frank essay, we alluded to as "the impossibility of discovering any absolute truth through language." For where a story told by a single voice can at least give the *illusion* of presenting the one authentic truth about a person or an action, a story told by more than one voice, from more than one point of view, automatically raises questions about the vexed relationship between narrative and truth, awakens fundamental doubts about the possibility of finding any words that correspond to reality. In *The Dickens Theatre*, Robert Garis, for example, explores the self-reflexiveness of Dickens's use of words, suggesting that in *Bleak House* the immediate and ongoing impression "is of a voice manipulating language with pleasure and pride in its own skill." And in "The Ghostly Signs of *Bleak House*," reprinted in this collection, Michael Ragussis displays a similar skepticism about language, examining as thematic the dissociation of words and objects in the novel.

The problem begins, Ragussis contends, where the book begins, with the title. Many readers have been troubled by the seeming inappropriateness of the name "Bleak House" for the John Jarndyce establishment, one of the few locales of action in the book that is ever *not* bleak; troubled, too, by the entire irrelevance of such a name for the cottage to which Esther Summerson moves at the end of the story. And because of what the critic calls this "divergence between name and place, between signifier and signified," readers are forced not only to speculate about the significance of the name "Bleak House" for the book itself but also to wonder about the trustworthiness of language in general in the novel. For, as Ragussis insightfully suggests, the fog that pervades the story is at least in part a fog of language, and Jo, the illiterate crossing-sweeper, estranged from language, thus becomes a key figure in the novel's thematic development, growing "into a symbol of linguistic disorder that touches everyone." That disorder, the essay goes on to assert, like the other, physical disease spread by Jo, infects the whole world of the story with a plague of namelessness centering on the "friendless, nameless, and unknown" Esther, who, lacking a father—a father who himself lacked a name—also lacks a personal identity. And it is the absence of personal identity, one aspect of the pervasive anomie of the fog-shrouded city, Ragussis concludes, that is the most serious side of the dissociation of language and reality in the novel.

The value of this anthology lies first in the excellence of the individual essays assembled here and then in the variety of critical approaches to *Bleak House* that those essays represent. The introduction has suggested ways in which some of those approaches seem related to one another, and there are other interests that two or more of the pieces share. Several of the critics, for example, focus on the book's double narrative. Janet Larson invokes the device of the two storytellers to help justify her reading of the novel as a contention between the biblical books of Esther and Job, Joseph Fradin finds the dialectical implications of his terms "will" and "society" specifically sanctioned by the novel's form, while both the Daleski and the Hutter articles are very centrally concerned with the split narration. Still, it is the manner in which these pieces differ, and the miscellaneousness of the collection that has resulted from those differences, that is likely to make this compilation most useful to students of Dickens's novel.

For readers interested in approaches to the story not included here or who seek a completer list of writings on *Bleak House*, several bibliographical resources are available. Both Joseph Gold's *The Stature of Dickens: A Centenary Bibliography* (Toronto: University of Toronto Press, 1971) and John J. Fenstermaker's *Charles Dickens, 1940–1975: An Analytical Subject Index to Periodical Criticism of the Novels and Christmas Books* (Boston: G. K. Hall, 1979) offer, within their stated ranges, full listings of critical studies. For information about articles and books published after 1975, useful volumes are *Victorian Fiction: A Second Guide to Research* (New York: MLA, 1978), edited by George Ford; Jeremy Hawthorn's *Bleak House* (Atlantic Highlands, N.J.: Humanities Press International, 1987); and the comprehensive yearly records of scholarship in *Dickens Studies Annual*. There are also the Korg, Dyson, and Bloom anthologies mentioned earlier, each with its selection of significant essays and its own bibliography.

ELLIOT L. GILBERT

University of California, Davis

Notes

1. *Victorian Fiction: A Second Guide to Research* (New York: Modern Language Association, 1978), 96.

2. Geoffrey Tillotson, afterword to *Bleak House* (New York: New American Library, 1980), 882.

3. Harold Bloom, ed., *Charles Dickens's "Bleak House"* (New York: Chelsea House, 1987), vii.

4. Hillis Miller, "The Interpretive Dance in *Bleak House*," reprinted in Bloom, *Dickens's "Bleak House,"* 13.

5. Norman MacKenzie and Jeanne MacKenzie, *Dickens: A Life* (New York: Oxford University Press, 1979), 45.

6. *Victorian Fiction*, 97.

7. Miller, "The Interpretive Dance," 13.

8. See *Bleak House*, Norton Critical Edition (New York: W. W. Norton & Co., 1977), 925.

9. Ibid., 934.

Bleak House

H. M. Daleski*

I

> What connexion can there be, between the place in Lincolnshire, the house in town, the Mercury in powder, and the whereabout of Jo the outlaw with the broom, who had that distant ray of light upon him when he swept the churchyard-step? What connexion can there have been between many people in the innumerable histories of this world, who, from opposite sides of great gulfs, have, nevertheless, been very curiously brought together! (p. 219)

Curious connections are so prominent in *Bleak House* that we scarcely deserve so rude an authorial nudging. Indeed, as we read the novel for the first time, the sense of connections being mysteriously made in a way that we cannot quite comprehend is what is principally offered to our bewilderment. (When we reread the novel, our awareness of the mastery with which the connections are prepared for and established is a constant source of pleasure.) Dickens's narrative technique, moreover, is designed to maintain our initial sense of expectant bewilderment, our alertness for connection. It is not merely that we are slowly led to see that "the whole bileing of people," in Mr. Bucket's phrase, is "mixed up in the same business" (p. 806), such an effect being common to any novel with an elaborate plot; the double narrative throughout quietly posits a large connection, a connection between the apparently exclusive worlds of Esther Summerson and Lady Dedlock, and testifies (with pre-Jamesian innocence) to the virtues in this instance of a mixed point of view. The nature of these virtues, however, has been so variously described[1] that it is worth considering in some detail how the double narrative functions.

It has been asserted that the Chancery case of Jarndyce and Jarndyce is at the centre of the plot, "almost every character" in one way or another being "caught up in [its] convolutions."[2] It seems to me, however, that the immediate effect of the double narrative is precisely to deny the existence of

*From *Dickens and the Art of Analogy* (New York: Schocken Books, 1970), 156–89. Reprinted by permission of the author and Faber & Faber, Ltd.

a single fixed centre. Though the narrative of the omniscient author opens with the evocation of Chancery in fog, it has little to say thereafter of Jarndyce and Jarndyce. The omniscient narrative is primarily concerned with "the world of fashion" (p. 8) and the world of squalor; and with Lady Dedlock, who mediates between the two and may be thought of as at the centre of this narrative. The first-person narrative, with Esther Summerson (the narrator) at its centre, is on the whole concerned with the Bleak House world of middle-class respectability, and it is in this narrative that the working of Chancery is most closely scrutinized.[3] The juxtaposition of the two narratives has a curious effect. Taking our bearings, as it were, by two different and alternating centres, following two different time sequences (the historic present of the omniscient narrative and the retrospective past of the first-person narrative), moving in strongly differentiated social circles, we are impressed with a sense of the distinctiveness and separateness of the worlds that cohere round the narrative centres; and our attention, moreover, is equally held by what we apprehend as two main actions, that concerned with Lady Dedlock's secret, and that related to the case of Jarndyce and Jarndyce. The narrative method thus ensures that our sense of unrelated parts, of dissociation, is far stronger than it is in a work such as *Middlemarch*, for instance, where Dorothea Brooke and Lydgate may be thought of as constituting analogous centres of interest but where the homogeneity of the narrative is never in doubt. At the same time the omniscient and first-person narratives, like two adjacent, intersecting circles, overlap, characters such as Miss Flite or Mr. Guppy appearing in both; and our initial impression of the structure is of two "round worlds" rather than one, as in *Dombey and Son*.

Once the novel gets under way, however, we become aware of a further characteristic of the narrative movement. On the one hand, the movement, centring alternately in Esther and Lady Dedlock, is in both cases strongly centrifugal; that is to say, we move out in an apparently random manner from Esther and Bleak House and Jarndyce and Jarndyce to the lives of characters such as the Skimpoles, the Turveydrops and the Jellybies; and, similarly, we move out from Lady Dedlock and her mansions in town and country to the world of such as Krook and the Smallweeds and the Snagsbies. On the other hand, the first-person narrative moves with ever-increasing urgency to repeated meetings between Esther and Lady Dedlock—to their first meeting, with its undertones of obscure significance, at the keeper's lodge (pp. 254–57); to their second meeting and the revelation of their relationship (pp. 508–13); and, finally, to Esther's discovery of her mother's body towards the end of the novel (pp. 811–12). This movement on the part of Esther and Lady Dedlock is, as it were, reciprocally centripetal, each moving toward the centre of the other's world, though to speak in such terms at once suggests the inadequacy of our initial conception of the structure. The narratives, we realize, not only overlap but converge; and the point at which they converge, the point at which the connection between Esther and Lady Dedlock is established, is seen to constitute the centre of a unified structure, of a circle that after all encompasses the "many circles within circles" of the two narratives in a single "round world."

The point at which the two narratives become inextricably linked is also the thematic centre of the novel. Since it is a point at which apparently exclusive worlds are symbolically shown to be kith and kin, the theme suggested is the inescapable oneness of various social classes or groups, Dickens revealing how an obsession with money may infest a whole society. *Bleak House*, therefore, is thematically continuous with *Martin Chuzzlewit* and *Dombey and Son*, but in it the theme is treated with a new and admirable comprehensiveness. For the first time in Dickens individual attitudes are related to those of organized society; and, furthermore, the likely fate of such a society is related to that of individuals in it. These connections are effected, as we might expect, by means of the analogical method, the method being used with great skill to link not only the manifold preoccupations of a large number of characters but also, and most strikingly, the representative public activity of Jarndyce and Jarndyce and the private drama of Lady Dedlock. The two main actions, which the double narrative leads us to apprehend as separate, are also shown, in the end, to converge.

The form of the novel is thus neither meretricious nor productive of merely minor felicities[4] but the necessary and indivisible expression of its substance. Indeed, though Esther is made to tell the story of the Jarndyces and Chancery, *her* story is an integral part of the narrative that is concerned with Lady Dedlock; the omniscient narrative, in other words, is also *Esther's* story, and once again what appears to be separate is not.[5] It is all one, and the plot, with its central revelation of the relationship between Esther and Lady Dedlock, is an organic part of the whole conception. Dickens's use of the plot, moreover, to evoke an atmosphere of mystery, which—like the fog—hangs over the novel to the end, should not be dismissed as evidence of an inferior art or tolerated as the price to be paid for other rewards by the adult reader, but should rather be regarded as contributive to the novel's imperative drive towards exposure—towards the exposure not only of Lady Dedlock and of Tulkinghorn's murderer and of Chancery practice but of the rottenness of a whole society, of which the large number of individual deaths is ominously symbolic.[6] The plot itself, that is to say, is a symbolic structure, and it tells us a great deal more what the book is about than the much-praised symbol of the fog. This should not be taken to suggest that it is fully meaningful and convincing. Woven into the brilliant imaginative design, there is the palpably melodramatic and distractingly irrelevant figure of an Hortense.

II

Discerning in Dickens a tendency, like that of Jacobean dramatists, to "episodic intensification," a tendency, that is, "to exploit to the full possibilities of any particular scene, situation or action without too much regard for the relevance of such local intensities to the total work of art," W. J. Harvey denies that *Bleak House* has the "organic unity" of a work such as *Great Expectations*. In *Bleak House,* he maintains, an "extreme tension" is set up between "the centrifugal vigour" of the parts and "the centripetal demands of the whole"; and the impression finally made by the book is one of "immense and potential anarchic energy being brought—but only just—under control."[7] This estimate, I feel, fails to do justice either to the imaginative coherence of the novel or to its smoothness. If part of the action does have a strongly centrifugal movement in the sense I have suggested, it is not by way of episodic intensification. The action that takes place at the periphery of the two main narrative areas is closely and directly related to that which proceeds more obviously at the centre of things. So careful is the organization, that an analysis of the function of circumferential figures leads us straight to the complex of ideas that is at the thematic centre of the novel, and that constitutes the nuclear analogue of its structure of analogies.

Harold Skimpole, to consider Esther's narrative first, would appear to be sufficiently remote from the central activities of this section of the book to make him a representative figure in this respect. A typical Dickens "character," of scant importance in the plot, Skimpole might be thought to have no particular business in *Bleak House* and to exist barefacedly as testimony to his creator's exuberance (if not to his ambivalence toward Leight Hunt). Yet Skimpole's first words prove—as we discover—to be of decided relevance to the large concerns of the novel:

> . . . he must confess to two of the oldest infirmities in the world: one was, that he had no idea of time; the other, that he had no idea of money. In consequence of which he never kept an appointment, never could transact any business, and never knew the value of anything! Well! So he had got on in life, and here he was! He was very fond of reading the papers, very fond of making fancy sketches with a pencil, very fond of nature, very fond of art. All he asked of society was, to let him live. *That* wasn't much. His wants were few. Give him the papers, conversation, music, mutton, coffee, landscape, fruit in the season, a few sheets of Bristol-board, and a little claret, and he asked no more. He was a mere child in the world, but he didn't cry for the moon. He said to the world, "Go your several ways in peace! Wear red coats, blue coats, lawn sleeves, put pens behind your ears, wear aprons; go after glory, holiness, commerce, trade, any object you prefer; only let Harold Skimpole live!" (pp. 69–70)

Skimpole, we see, opposes to the pursuit of money in the world of commerce and trade the satisfaction of his cultivated tastes (which range, with fine impartiality, over realms of both flesh and spirit). Since the world that he bids go its way in peace is the world, among other things, of Chancery and Jarndyce and Jarndyce, his opting out of its commitments has a certain charm; and his dilettantism seems relatively harmless. But, as Esther and Richard very soon discover, his demand that the world at large "let Harold Skimpole live" turns out to be more sharply directed to that portion of it with cash to spare—and to mean: "Let Harold Skimpole live by letting him live on you." By presenting himself as "a mere child in the world," Skimpole further-more absolves himself from all responsibility for his actions, leaving himself the freedom not only to practise but (in a subsequent "discourse about Bees") to preach "the Drone philosophy" (p. 93). His pained withdrawal from the world, it is apparent, is simply a strategy for accosting it by other means, and his twin "infirmities" are no more otherworldly than the Court of Chancery, which proceeds with a comparable indifference to time and the conservation of other people's money.

Skimpole's oblivious self-centredness is perhaps most strikingly indi-cated when he secretly hands the sick Jo over to Bucket. His response, when his part in Jo's strange disappearance is revealed and Esther taxes him with it, is a marvel of perverted logic:

> "Observe the case, my dear Miss Summerson. Here is a boy received into the house and put to bed, in a state that I strongly object to. The boy being in bed, a man arrives—like the house that Jack built. . . . Here is the Skimpole who accepts the banknote produced by the man who de-mands the boy who is received into the house and put to bed in a state that I strongly object to. Those are the facts. Very well. Should the Skimpole have refused the note? *Why* should the Skimpole have refused the note? Skimpole protests to Bucket; 'what's this for? I don't understand it, it is of no use to me, take it away.' Bucket still entreats Skimpole to accept it. Are there reasons why Skimpole not being warped by prejudices, should ac-cept it? Yes. Skimpole perceives them. What are they? Skimpole reasons with himself, this is a tamed lynx, an active police-officer, an intelligent man . . . [who] has acquired, in the exercise of his art, a strong faith in money; he finds it very useful to him, and he makes it very useful to society. Shall I shake that faith in Bucket, because I want it myself; shall I deliberately blunt one of Bucket's weapons; shall I positively paralyse Bucket in his next detective operation? And again. If it is blameable in Skimpole to take the note, it is blameable in Bucket to offer the note—much more blameable in Bucket, because he is the knowing man. Now, Skimpole wishes to think well of Bucket; Skimpole deems it essential, in its little place, to the general cohesion of things, that he *should* think well of Bucket. The State expressly asks him to trust to Bucket. And he does. And that's all he does." (p. 830)

If, in his juggling of "the facts," Skimpole here clearly enjoys playing Falstaff after Gadshill, his self-exposure is complete. The logical extension of his parasitism, of his readiness to snap up all unconsidered trifles, is an insidious moral corruption, of which his acceptance of Bucket's bribe is only one instance, for he also evidences a like fondness for five-pound notes in reliev-ing Vholes of one in return for introducing him to Richard (p. 533). Un-warped by prejudice, Skimpole contrives both to have his cake and eat it, to admit the facts and yet to evade all moral responsibility for his behaviour by denying it to be questionable, and then by anyway fixing responsibility, with impeccable logic, on Bucket. His attitude, in this respect, is of a piece with his initial refusal to take responsibility for Jo, with his placid indifference to his fate. By confining the matter at issue to his acceptance of the money, moreover, he also manages to ignore other implications of his handing over of Jo, to ignore the fact that his action is a betrayal of his host's confidence, as Esther tells him (p. 829); and, still more important, that it represents, as we see, a betrayal of the sick boy himself. Skimpole's betrayal of Jo is a specific dramatization, an enactment in miniature, as it were, of the large breach of faith in respect of Jo that is perpetrated by the society he lives in; and that breach of faith, I shall argue, is likewise attributable to a moral corruption that is associated with parasitism and an evasion of responsibility. An apparently peripheral figure such as Skimpole, in other words, is of central importance, and the way in which Dickens handles him is some evidence of the "organic unity" of the novel.

A figure in the omniscient narrative who might be thought of as occupying an analogous position to that of Skimpole in Esther's narrative is Grandfather Smallweed, though it is true that, serving as Tulkinghorn's instrument, he has a more clearly defined function in the plot. If Skimpole is a typical Dickens "character," Smallweed is one of Dickens's typical grotesques, "a mere clothes-bag with a black skull-cap on the top of it," constantly requiring to undergo at the hands of his granddaughter "the two operations . . . of being shaken up like a great bottle, and poked and punched like a great bolster" in order to be restored to some animation, and constantly discharging missiles at "the venerable partner of his respected age whenever she makes an allusion to money" (p. 289). But Smallweed, we soon perceive, has not simply strayed out of *The Old Curiosity Shop*. His occupation, for one thing, has the authentic *Bleak House* stamp. A moneylender, living on other people with the persistence if not the suavity of Skimpole—George complains that he has paid him "half as much again as [the] principal, in interest and one thing and another" (p. 473)—Smallweed engages in a business which we may regard as the archetype of parasitic activity in the novel. Appropriately, making use of the kind of image that we will find recurring in other contexts, Phil Squod (when George makes his complaint) proclaims Smallweed to be "a leech in his dispositions." And the moneylender's eagerness (like that of a large number of characters in the book) to lay his hands on someone else's property is not confined to the call of professional duty, as he reveals in a memorable gesture when he asserts his right to inherit the worldly remains of the late Mr. Krook: "I have come down," repeats Grandfather Smallweed, hooking the air towards him with all his ten fingers at once, "to look after the property" (p. 465).

Smallweed, furthermore, is as prone to passing the buck as Skimpole, habitually seeking to evade responsibility for the squeezing of his clients by maintaining that he is merely the agent of a "friend in the city"—a prefigurement, this, of the more involved game that Fledgeby plays with Riah in *Our Mutual Friend*. Nor is integrity one of Smallweed's virtues. He is not at all averse (under Tulkinghorn's direction) to breaking faith with George, for instance, leaving the trooper with a sense of having been unaccountably betrayed: "There has always been an understanding that this bill was to be what they call Renewed," George tells Phil. "And it has been renewed, no end of times" (p. 473). The way in which Smallweed brings pressure to bear on George, moreover, is a prelude to his open blackmailing of Sir Leicester when he obtains possession of Lady Dedlock's letters to Hawdon (pp. 730–2).

The narrative excursions, then, are designed to evoke a varied but recurring image of a corrupt and parasitic society, of a society in which people do not so much live with one another as on one another. On the periphery of things, Skimpole and Smallweed are simply the most striking instances of a widespread tendency. There is also, for instance, Mr. Turveydrop, who having suffered his wife to work herself to death "to maintain him in those expenses which were indispensable to his position," not only allows his small, shabby, hard-working son to keep him but seems, in his fat resplendence, to be absorbing his son's substance; a distinguished man, he does "nothing whatever" but serve as "a model of Deportment" (pp. 191–2). There are, too, the Dedlock relations, foremost among them being that *memento mori*, Miss Volumnia, who lives "slenderly" in Bath "on an annual present from Sir Leicester," making "occasional resurrections in the country houses of her cousins" (p. 390); and the Honourable Bob Stables, who in his desire "to serve his country in a post of good emoluments, unaccompanied by any trouble or responsibility" (pp. 390–1) looks ahead to the Barnacles of *Little Dorrit*.[8] There are, in addition, the philanthropists, those acquaintances of Mr. Jarndyce, who are ready "to do anything with anybody else's money" (p. 99). Of these the most notable for "rapacious benevolence" is Mrs. Pardiggle, "a formidable style of lady," who has the effect "of wanting a great deal of room," swelling, it would seem, on the enforced contributions to good causes of her "weazened and shrivelled" children; in the world of commerce and trade that Skimpole rejects she makes a show "of doing charity by wholesale, and of dealing in it to a large extent" (pp. 100–1, 108). There are Mr. Quale and Mr. Gusher, who originate testimonials to each other, soliciting donations from "charity schools of small boys and girls, who [are] specially reminded of the widow's mite, and requested to come forward with halfpence and be acceptable sacrifices" (p. 204). The extent to which parasitism is corrupting is not demonstrated, in respect of the instances of it that have just been noted, with the finality that characterizes the presentation of Skimpole and Smallweed, but it is firmly enough implied; it is further indicated in the depiction of the institutions of the society of which Mr. Turveydrop, the Dedlock relations and Mrs. Pardgiggle are respected members.

III

The most prominent institution of this society is, of course, Chancery, and the representative example of its procedure its handling of the cause of Jarndyce and Jarndyce. Jarndyce and Jarndyce, it is at once brought to our notice, is a rich picking for the lawyers engaged in the suit, "some two or three of whom have inherited it from their fathers, who made a fortune by it" (p. 2). Jarndyce and Jarndyce, indeed, exemplifies that "the one great principle of the English law is, to make business for itself" at the expense of "the laity" (p. 548). The practice of law, in other words, has little to do with justice and is simply a socially condoned form of parasitism—as is graphically confirmed by the eventual lot of the Jarndyce estate, which is eaten up in costs (another instance, this, of the symbolic dimensions of the plot). This view of the legal process is reinforced by that taken of lawyers in a series of images. The house Tulkinghorn lives in is divided into sets of chambers in which "lawyers lie like maggots in nuts" (p. 130). The quintessential lawyer is Vholes, and his name, as Louis Crompton has pointed out,[9] evokes that of the parasitic field mouse that destroys crops. There is "something of the Vampire" in Vholes (p. 820); he looks at Richard "as if he were making a lingering meal of him with his eyes as well as with his professional appetite" (p. 550), and, when Jarndyce and Jarndyce has run its course, he gasps "as if he [has] swallowed the last morsel of his client" (p. 867). The toleration by "the laity" of this legal voraciousness, albeit with some grumbling, is seen as an insane condonation of social cannibalism: "As though, Mr. Vholes and his relations being minor cannibal chiefs, and it being proposed to abolish cannibalism, indignant champions were to put the case thus: Make man-eating unlawful, and you starve the Vholeses!" (p. 549)

An essential condition of this legal parasitism being the protraction of proceedings, it is not unexpected that Jarndyce and Jarndyce should appear to be "an endless cause" (p. 2). But the dilatoriness of Chancery also points to its evasiveness, to its failure to take decisions, its failure, that is, to fulfil its social function of taking responsibility in issues brought before it. And this evasiveness ramifies, for "shirking and sharking, in all their many varieties" are "sown broadcast by the ill-fated cause" (p. 5); and the Lord Chancellor and the lawyers, as Gridley complains, assert that they are not responsible for injustices—"It's the system" (p. 215). If the system of justice that "gives to monied might, the means abundantly of wearying out the right" (p. 3) is clearly rotten at the core, we are also shown (moving yet once again, as it were, from centre to fringe) how the corruption spreads. We see this notably in the equivocal position of Bucket, that amiable representative of the forces of law and order, the "tamed lynx" of Skimpole's disquisition. Bucket is as efficient and decisive as Chancery is confusedly procrastinatory, and he is capable of adhering with some delicacy to a code of honour (as when he delays George's arrest at the Bagnet birthday); but he is also not above lying to Snagsby (with "an engaging appearance of frankness") about the nature of Tulkinghorn's interest in Jo's encounter with the lady (p. 309); nor above bribing Skimpole and abducting the sick Jo; nor bargaining with Smallweed about the sum he aims to extort from Sir Leicester (pp. 732, 735); nor recommending to that baronet that he capitulate to the blackmail (p. 735).

If this, then, is the way in which the Court of Chancery is presented to us, it is important to note two further points relative to that presentation. First, though Dickens's case against Chancery may appear to be poetically heightened, it was not untrue to the facts. Jarndyce and Jarndyce was suggested, says Edgar Johnson, by "the notorious Jennings case, involving the disputed property of an old miser of Acton who had died intestate in 1798, leaving almost £1,500,000. When one of the claimants died in 1915 the case was still unsettled and the costs amounted to £250,000."[10] Second, it should be clear that the attack on Chancery is intended to be more than an attack on a single antiquated institution.[11] Chancery is throughout presented as a representative national establishment: as such, as "a slow, expensive, British, constitutional kind of thing," it commands Sir Leicester's tacit support (p. 13); and as such it evokes Mr. Kenge's defensive pride: "We are a great country, Mr. Jarndyce, we are a very great country. This is a great system, Mr. Jarndyce, and would you wish a great country to have a little system?" (p. 844). To regard Chancery as being at the heart not only of the fog that covers London at the beginning of the novel but of a whole social system, to regard it, that is, as symbolic of the functioning of a parasitic society, is to register the difference between Dickens's social criticism in *Bleak House* and that in *Nicholas Nickleby*, for instance, with its restricted attack on Dotheboys Hall; and also that, as we have seen, in *Oliver Twist*, with its more limited denunciation of the workhouse. To see that Chancery, and not the fog, is the central symbol of *Bleak House* is both to recognize the opening move in the analogical strategy of the late novels and to do justice to the nature and scope of Dickens's first major assault on the England of his day.

That Chancery is intended to have this kind of representative significance is borne out not alone (as I shall indicate) by the development of the action that connects it with Jo and Tom-all-Alone's but by the glancing reflection of its image in another central institution of state—parliament. The politicians, it emerges, are also not concerned with exercising the responsibilities of their office but only, again like the lawyers, with graciously living on the "people," the "supernumeraries" of the drama that is enacted between Boodle and Buffy and their retinues, of the drama that makes politics the art of providing for Noodle (p. 161). To ensure that he and his are provided for, moreover, Sir Thomas Doodle finds, during an election, that he "must throw himself upon the country—chiefly in the form of sovereigns and beer," the "auriferous and malty shower" being later "unpleasantly connected with the word bribery" in some two hundred election petitions (pp. 562–8). In addition, it is perhaps not irrelevant to mention that in the industrial society in which Chancery and Parliament so effectively maintain themselves smoke is described (in a passing reference) as "the London ivy," and "affectionate parasite" that wreathes itself so clingingly round the sign PEFFER (later PEFFER and SNAGSBY) as to "overpower" it (p. 127).

Smoke, together with mud and fog, is also linked to Chancery in the much-discussed description with which the novel begins, the description in which Chancery (by means of a richness of association that has not perhaps had its due) is given a memorable habitation:

> London. Michaelmas Term lately over, and the Lord Chancellor sitting in Lincoln's Inn Hall. Implacable November weather. As much mud in the streets, as if the waters had but newly retired from the face of the earth, and it would not be wonderful to meet a Megalosaurus, forty feet long or so, waddling like an elephantine lizard up Holborn Hill. Smoke lowering down from chimney-pots, making a soft black drizzle, with flakes of soot in it as big as full-grown snowflakes—gone into mourning, one might imagine, for the death of the sun. Dogs, undistinguishable in mire. Horses, scarcely better; splashed to their very blinkers. Foot passengers, jostling one another's umbrellas, in a general infection of ill-temper, and losing their foot-hold at street-corners, where tens of thousands of other foot passengers have been slipping and sliding since the day broke (if this day ever broke), adding new deposits to the crust upon crust of mud, sticking at those points tenaciously to the pavement, and accumulating at compound interest.
>
> Fog everywhere. Fog up the river, where it flows among green aits and meadows; fog down the river, where it rolls defiled among the tiers of shipping, and the waterside pollutions of a great (and dirty) city. . . .
>
> The raw afternoon is rawest, and the dense fog is densest, and the muddy streets are muddiest, near that leaden-headed old obstruction, appropriate ornament for the threshold of a leaden-headed old corporation: Temple Bar. And hard by Temple Bar, in Lincoln's Inn Hall, at the very heart of the fog, sits the Lord High Chancellor in his High Court of Chancery.
>
> Never can there come fog too thick, never can there come mud and mire too deep, to assort with the groping and floundering condition which this High Court of Chancery, most pestilent of hoary sinners, holds, this day, in the sight of heaven and earth. (pp. 1–2)

Bearing in mind the complacency of mid-century optimism about progress, we cannot help being struck by the dark harshness of this evocation of the Victorian scene. What is suggested, indeed, is the difficulty of making any progress at all in the fog and smoke and mud, the predicament of a "groping and floundering condition" being general. The ramifications of this condition are far-reaching. In the first place the mud, which is in part responsible for it, is associated with an accumulation "at compound interest," and with a state in which "it would not be wonderful to meet a Megalosaurus"; the accumulation of money, that is, is tacitly associated with a reversion to a lower form of life, and (by a further extension of the image) with a retrogressive Chancery, which is situated where "the muddy streets are muddiest." Second, the mud is linked, in terms of the imagery, with a "black drizzle" of smoke and soot, those emblems of industrial civilization; and what this posits is not just a retrogression but a blotting out of life, for one might imagine the flakes of soot mourning "the death of the sun," and it is doubtful "if this day ever broke." Chancery itself, it hardly needs saying, is "at the very heart of the fog"; and the court is "dim", with "wasting candles here and there" and fog hanging "heavy" in it and stained-glass windows that "admit no light of day into the place" (p. 2). Third, the dual movement of the narrative as a whole is reflected in the development of one of the images in this passage. The fog that is "defiled" by the "waterside pollutions" of the great city is responsible, together with the mud and the smoke, for a general "infection" of ill-temper among foot passengers; at the centre of the fog, where "the dense fog is densest," there is the Court of Chancery, that most "pestilent" of sinners. Moving out from that centre to the country at large, we are told that Chancery "has its decaying houses and its blighted lands in every shire" (pp. 2–3), and that Jarndyce and Jarndyce "has stretched forth its unwholesome hand to soil and corrupt" untold numbers of people (p. 5). Chancery, that is, is from the outset associated with the spread of a noxious infection and corruption in the body politic. If Dombeyism, as we have seen, is the blight of domestic life, then Chancery and all its works is presented as the blight of public life, the parasite that consumes the social organism.[12]

The image that radiates from the pestilent sinner should be related to a passage in which Mr. Jarndyce tells Esther of the decay of some Jarndyce property in London:

> "There is, in that city of London there, some property of ours, which is much at this day what Bleak House was then [i.e., in the time of Tom Jarndyce]—I say property of ours, meaning of the Suit's, but I ought to call it the property of Costs; for Costs is the only power on earth that will ever get anything out of it now, or will ever know it for anything but an eyesore and a heartsore. It is a street of perishing blind houses, with their eyes stoned out; without a pane of glass, without so much as a windowframe, with the bare blank shutters tumbling from their hinges and falling asunder; the iron rails peeling away in flakes of rust; the chimneys sinking in; the stone steps to every door (and every door might be Death's Door) turning stagnant green; the very crutches on which the ruins are propped, decaying. Although Bleak House was not in Chancery, its master was, and it was stamped with the same seal. These are the Great Seal's impressions, my dear, all over England—the children know them!" (pp. 96–7)

Here, figured persistently in detail after detail of the imagery, is plainly a manifestation of social blight, of Chancery's "decaying houses and blighted lands." And the property referred to, though Mr. Jarndyce does not mention its name, is equally clearly Tom-all-Alone's, the London slum in dispute in Jarndyce and Jarndyce and the home of Jo. Mr. Jarndyce's sudden reference to children implies one of the most disturbing aspects of the Great Seal's imprint—the blighting of the lives of children (like Jo) who are born and bred in such slums. It is, indeed, in his exposure of the way in which the lives of the innocent are blighted that Dickens's attack on Chancery (and the society of his day) is centred. Certainly Tom-all-Alone's is at the centre of the world of *Bleak House*, it being no coincidence that a surviving list of projected titles of the novel should so insistently point to it. John Forster notes the following titles which were "successively proposed for *Bleak House*. 1. "Tom-all-Alone's. The Ruined House"; 2. "Tom-All-Alone's. The Solitary House that was always shut up"; 3. "Bleak House Academy"; 4. "The East Wind"; 5. "Tom-all-Alone's. The Ruined [House, Building, Factory, Mill] that got into Chancery and never got out"; 6. "Tom-all-Alone's. The Solitary House where the Grass grew"; 7. "Tom-all-Alone's. The Solitary House that was always shut up and never Lighted"; 8. "Tom-all-Alone's. The Ruined Mill, that got into Chancery and never got out"; 9. "Tom-all-Alone's. The Solitary House where the Wind howled"; 10. "Tom-all-Alone's. The Ruined House that got into Chancery and never got out"; 11. "Bleak House and the East Wind. How they both got into Chancery and never got out"; 12. "Bleak House."[13]

If Mr. Jarndyce's description of Tom-all-Alone's points predominantly to its deterioration as property, the omniscient narrative gives us some indication of the condition of its human inhabitants:

> Jo lives—that is to say, Jo has not yet died—in a ruinous place, known to the like of him by the name of Tom-all-Alone's. It is a black, dilapidated street, avoided by all decent people; where the crazy houses were seized upon, when their decay was far advanced, by some bold vagrants, who, after establishing their own possession, took to letting them out in lodgings. Now, these tumbling tenements contain, by night, a swarm of misery. As, on the ruined human wretch, vermin parasites appear, so these ruined shelters have bred a crowd of foul existence that crawls in and out of gaps in walls and boards; and coils itself to sleep, in maggot numbers, where the rain drips in; and comes and goes, fetching and carrying fever, and sowing more evil in its every footprint than Lord Coodle, and Sir Thomas Doodle, and the Duke of Foodle, and all the fine gentlemen in office, down to Zoodle, shall set right in five hundred years—though born expressly to do it. . . .
>
> This desirable property is in Chancery, of course. It would be an insult to the discernment of any man with half an eye, to tell him so. Whether "Tom" is the popular representative of the original plaintiff or defendant in Jarndyce and Jarndyce; or whether Tom lived here when the suit had laid the street waste, all alone, until other settlers came to join him; or whether the traditional title is a comprehensive name for a retreat cut off from honest company and put out of the pale of hope; perhaps nobody knows. Certainly, Jo don't know.
>
> "For *I* don't," says Jo, "*I* don't know nothink." (pp. 219–20)

It is a further measure of the organic unity of the novel that in this centrally significant passage there should appear the simile of the vermin parasites. In terms of the simile, the "crowd of foul existence" that the slum has bred "in maggot numbers" is clearly a crowd of human parasites, of miserable mendicants whose begging exemplifies the most primitive and precarious form of social parasitism. Of such a tribe is Jo, dumbly sweeping his crossing and depending on the charity of men like Hawdon and Snagsby. Of such is Jo, who, like "the other lower animals," gets on as well as he can in "the unintelligible mess" of city life; who, listening to "a band of music" together with a drover's dog, is said to derive "probably . . . the same amount of animal satisfaction" as the dog and to be "probably upon a par" with it "as to awakened association, aspiration or regret, melancholy or joyful reference to things beyond the senses," but to be "otherwise" far beneath "the brute": "Turn that dog's descendants wild, like Jo, and in a very few years they will so degenerate that they will lose even their bark—but not their bite" (pp. 221–2). In his low, degenerate state, in other words, Jo (tiny parasite) points to the existence of a muddy Megalosaurus at the heart of civilization.[14]

Orphaned, defenceless, knowing nothink, Jo is an inevitable victim of exploitation. He, and others like him, it is implied, are in their turn parasitically battened on by the "bold vagrants" who have "seized" the houses in Tom-all-Alone's and let them out in lodgings. And the vagrants remain undisturbed in their illegal possession of the houses, of course, because the property is "in Chancery," because, consequently, it as good as belongs to no one and no one is to be found both willing and able to take responsibility for it. Certainly not the lawyers, for those maggots in nuts are not only far removed from the maggot numbers of Tom-all-Alone's but otherwise engaged in the consuming suit of Jarndyce and Jarndyce. Certainly not the politicians, for though Lord Coodle and Sir Thomas Doodle and their fellows participate in "much mighty speech-making . . . both in and out of Parliament, concerning Tom," they are really preoccupied with providing for Noodle; and "Tom" is accordingly left to go "to perdition head foremost in his old determined spirit" (p. 627). The street is "laid waste" under the joint auspices, as it were, of legislature and judiciary. The image of being of this society, it becomes clear, is a chain of parasites.

Since it is Chancery that is responsible, in the first instance, for the desolation of Tom-all-Alone's, and since Jo is viewed as having been "bred" by the "ruined shelters," it seems reasonable to regard him as the direct responsibility of Chancery. Jo, we might say, the poor naked wretch who has to bide the pelting of the storm, is as much a ward of Chancery as Ada and Richard. Yet the long arm of the law, when it concerns itself with Jo at all, is intent only to push him out of sight: the police constable's instructions, as the wistful Snagsby is informed, are that Jo is "to move on" (p. 265). The injunction is a concise indication of the way in which the authorities evade their obligation towards Jo; and this passing of the buck typifies the official response he meets with elsewhere when he moves on. Worn-out and ill, he is befriended by the brickmakers' women at St. Albans, but they can find no "proper refuge" for him (as Esther reports):

> The friend had been here and there, and had been played about from hand to hand, and had come back as she went. At first it was too early for the boy to be received into the proper refuge, and at last it was too late. One official sent her to another, and the other sent her back again to the first, and so backward and forward; until it appeared to me as if both must have been appointed for their skill in evading their duties, instead of performing them. (pp. 431–2)

And when Allan Woodcourt later finds Jo in London, so "deplorably low and reduced" as probably to be "too far gone to recover" (p. 640), he reflects (considering where to "bestow" him) on the "strange fact" that "in the heart of a civilised world this creature in human form should be more difficult to dispose of than an unowned dog" (p. 636). The failure on the part of organized society to provide for Jo (as distinct from providing for Noodle) amounts to a betrayal of him, to a betrayal of the trust reposed in it to care for a ward; and this failure, as Woodcourt's thought implies, is symptomatic of that of the "civilised world" which will not own him.

The immediate consequence for Jo of this failure is his untimely death. Taken in, eventually, by George, he is not prepossessing: "Homely filth begrimes him, homely parasites devour him, homely sores are in him, homely rags are on him: native ignorance, the growth of English soil and climate, sinks his immortal nature lower than the beasts that perish" (p. 641). Jo, we realize, has been devoured by a parasitic society as well as by the homely parasites. And his death, Dickens insists, is representative, exemplifying the fate of the unprotected in such a society:

> Dead, your Majesty. Dead, my lords and gentlemen. Dead, Right Reverends and Wrong Reverends of every order. Dead, men and women, born with Heavenly compassion in your hearts. And dying thus around us every day. (p. 649)

The tone of this is uncertain (though even its mixture of effects is preferable to the sentimentality of that recital of the Lord's Prayer which it follows), but its emphasis is unmistakable: it is a whole society that shares in the guilt of Jo's death.

The general social consequences of the existence of a slum such as Tom-all-Alone's are first adverted to in the passage (quoted on p. 171 above) in which the "crowd of foul existence" is said to come and go, "fetching and carrying fever, and sowing more evil in its every footprint" than the Lord Coodles can ever set right. These consequences are elaborated on in the description of the revenge "Tom" takes on being left to go to perdition:

> But he has his revenge. Even the winds are his messengers, and they serve him in these hours of darkness. There is not a drop of Tom's corrupted blood but propagates infection and contagion somewhere. It shall pollute, this very night, the choice stream (in which chemists on analysis would find the genuine nobility) of a Norman house, and his Grace shall not be able to say Nay to the infamous alliance. There is not an atom of Tom's slime, not a cubic inch of any pestilential gas in which he lives, not one obscenity or degradation about him, not an ignorance, not a wickedness, not a brutality of his committing, but shall work its retribution, through every order of society, up to the proudest of the proud, and to the highest of the high. Verily, what with tainting, plundering, and spoiling, Tom has his revenge. (pp. 627–8)

The central image of the insidious contagion which is Tom's revenge is the actual disease that is disseminated by the slum, "Tom's corrupted blood . . . [propagating] infection and contagion" in the society that has propagated it. The image admirably conveys a number of related significances. The infection and contagion are, first, a direct physical manifestation of the "alliance" (no matter how "infamous") of "every order of society," of their interdependence; the image, in other words, points directly to what is indirectly insisted on by the narrative method. The spread of the disease also demonstrates what the alliance entails: it is a dramatic assertion that a gangrened limb cannot safely be left unattended, that a society which leaves its slums to go to perdition head foremost will ineluctably be dragged down after them. But the fact that the society which disregards the signs of its own disorder in this way is a "pestilent sinner" at heart, and the fact that the disease which corrupts its blood originates in Tom-all-Alone's suggest, furthermore, that the infection and contagion are symbolic of the specific disease that is Chancery. The spread of the disease, that is, symbolizes the way in which Chancery functions to blight the lives of those it touches, irrespective of how remote their connection with it may appear to be. In the plot this process is directly exemplified by the career of Richard (which I shall discuss later); it is symbolized by Jo's contraction of the (unnamed) disease and by the way he infects Esther and Charley. Esther and Jo (the latest in a line of victims that starts with Pickwick) are both equally innocent victims of Chancery. Finally, the spread of the infectious disease is intended to represent in tangible physical terms the analogous spread in such a society of a moral corruption, of what Dickens in *Dombey and Son* calls a "moral pestilence." The dissemination of this pestilence is shown to have a characteristic dual movement. It is Chancery that produces the specific parasitic blight of Tom-all-Alone's; stewing in its corruption, it is the slum that pours back into society the more general (but equally contaminating) mess of "obscenity" and "degradation," of "ignorance," "wickedness" and "brutality."

In *Barnaby Rudge* there is an interesting parallel to this vein of imagery. The Gordon rioters are described as follows:

> One other circumstance is worthy of remark; and that is, that from the moment of their first outbreak at Westminster, every symptom of order or preconcerted arrangement among them vanished. When they divided into parties and ran to different quarters of the town, it was on the spontaneous suggestion of the moment. Each party swelled as it went along, like rivers as they roll towards the sea; new leaders sprang up as they were wanted, disappeared when the necessity was over, and reappeared at the next crisis. Each tumult took shape and form from the circumstances of the moment; sober workmen, going home from their day's labour, were seen to cast down their baskets of tools and become rioters in an instant; mere boys on errands did the like. In a word, a moral plague ran through the city. The noise, and hurry, and excitement, had for hundreds and hundreds an attraction they had no firmness to resist. The

> contagion spread like a dread fever: an infectious madness, as yet not near
> its height, seized on new victims every hour, and society began to tremble
> at their ravings. (p. 403)

Since Dickens's preoccupation with the eighteenth-century Gordon riots
reflects, at least in part, a concern with the Chartist agitation of his own day,
as Edmund Wilson has pointed out,[15] the quoted passage suggests the possibility of another dimension to the disease imagery that is central in *Bleak
House*. Are we to understand, that is to say, that the continued disregard of
Tom may lead to the violent eruption of his corrupted blood, to insurrection?
There is certainly at least one passage that hints at this:

> Twice, lately, there has been a crash and a cloud of dust, like the
> springing of a mine, in Tom-all-Alone's; and, each time, a house has fallen.
> These accidents have made a paragraph in the newspapers, and have filled
> a bed or two in the nearest hospital. The gaps remain, and there are not
> unpopular lodgings among the rubbish. As several more houses are nearly
> ready to go, the next crash in Tom-all-Alone's may be expected to be a
> good one. (p. 220)

The collapse of slum houses, it may be argued, is not an uncommon occur-
rence, but the opening simile is so forcefully evocative of violent and unnatu-
ral explosion as to charge the reference to "the next crash in Tom-all-Alone's"
with ominous threat. The explosive potentiality of the slum, however, is not
further developed; the representative inhabitant of Tom-all-Alone's is poor,
defenceless Jo, and adult residents are only dimly seen as skulking figures in
the dark.

Though Dickens, therefore, does not ignore the possibility of revolution, he posits a rather different fate for this unregenerate society. Characteristically, he communicates his sense of this fate through a daring and
grotesque image, an image, however, that subtly combines elements of two
other major images—those of the corrupted blood and the parasite—the
image of Krook's death by Spontaneous Combustion. Krook's representative
significance is baldly asserted: Miss Flite tells Esther's party that "among the
neighbours" Krook is called "the Lord Chancellor," and that his junk-shop is
called "the Court of Chancery" (p. 51). His physical appearance is clearly
intended to evoke the aura of his illustrious namesake at the heart of the mud
and the fog: he is "short, cadaverous, and withered" (p. 50); he spreads his
lean hands "like a vampire's wings" (p. 138). His breath, moreover, issues "in
visible smoke from his mouth, as if he were on fire within" (p. 50)—a phenomenon that leads straight to his later grisly disintegration:

> The Lord Chancellor of that Court, true to his title in his last act, has died
> the death of all Lord Chancellors in all Courts, and of all authorities in all
> places under all names soever, where false pretences are made, and where
> injustice is done. Call the death by any name Your Highness will, attribute
> it to whom you will, or say it might have been prevented how you will, it is
> the same death eternally—inborn, inbred, engendered in the corrupted

humours of the vicious body itself, and that only—Spontaneous Combustion, and none other of all the deaths that can be died. (pp. 455–6)

Though George Henry Lewes at once roundly declared that no authoritative
organic chemist would countenance the possibility of spontaneous combustion (in which Dickens sincerely believed),[16] Krook's death retains the imaginative, if not the scientific, validity it was originally intended to have. "Inborn,
inbred, engendered in the corrupted humours of the body itself," Krook's
death leaves him, as it were, self-consumed, "represented" only by what looks
like "the cinder of a small charred and broken log of wood sprinkled with white
ashes" (p. 455). This, then, rather than revolution, is the postulated end of a
world that condones Chancery and Tom-all-Alone's—as though the parasitic
society were at last to turn universal wolf and eat up itself.

IV

The way in which Chancery blights all it touches is directly exemplified,
as I have remarked, by the case of Richard. Richard, indeed, is rather too
much of a "case," too predictable in his behaviour, to be really interesting;
but as an *exemplum* to what is said more imaginatively elsewhere in the
novel, he has his place. His place, from birth, is in Chancery:

> "My dear Esther, I am a very unfortunate dog not to be more settled, but
> how *can* I be more settled? If you lived in an unfinished house, you
> couldn't settle down in it; if you were condemned to leave everything you
> undertook, unfinished, you would find it hard to apply yourself to any-
> thing; and yet that's my unhappy case. I was born into this unfinished
> contention with all its chances and changes, and it began to unsettle me
> before I quite knew the difference between a suit at law and a suit of
> clothes; and it has gone on unsettling me ever since; and here I am now,
> conscious sometimes that I am but a worthless fellow to love my confiding
> cousin Ada." (p. 322)

Richard's words reveal that the heritage he has come into as one of the heirs
to the disputed estate in Jarndyce and Jarndyce clearly bears the imprint of
the Great Seal. Born into the "unfinished contention," as if into original sin,[17]
he is "condemned" to be unsettled; is condemned, that is, as Mr. Jarndyce
says, to "a habit of putting off—and trusting to this, that, and the other
chance, without knowing what chance" (p. 167); is condemned, like Jo, to
move on. Richard moves on to some effect, abandoning Bayham Badger and
medicine for Kenge and Carboy and the law, and them for the army and
soldiering, and that for Vholes and Jarndyce and Jarndyce. His indecisive-
ness, his inability to take responsibility for the future course of his life,
resembles nothing so much as a Chancery-begotten propensity to "shirk and
shark": "It's not," he says, "as if I wanted a profession for life. These proceedings will come to a termination, and then I am provided for" (p. 323).
Richard's last remark has the true parasitic stink, aligning him as it does with

Noodle and the politicians, with the lawyers and Vholes (that conscientious provider, with three daughters and a father in the Vale of Taunton), with Skimpole and with Mr. Turveydrop and with all the other characters in *Bleak House* who are analogously in search of a host. We are not surprised, therefore, that Esther's response to the communication of his modest aspiration is to wonder how he will end "when so soon and so surely all his manly qualities" have been touched "by the fatal blight" that ruins everything it rests on (p. 324).

Having been touched by the fatal blight, Richard succumbs, as in a moral pestilence, to the suspicion and distrust bred by Jarndyce and Jarndyce—the suspicion that Mr. Jarndyce has anticipated and attempted to fight against in applying to Chancery to have Richard and Ada live with him. Richard's distrust fixes itself, to start with, on Mr. Jarndyce. He comes to view Jarndyce's constant admonitions to him to have nothing to do with the suit as the tactics of self-interest, a design to keep him in indifferent ignorance of the proceedings (p. 524). Nor is he at a loss to account for so uncharitable an explanation of Jarndyce's motives:

> "Come, sister, come," said Richard, a little more gaily, "you will be fair with me at all events. If I have the misfortune to be under that influence, so has he. If it has a little twisted me, it may have a little twisted him, too. I don't say that he is not an honourable man, out of all this complication and uncertainty; I am sure he is. But it taints everybody. You know it taints everybody. You have heard him say so fifty times. Then why should *he* escape?" (p. 525)

The distinctive tone of this, I think we are meant to recognize, is that of Harold Skimpole, it being noteworthy that Richard has just before been in Skimpole's company and confessed to a liking for him: "He does me more good than anybody," he tells Esther (p. 521). Richard's statement is characterized by the kind of specious logic we associate with Skimpole's description of his encounter with Bucket. Intent on making his point, moreover, Richard reveals a Skimpole-like indifference to the "taint" he has admitted.

Mr. Jarndyce is magnanimous enough to acquit Richard of responsibility for his suspicions—he tells Esther that "it is in the subtle poison of [abuses such as Chancery] to breed such diseases. His blood is infected, and objects lose their natural aspects in his sight. It is not *his* fault" (p. 492)—but Richard's corrupted blood, like that of Tom-all-Alone's, only spreads the infection. Fearing betrayal wherever he turns, he becomes suspicious, next, of Vholes, even drawing comfort from the failure of his military venture at the prospect of continued proximity to the lawyer: "Why, if this bubble hadn't broken now . . ." he says, "I must have been ordered abroad; but how could I have gone? How could I, with my experience of that thing, trust even Vholes unless I was at his back?" (p. 620). Even Ada, in the end, is involved in his presumption. Esther has previously suspected that he is "postponing his best truth and earnestness" in his feeling for Ada "until Jarndyce and

Jarndyce should be off his mind" (p. 523); that there are grounds for her uneasiness is revealed when (at the time of his crisis in the army) she is the bearer of a letter to him from Ada in which his cousin offers him "the little inheritance she is certain of so soon" in order that he may "set [himself] right with it, and remain in the service." He is deeply affected by the offer, but his distrust of Jarndyce is so great that, without his being aware of it, it contaminates even his love for Ada: "And the dear girl," he says, "makes me this generous offer from under the same John Jarndyce's roof, and with the same John Jarndyce's gracious consent and connivance, I dare say, as a new means of buying me off" (pp. 620–1).

With his heart "heavy with corroding care, suspense, distrust, and doubt," Richard is one day observed in the neighbourhood of Vholes's office by Mr. Guppy and Mr. Weevle. "William," says Weevle, as Richard passes, "there's combustion going on there! It's not a case of Spontaneous, but it's smouldering combustion it is" (pp. 555–6). Just as Krook, in other words, is consumed by the corrupted humours of his own vicious body; just as the estate in Jarndyce and Jarndyce (together with all Richard's and all Ada's money) is consumed in costs; so does Richard consume himself with the care and suspense and distrust and doubt engendered by Chancery. As he obviously sickens, Woodcourt can diagnose "no direct bodily illness" (p. 814); his illness is "of the mind" (p. 864). On the day that Jarndyce and Jarndyce ends, his mouth fills with blood in the court, and, quite "worn away" (p. 868), he is taken home to die. The blight of Chancery thus again falls on innocent victims, on his patient wife and on his unborn child, who—like Esther—is left to grow up without ever knowing a father.

V

That Esther's life is in this respect analogous to that of Richard's child suggests that there may perhaps be a connection between the fate of Richard and that of Lady Dedlock. Certainly the narrative method, we remember, implies some connection between Jarndyce and Jarndyce and Lady Dedlock's secret. The opening of the novel, moreover, firmly links the muddy, foggy world of Chancery and the wet world of fashion:

> It is but a glimpse of the world of fashion that we want on this same miry afternoon. It is not so unlike the Court of Chancery, but that we may pass from the one scene to the other, as the crow flies. Both the world of fashion and the Court of Chancery are things of precedent and usage; oversleeping Rip Van Winkles, who have played at strange games through a deal of thundery weather . . .
>
> It is not a large world. . . . There is much good in it . . . But the evil of it is, that it is a world wrapped up in too much jeweller's cotton and fine wool, and cannot hear the rushing of the larger worlds, and cannot see them as they circle round the sun. It is a deadened world, and its growth is sometimes unhealthy for want of air.

> . . . My Lady Dedlock has been down at what she calls, in familiar
> conversation, her "place" in Lincolnshire. The waters are out in Lin-
> colnshire. An arch of the bridge in the park has been sapped and sopped
> away. The adjacent low-lying ground, for half a mile in breadth, is a stag-
> nant river, with melancholy trees for islands in it, and a surface punctured
> all over, all day long, with falling rain. . . . On Sundays, the little church
> in the park is mouldy; the oaken pulpit breaks out into a cold sweat; and
> there is a general smell and taste as of the ancient Dedlocks in their
> graves. . . . (p. 8–9)

What links the world of Chancery (where flakes of soot mourn the death of
the sun) and the world of fashion, it is evident, is a common deadness. The
description of the scene in Lincolnshire evokes a flooded world, a world in
which everything stands stagnant, being slowly "sapped and sopped away"
like the arch of the bridge, suggestively evokes, in a word, the "deadened
world" that the world of fashion is explicitly said to be. This sense of deadness
is associated with a number of characteristics of the world of fashion, and it is
also related, as we slowly discover, to some aspects of Lady Dedlock's predicament. The deadness is associated, first, with a "want of air," with a sense,
that is, of unhealthy enclosure, with a narrow exclusiveness that takes no
heed of "larger worlds"; it seems to be the price paid for the suffocating
embrace of soft jeweller's cotton and wool. Second, the deadness is associated with the influence of the past. Bound by "precedent and usage," the
world of fashion (an "oversleeping Rip Van Winkle") is outmoded—and so
denies itself, as it were. The dead past, moreover, like "the ancient Dedlocks
in their graves," infuses its "general smell and taste" into the present.

    This, then, is the world of fashion of which Lady Dedlock is the arbiter.
"Bored to death," she appears to be at one with her environment:

> My Lady Dedlock (who is childless), looking out in the early twilight from
> her boudoir at a keeper's lodge, and seeing the light of a fire upon the
> latticed panes, and smoke rising from the chimney, and a child, chased by
> a woman, running out into the rain to meet the shining figure of a
> wrapped-up man coming through the gate, has been put quite out of
> temper. My Lady Dedlock says she has been "bored to death." . . .
>   Sir Leicester is twenty years, full measure, older than my Lady. . . .
> He is ceremonious, stately, most polite on every occasion to my Lady, and
> holds her personal attractions in the highest estimation. His gallantry to
> my Lady, which has never changed since he courted her, is the one little
> touch of romantic fancy in him.
>   Indeed, he married her for love. A whisper still goes about, that she
> had not even family; howbeit, Sir Leicester had so much family that per-
> haps he had enough, and could dispense with any more. But she had
> beauty, pride, ambition, insolent resolve, and sense enough to portion out
> a legion of fine ladies. Wealth and station, added to these, soon floated her
> upward; and for years, now, my Lady Dedlock has been at the centre of
> the fashionable tree.
>   How Alexander wept when he had no more worlds to conquer, every-

body knows—or has some reason to know by this time, the matter having been rather frequently mentioned. My Lady Dedlock, having conquered *her* world, fell, not into the melting, but rather into the freezing mood. An exhausted composure, a wornout placidity, an equanimity of fatigue not to be ruffled by interest or satisfaction, are the trophies of her victory. She is perfectly well-bred. If she could be translated to Heaven to-morrow, she might be expected to ascend without any rapture. (pp. 9–10)

The nature of Lady Dedlock's deadness is defined by that which (disturbingly) bores her to death—the signs of animation she sees as she gazes from her window at the keeper's lodge. In the cold, stagnant, soggy scene the lodge (with its fire and movement and the "shining" figure of the man) is a place of warmth and life; the warmth and life are associated, furthermore, with the love that seems to bind man, woman and child together and that apparently communicates itself to Lady Dedlock, ("who is childless"), and married to a man twenty years her senior. Lady Dedlock's deadness, it is implied, is connected with the sterility of her marriage, its emotional as well as physical sterility, for if Sir Leicester has "married her for love," she (in her ambition and insolent resolve) has married "wealth and station." The coldness of her choice, indeed (like that of Edith Dombey), is suggested by her "freezing mood," the rigidity of which marks her posture in the "deadened world." Her posture is also one of composure and placidity and equanimity, but if these are the visible "trophies of her victory" over "society," they silently point (together with the affectation of exhaustion) to the cost of victory over herself, to her ever-present, unrelaxed need of repressing feeling.

The feeling Lady Dedlock principally has to repress, of course, is that connected with her past. Having chosen, like so many characters in *Bleak House* to be provided for (to be a maggot in her own particular kind of nut, as it were), she has, in defence of her position, to suppress all suggestion of her illicit association with Hawdon and of the illegitimate birth of their daughter. To judge, moreover, by her response when she catches sight of Hawdon's handwriting some twenty years after she has broken with him, we may assume that she had had to contend with a strong feeling for him, a feeling that remains as alive as the child she thinks dead. Having denied Hawdon and betrayed his love, Lady Dedlock, beneath her perfectly well-bred manner, has constantly to deny herself.

Though Lady Dedlock does not bequeath an estate to her daughter (companion to one of the parties to Jarndyce and Jarndyce), she leaves her to a future that promises to be as dark as any shadowed by the Court of Chancery. One of Esther's early memories is of her mother's sister exploiting the occasion of a birthday to say to her:

"Your mother, Esther, is your disgrace, and you were hers. . . . For yourself, unfortunate girl, orphaned and degraded from the first of these evil anniversaries, pray daily that the sins of others be not visited upon your head, according to what is written. Forget your mother, and leave all

other people to forget her who will do her unhappy child that greatest
kindness. . . ."

"Submission, self-denial, diligent work, are the preparations for a life
begun with such a shadow on it. You are different from other children,
Esther, because you were not born, like them, in common sinfulness and
wrath. You are set apart." (pp. 17–18)

Miss Barbary's injunction to Esther is to pray that the sins of others be not
visited on her head; her words make manifest how they are. The novel as a
whole, however, suggests (with firm moral unconventionality) that Lady
Dedlock's sin is not what her sister takes it to be,[18] the novel suggests, that
is, that her "sin" is not illicit love but a loveless marriage, not the bearing of
an illegitimate child but the failure to live up to the love that brought the
child into being. And the consequence of this failure is the blighting of the
life of the child, the life that is "begun with such a shadow on it," the child
who from birth is "set apart"; for Lady Dedlock is not exonerated by her
ignorance of the child's fate—she knowingly abandoned its father and is
responsible both for that betrayal and its effects.

It is, indeed, in the twice-enacted blighting of Esther's life that Lady
Dedlock's past and Jarndyce and Jarndyce are most conspicuously connected. Her life blighted in infancy, the innocent victim of her mother's
abandonment of her father, Esther survives to win happiness at Bleak House
only to be struck down in young womanhood, the innocent victim of society's
abandonment of Jo. In both cases, moreover, the complex of reasons that
underlies the abandonment is not dissimilar. That we are meant to make this
connection is confirmed, I think, by the way in which Dickens suggests that
Jo's infection may be traced to two possible sources. It might well seem, as I
have previously indicated, that it is the corrupted blood of Tom-all-Alone's
that infects Jo (and so infects Esther); it is made just as likely that he contracts
the disease when he visits the churchyard in which Esther's father is buried:
the churchyard is "pestiferous and obscene," and communicates "malignant
diseases . . . to the bodies of our dear brothers and sisters who have not
departed"; when Hawdon is lowered down "a foot or two," he is sown "in
corruption" only "to be raised in corruption"; the "poisoned air deposits its
witch-ointment slimy to the touch" on the iron gate of the churchyard (p.
151). When Jo takes the disguised Lady Dedlock to the churchyard, he
excitedly watches the progress of a rat among the graves, while she
"shrinks . . . into a corner of [the] hideous archway, with its deadly stains
contaminating her dress" (p. 225)[19] If Dickens is thus at some pains to make it
an open question as to where Jo is infected, the uncertainty suggests it is the
same blight, ultimately, of which Esther is the victim.

Esther, that is to say, is a victim of the corruption of both her mother
and the society in which she lives; and with this kind of relation established,
Lady Dedlock's fate—like that of Krook—is seen to have wider implications.
Lady Dedlock, in the full maturity of experience, is forced to make a crucial

choice when she discovers that Esther is her daughter, when she discovers, so to speak, that the world of fashion is more closely related than she has suspected to the larger worlds it habitually ignores. The alternatives she faces, it might seem, are either to accept the relation fully or to deny it. In the event, she temporizes and does neither. She reveals herself to Esther, but insists that the relation be kept secret, and that thenceforth they neither associate nor communicate (p. 510). She insists on the secrecy, she says, for the sake of both Sir Leicester and Esther herself, but this clearly is a rationalization; for Sir Leicester, it is later shown, needs no protecting, and Esther has no personal interest in keeping the secret. Lady Dedlock simply cannot face up to taking responsibility for the relation, cannot contemplate bearing the disgrace which she imagines the admission of her past conduct will entail. She parts from Esther to return, as she says, to "the dark road" of her choice: "The dark road I have trodden for so many years will end where it will. I follow it alone to the end, whatever the end be. It may be near, it may be distant; while the road lasts, nothing turns me" (p. 511). The dark road is the road of continued evasion, of continued fencing with Tulkinghorn, the road of her final flight and the last evasive tactic of the exchange of clothes with the brickmaker's wife. But Lady Dedlock's choice of this road means, in the end, that she is driven to her death, for she is utterly worn out by her flight; and twist though it may, the road leads her back to the pestiferous churchyard in which Hawdon is buried, leads her back, that is, to an admission of the relation she has so long denied; leads her, if only in death, to a true identity, for Esther, seeing before her a woman dressed in Jenny's clothes, sees "the mother of the dead child" (p. 811).

VI

How radical, then, is Dickens's attack on mid-Victorian England? Commenting on the symbolism of Krook's death, Edgar Johnson says "the injustices of an unjust society" are no longer seen as "subjects for local cure or even amputation": "Nothing will do short of the complete annihilation that they will ultimately provide by blowing up of their own corruption";[20] while Monroe Engel (also in relation to Krook's "[dissolving] of spontaneous combustion") maintains that "a kind of inevitable dissolution is the hope," though "it is clear that Dickens has grave doubts that enough will happen by peaceful process."[21] It seems to me, however, that at this stage of his career (and *Bleak House* should be regarded as his first major attempt to come to grips with the society in which he lived) Dickens was neither as radical nor as pessimistic as these pronouncements suggest. Though it is true that the novel presents an image of possible social collapse—presenting it not alone through the death of Krook but through the equally representative deaths of Richard and Lady Dedlock and through the pervasive disease imagery—the collapse is neither prescribed nor hoped for. It is presented as a warning, a prophetic warning of what will inevitably come to pass if a stiff-necked people refuses to change its ways. But the way to change, to peaceful recuperation, as it were, is throughout presented as both clear and accessible.

Since the two major factors in the diagnosis of what has caused the corruption of Tom's blood are shown to be parasitism and the evasion of responsibility by properly constituted authority, it would seem to follow that all that is required in such a society is a readiness to make one's own way and to accept responsibility. Such, at any rate, is the cure apparently propounded in *Bleak House*. Anticipating Samuel Smiles, Dickens sets against the horde of parasites, as George H. Ford has pointed out,[22] some representative exemplars of self-help: the young Turveydrop, Rouncewell the ironmaster, Allan Woodcourt, and of course Esther Summerson. And against widespread dereliction he places the ubiquitous benevolence of Mr. Jarndyce. Since these characters epitomize qualities that Dickens may be taken to recommend, it is a drawback that they are not presented with greater imaginative vitality; Woodcourt, for instance, remaining pale for all his goodness, and the more robust presence of Mr. Jarndyce being a little too benign for ordinary flesh and blood. It is a further drawback that goodness should sometimes appear as the mask of the prig, as all too often in the case of Esther, or of smugness, as in the case of Rouncewell. Dickens, it seems, like so many artists, is more at home in the mud and mire and fog than in the pure empyrean. Nevertheless, the virtue of these characters, especially that of Mr. Jarndyce and Esther, has an important function in the novel.

Mr. Jarndyce is viewed as a kind of natural guardian (as other men are natural athletes), and he is called Guardian not alone by Esther but also by Ada (after Richard's death and at his insistence) and by Esther's children, who "know him by no other name" (p. 877). He is viewed, that is, as performing functions on a personal level that are supposedly fulfilled by institutions (such as Chancery and Parliament) on a national level. Characteristically, he takes responsibility for all the weak and the needy with whom he comes in contact, though the typical object of his attentions (the symbolic object) is the orphan. Thus it is that he successively takes responsibility for Esther, for Ada and Richard, for Charley and Coavinses' other children, and for Jo. And he does so, of course, without in any way neglecting other responsibilities, being strongly differentiated from Mrs. Jellyby, whose assumption of responsibility in regard to the families of those who are to cultivate coffee and educate the natives of Borrioboola-Gha covers a multitude of evasions in regard to her own family; and from Mrs. Pardiggle, who arms herself with uplifting tracts and "[pounces] upon the poor . . . applying benevolence to them like a strait-waistcoat" (p. 423) while their children (as in the case of Jenny's baby) die round her; and he is equally differentiated from Harold Skimpole, who is only "a mere child in the world."

Mr. Jarndyce, moreover, typically helps those in need by enabling them to help themselves. "Trust in nothing but in Providence and your own efforts," he tells Richard (p. 180); and it is in this spirit that he providentially offers his services to others—as in the case of Esther, the representative instance. He is no sooner aware of the predicament of the unknown orphan than he willingly assumes responsibility for her, but with the "expectation" that Conversation Kenge (intimitably) details:

> "Mr. Jarndyce," he pursued, "being aware of the—I would say, desolate—position of our young friend, offers to place her at a first-rate establishment; where her education shall be completed, where her comfort shall be secured, where her reasonable wants shall be anticipated, where she shall be eminently qualified to discharge her duty in that station of life unto which it has pleased—shall I say Providence?—to call her." . . .
>
> "Mr. Jarndyce," he went on, "makes no condition, beyond expressing his expectation that our young friend will not at any time remove herself from the establishment in question without his knowledge and concurrence. That she will faithfully apply herself to the acquisition of those accomplishments, upon the exercise of which she will be ultimately dependent. That she will tread in the paths of virtue and honour, and—the—a—so forth." (pp. 21–2)

What Mr. Jarndyce requires of Esther, we see, is quite simply that she keep faith with him, the expectation (and demonstration) of fidelity being as much a concomitant of the assumption of responsibility as betrayal is shown to be a consequence of its evasion. Having kept faith, Esther is rewarded not only by being given the chance to stand on her own feet but by being delegated her own area of responsibility: on becoming housekeeper at Bleak House, she stands looking at the basket of keys—the keys of office, as it were—with which she has been presented, "quite lost in the magnitude of [her] trust" (p. 68).

Esther consolidates her position at Bleak House, becoming, as Skimpole puts it, "the very touchstone of responsibility":

> "Now when you mention responsibility," he resumed, "I am disposed to say, that I never had the happiness of knowing any one whom I should consider so refreshingly responsible as yourself. You appear to me to be the very touchstone of responsibility. When I see you, my dear Miss Summerson, intent upon the perfect working of the whole little orderly system of which you are the centre, I feel inclined to say to myself—in fact I do say to myself, very often—*that's* responsibility!" (p. 531)

Skimpole's evasive pleasantry should not be taken to invalidate the truth of his description of Esther's position. His account of her achievement, indeed, suggests how central (from yet another point of view) Esther's role in the novel is. If her success at Bleak House (a success which is capped, if not crowned, by Mr. Jarndyce's proposal of marriage to her) sets her as far apart as her social class from Jo, the abandoned orphan of the slums who is lower than a drover's dog; we cannot help reflecting that it is to Tom-all-Alone's—or thereabouts—that she would certainly have gone on the death of Miss Barbary if not for the grace of Mr. Jarndyce. Esther's success (with Mr.

Jarndyce's aid), that is, is meant to be representative of what can be done through a combination of effort and due assumption of responsibility. Moreover, having achieved "the perfect working of the whole little orderly system" of which she is the centre, and having achieved it through assuming responsibility in her turn, Esther also in effect demonstrates what is required for the efficient running of the "great country" and the "great system" of which Conversation Kenge boasts to Mr. Jarndyce, and of which Parliament and Chancery are the centres. Dickens, in other words, far from being a revolutionary, is calling in *Bleak House* for nothing more subversive than a change of housekeepers.

It is now clear, I think, why Dickens hesitated between a variant of Tom-all-Alone's and of Bleak House in choosing his title. Ruin and perfect system, disease and health—the question is which shall be bequeathed to the children of England. The choice of Bleak House as the title, the name of the house redeemed by Mr. Jarndyce from the ravages of Chancery, must be taken to point to the author's faith in the possibility of renovation, to his hope that a Jo, having made his way from Tom-all-Alone's to Bleak House, will find his permanent home there. Such a hope, of course, ignores the presence—even in a Bleak House—of a Skimpole. The Skimpoles remain impervious even to a Jarndyce; they are not willing to keep faith. It is only when Dickens perceives the limitations of Mr. Jarndyce's position, perceives the limits of his redemptive capacity, tht he begins to think in terms of transformation rather than rehabilitation. In the closing pages of the novel we are given some idea of the kind of transformation he will steadily come to evisage: Esther reports that, despite the loss of her "old looks," her husband thinks she is "prettier" than she ever was (p. 880). If it is Mr. Jarndyce's benevolence that counteracts the blight of her childhood, it is Woodcourt's love, we see, that transforms the blight of Chancery.

Notes

1. See, most notably, the analyses of the narrative technique in J. Hillis Miller, *Charles Dickens*, pp. 164, 176–9; W. J. Harvey, "Chance and Design in *Bleak House*," *Dickens and the Twentieth Century*, ed. John Gross and Gabriel Pearson, pp. 147–53; and Morton Dauwen Zabel, "*Bleak House*," *Craft and Character in Modern Fiction* (New York, 1957), pp. 38–40.

2. Edgar Johnson, *Charles Dickens*, II, 764.

3. Dickens is not altogether consistent in his handling of the two narratives. Though Richard's history is throughout traced by Esther in her narrative, the account of one meeting between Richard and Vholes (pp. 547–55) is arbitrarily assigned to the omniscient narrative, it being difficult to justify the departure from a well-defined narrative "area" on the grounds of the narrator's omniscience. This kind of carelessness is also manifest in the way in which Dickens sometimes fails to maintain Esther's distinctive style, lapsing into sudden vividness—as W. J. Harvey has pointed out. See "Chance and Design in *Bleak House*", *loc. cit.*, p. 147.

4. One of the intermittent and paradoxical products of the employment of a mixed point of view is an increased verisimilitude in the area where the narratives overlap. Having become accustomed, for instance, to the way in which the delightful Snagsby is presented by the

omniscient author, it is with a recognition of the kind we experience in real life when we suddenly see someone we know well in a new light that we respond to Esther's view of him toward the end of the novel: "In the passage behind the door, stood a scared, sorrowful-looking little man in a grey coat, who seemed to have a naturally polite manner, and spoke meekly" (p. 805).

5. I am indebted for this suggestion to a student of mine, Mrs. Lillian Reichstein.

6. If we include the deaths (off-stage, so to speak) of Tom Jarndyce and Miss Barbary, there are altogether eleven deaths in the novel: in addition to these two, there are those of Hawdon, the brickmaker's baby, "Coavinses" (Charley's father), Gridley, Krook, Jo, Tulking-horn, Lady Dedlock, and Richard.

7. "Chance and Design in *Bleak House*," *loc. cit.*, pp. 145–6.

8. As does Sir Thomas Doodle, who "comes in" after Lord Coodle has gone out, "bringing in with him all his nephews, all his male cousins, and all his brothers-in-law" (p. 562).

9. "Satire and Symbolism in *Bleak House*," *Nineteenth-Century Fiction*, 12 (March 1958), 300.

10. *Charles Dickens*, II, 771. Dickens himself, in his Preface to the novel, insists on the truth of his account: ". . . I mention here that everything set forth in these pages concerning the Court of Chancery is substantially true, and within the truth" (p. xiii); and John Butt and Kathleen Tillotson quote a passage from *The Times* of 28th March 1851 that lends support to his insistence. See *Dickens at Work*, p. 185.

11. A typically defensive reaction of some of Dickens's contemporaries was both to attempt to localize the attack in this way and to discredit it by asserting its redundance. George H. Ford refers to a review of *Little Dorrit* by Fitzjames Stephen (the elder brother of Leslie Stephen) in 1857, in which Stephen "makes one hit against the social criticism which was to persist among later critics: that Dickens was simply whipping dead horses. He seems . . . to get his first notions of an abuse from the discussions which accompany its removal. . . . This was his course with respect both to imprisonment for debt and to Chancery reform." *Dickens and His Readers*, p. 105. Edgar Johnson quotes Lord Chief Justice Denman's description of the attack on Chancery as "belated and now unnecessary." *Charles Dickens*, II, 760.

12. This effect is strengthened by the repetition of the same image in the first-person narrative: Esther thinks of Jarndyce and Jarndyce as "that blight" (p. 523), this being the typical term used by Mr. Jarndyce as well as Esther to refer to the suit.

13. *Charles Dickens*, Vol. III (London, 1874), pp. 31–2.

14. Another (related) aspect of the retrogressive tendency of this society is pointed to in the description of the churchyard in which Hawdon is buried. "With houses looking on, on every side, save where a reeking little tunnel of a court gives access to the iron gate—with every villainy of life in action close on death, and every poisonous element of death in action close on life—here, they lower our dear brother down a foot or two: here, sow him in corruption, to be raised in corruption: an avenging ghost at many a sick bedside: a shameful testimony to future ages, how civilisation and barbarism walked this boastful island together" (p. 151).

15. See "Dickens: The Two Scrooges," *The Wound and the Bow*, p. 16.

16. See Gordon S. Haight, "Dickens and Lewes on Spontaneous Combustion," *Nineteenth-Century Fiction*, 10 (June 1955), 53–63. Cf. Dickens: "I am very truly obliged to you for the loan of your remarkable and learned Lecture on Spontaneous Combustion; and I am not a little pleased to find myself fortified by such high authority. Before writing that chapter of *Bleak House*, I had looked up all the more famous cases you quote. . . ; but three or four of those you incidentally mention . . . are new to me—and your explanation is so beautifully clear, that I could particularly desire to repeat it several times before I come to the last No. and the Preface. . . .

"It is inconceivable to me how people can reject such evidence, supported by so much familiar knowledge, and such reasonable analogy. But I suppose the long and short of it is, that they don't know, and don't want to know, anything about the matter." Letter to Dr. John

Elliotson, 7.2.1853, *The Letters of Charles Dickens*, ed. Walter Dexter (Bloomsbury, 1938), II, 446–7. See, too) Preface to *Bleak House*, p. xiv.

17. Mark Spilka argues the analogy in all earnestness in *Dickens and Kafka: A Mutual Interpretation* (London, 1963), pp. 215, 218.

18. Nor what a modern critic takes it to be either: Robert Garis considers Dickens's treatment of Lady Dedlock to be "insufficient" and even "rather offensive," but he regards her sin as that of "the woman taken in adultery." See *The Dickens Theatre: A Reassessment of the Novels* (Oxford, 1965), pp. 138–40.

19. Mark Spilka takes the same view. He says Jo's illness "might stem as much from the grave as from the slum," *Dickens and Kafka*, p. 214. J. Hillis Miller seems to think there is no doubt that Jo contracts the disease in the churchyard, but allows for its origin in the slum. He talks of the disease "which is bred in the "poisoned air" . . . of Tom-all-Alone's, and spreads from Nemo's graveyard to Jo the crossing sweeper . . ." *Charles Dickens*, p. 209.

20. *Charles Dickens*, II, 782.

21. *The Maturity of Dickens* (Cambridge, Massachusetts, 1959), p. 122.

22. 'Self-Help and the Helpless in *Bleak House*', *From Jane Austen to Joseph Conrad*, ed. Robert C. Rathburn and Martin Steinmann (Minneapolis, 1958), pp. 97–100.

Will and Society in *Bleak House*   By Joseph I. Fradin*

Lionel Trilling has observed that *Little Dorrit* is "about the will and society" and that "the whole energy of the imagination in the novel is directed toward finding the nonpersonal will in which shall be our peace." Little Dorrit is "not only the Child of the Marshalsea . . . but also the Child of the Parable, the negation of the social will."[1] Professor Trilling's comment, enlightening over a large area of Dickens' work, seems to me especially applicable to the first and most germinal of Dickens' "dark novels," *Bleak House;* and I want here to approach *Bleak House* through Dickens' analysis of will and society.

Like *Little Dorrit*, *Bleak House* is "about" other things, too, and such an approach will involve certain losses. But I know of no single reading or schematization of *Bleak House* which succeeds in yielding all of the novel's riches; and I need, perhaps, say only this: that I am aware that the narrative action, the complex and wonderfully done plot, backed by the full resources of Dickens' genius for satiric comedy and made resonant by a brilliant texture of symbol and allusion, itself compels us toward the novel's meanings; and the plot gets little attention in this essay.[2]

On the other hand, to approach *Bleak House* through the question of "will and society" has, by virtue of the dialectic implied in the question, the immediate sanction of the novel's form: the two separate narratives and the debate between them of which the novel is composed. For what makes the

*Reprinted by permission of the Modern Language Association of America from *PMLA* 81, no. 1 (March 1966): 95–109.

first impact on us is not, after all, a matter of plot but of rhythm, a powerful and insistent beat created by the double narrative technique, the changing back and forth between the impersonal, ironic third person voice and the emotional, committed voice of Esther Summerson.

This rhythm establishes itself immediately and indelibly in the opening chapters. The novel begins in a much-praised passage (its freshness and power remain undimmed) in which Dickens creates in fragmentary strokes a vision of his own

> Unreal City,
> Under the brown fog of a winter dawn

where "chance people on the bridges peep . . . over the parapets into a nether sky of fog, with fog all round them." We move then from the fog and mud, the Megalosaurus-Leviathan, the piles of dead things of Chancery and dying things of Chesney Wold, from the city swallowing lives ("I had not thought death had undone so many") and Lady Dedlock feeling "the faintness of death" upon her to Esther Summerson's doll, armchair, church, and her memories of being brought up "like some of the princesses in the fairy stories" by her godmother, a "good, good woman." Beating steadily through the novel, this rhythm echoes dramatically at its heart, when Esther, having caught a fever originating in the hell of Tom-all-Alone's, becomes blind, and we hear the resigned tones of her acceptance—"and now come and sit beside me . . . touch me with your hand. For I cannot see you, Charlie; I am blind"— followed at once in the next chapter by the somber, angry tones of the third person narrator's vision of night in Lincoln's Inn. And the rhythm is there at the end of the novel, relentless and uncompromising. The third person narrative ends "down in Lincolnshire" at Chesney Wold, where there are "no visitors to be the souls of pale cold shapes of rooms" and "where a maid screams if an ash drops from the fire"; and while that scream, so perfect a concluding sound for the anonymous narrative, is still in our ears, Esther's familiar voice, deepened a bit, perhaps, but still the voice of Chapter Three, concludes, "Full seven happy years I have been the mistress of Bleak House."

In a word, the double narrative technique, which carries the dialectic between self and society, between Esther's subjective vision and the nervous chaos-without-meaning that is the third person world, is not a gratuitous device. (I do not mean that the separation is absolute or perfectly handled. Esther does see the darkness and the suffering, and much of what *we* see comes through her.) It is, rather, the embodiment of the radical dilemma which informs the novel. This is the conflict between intelligence and feeling or, here, between denial and affirmation, where denial has behind it the weight of intellect and dispassionate observation, and affirmation the whole complex of human need, hope, and feeling. The form of *Bleak House*, that is, becomes a metaphor of the divided modern consciousness, and the problem implied by the form is poignantly contemporary. Given: a world which the detached critical intelligence sees as hastening toward disintegration; in which, before tremendous and indifferent forces of cruelty and injustice, the human spirit seems to count for little or nothing, in which social or public action tends to be coercive, and therefore at best ambiguous, at worst evil, given, in short, a world which the twentieth century finds pressing heavily upon itself, to define the condition of the will and the mode of action which will prevent this world from destroying individual moral energy and the impulse toward human engagement.

The "given" in the above scheme is handled with great brilliance; from the beginning the pestilential and decaying world of *Bleak House* powerfully attacks our feelings:

> There . . . is a street of perishing blind houses, with their eyes stoned out; without a pane of glass, without so much as a window-frame, with the bare blank shutters tumbling from their hinges and falling asunder; the iron rails peeling away in flakes of rust; the chimneys sinking in; the stone steps to every door (and every door might be Death's Door) turning stagnant green; the very crutches on which the ruins are propped, decaying. (Ch. viii)

It is a dark world in which children are lost and brutalized; and the innocent are like beasts driven against stone walls:

> The blinded oxen, over-goaded, over-driven, never guided, run into wrong places and are beaten out; and plunge, red-eyed and foaming, at stone walls; and often sorely hurt the innocent, and often sorely hurt themselves. Very like Jo and his order; very, very like! (Ch. xvi)

It is a world in which good men like Richard Carstone or Gridley are caught in the nightmare of Chancery, Gridley fighting blindly for justice, and Richard for something between an impossible justice and debilitating expectations: "But, you know I made a fight for it," the dying Gridley says, "you know I stood up with my single hand against them all, you know I told them the truth to the last, and told them what they were, and what they had done to me" (Ch. xxiv). And Richard's last attempt at the Court leaves us with a frightening Kafkaesque image: "Allan had found him sitting in the corner of the Court . . . like a stone figure. On being roused, he had broken away, and made as if he would have spoken in a fierce voice to the Judge. He was stopped by his mouth being full of blood, and Allan had brought him home" (Ch. lxv).[3]

Only the second of these passages is in the voice of the third person narrator, yet in each of them the very cadences as well as the images seem to hold the echo of larger meanings: Dickens' imagination thrusts the *Bleak House* world beyond the topical,[4] beyond "social criticism," toward a deeply felt vision of the human predicament.

Esther Summerson herself, the chief exemplar of the way to individual salvation, is of course a more difficult matter. Any open-minded reading of *Bleak House* must find Esther unsatisfactory at best and preposterously sweet and self-effacing at her worst. But at the same time no open-minded reader can any longer dismiss her as a merely sentimental indulgence on Dickens' part, and one of the advantages of seeing her against the kind of background I have sketched here is that it enables us to judge more fairly the nature both of the achievement and the failure which Esther represents (we shall return to this later). When we view the novel as the confrontation of Esther's world and the world of the third person narrator, it becomes clear that, whatever Esther's inadequacies, the novel escapes a final sentimentality precisely because the two worlds end as they begin: essentially separate. Although the temptation must surely have been present, there is no specious bridging of the gap, no attempt to impose a false wholeness of view. The debate between the two voices carries, without the genuine possibility of resolution, beyond the conclusion, and the limitations, of the story they tell. Esther's voice runs parallel to the maid's scream at the end of the novel; beyond the narrative itself, the scream, echoing toward us with unmitigated force, becomes the very context of Esther's happy voice. In a word, Esther does not triumph, she merely saves herself. The new Bleak House arises not from the ashes of the old but (metaphorically) beside it and surrounded by the dust of the wasteland. The ending of *Bleak House*, that is, though it cannot call forth so immediately satisfying a response, is not so different in kind from the conclusion of *Little Dorrit*, in which Arthur and Little Dorrit, "inseparable and blessed," go "quietly down into the roaring streets."

All this is not to say that Esther avoids sentimentality. Her unfailingly sunny disposition in adversity, her self-conscious innocence borne all too bravely under the burden of her childhood, her coy modesty as she reflects and transmits the chorus of approval poured on her from all sides—Dame Durden's whole manner offends our sensibilities. We squirm where the Victorians wept. (We continue, I think, to be uncomfortable about Esther even when we are willing to recognize that her need to be loved and to report the praises which are the signs of love is itself one of her scars.)

A good deal of the sentimentality arising from these things, however, is a matter of taste, or of outmoded attitudes and conventions. That is to say, it is, though annoying, superficial. Not altogether so: for not only has the language of feeling radically changed, but Esther's moral vocabulary is no longer our own. Freud has made it impossible for us to believe in uncomplicated human goodness, as science has made it difficult to ground individual goodness, as Esther so easily does, in a purposeful Good. Part of our dissatisfaction with Esther comes about consesquently because Dickens' moral vocabulary is inadequate to express our full sense of ourselves, of our real condition.

But in recognizing the superiority of our moral language, which can probe more subtly and with greater discrimination over a wider range of human experience, we fail, I think, to see how much it has decayed in those areas where Dickens most demands—and justifiably—sympathetic reading. The great and simple words by which men have lived make us self-conscious; when sentiment is attached to them they tend to embarrass us, and they embarrass us especially when they are frankly explicit, as they are in Esther. We have no ready and uninhibited language—Dickens himself had trouble—to describe the kind of positive selflessness that is Esther's. The "good" men in our serious fiction must be ambiguous, at least. Almost always failures, outsiders, rebels against conventional moral standards, they do not convince us unless they bear the visible scars of the struggle against their own natures. (Esther's scarred face is a sign of her involvement in the universal guilt, but we see no internal struggle. Like her goodness, her scars come unearned.) Their vision of the world must be troubled, and it must be embodied in acts of sympathy and love which, since their view of themselves is ambivalent, often come disguised as guilt or sin. But, again, while it may be necessary that our good men be, like the saints of Graham Greene, adulterers, bad priests, thieves, men-of-violence of one kind or another, one may yet wonder if what seems to us the inevitable form of a truth we have painfully discovered may not seem to another generation a convention of our own. I do not wish to argue the point here: it is worth bringing up only to the extent that it may make us more willing to acknowledge the possibility of a genuine moral vocabulary like Esther's even though we are no longer at home in it, in order to allow without uneasiness the large claim that must be made for her. In Esther as in Little Dorrit, Dickens intends to create a central character who draws her goodness and her peace from sources which the world cannot contaminate, a character whose connection with the world, as an expression of her essential nature, is not will but love—in other words a saint.

The hard core of Esther's character lies in the way she reacts to suffering—that is to say, with a calm compassion that comes from her faith and her sense of final purpose, and translates itself spontaneously into duty without the expectation of reward. The obscure guilt which she feels reinforces in principle what she does out of natural kindness; her duty and her love are one.

The novel is full of occasions which bear this out. A minor but memorable moment comes when, on the visit to the bricklayer's, Ada bends down to touch the wife's baby and the child dies (it is one of those moments when the submerged evil flickers to the surface to reinforce the social horror):

> Such compassion, such gentleness, [Esther writes] as that with which she bent down weeping, and put her hand upon the mother's, might have softened any mother's heart that ever beat. The woman at first gazed at her in astonishment, and then burst into tears.
>
> Presently I took the light burden from her lap; did what I could to make the baby's rest the prettier and gentler; laid it on a shelf, and covered it with my own handkerchief. We tried to comfort the mother, and we whispered to her what Our Saviour said of children. She answered nothing, but sat weeping—weeping very much. (Ch. viii)

Ada cries bitterly; Esther participates in the feeling, which then expresses itself in the grace and simplicity of the necessary action.

That this comes from something more than the Dame Durden in her becomes clear when Esther turns her attention away from herself and her relations with people, outward to nature and what lies beyond nature. From the beginning Esther is given the capacity to find beauty where the third person narrator might have found something menacing or lifeless:

> I sat . . . watching the frosty trees, that were like beautiful pieces of spar; and the fields all smooth and white with last night's snow; and the sun, so red but yielding so little heat; and the ice, dark like metal, where the skaters and sliders had brushed the snow away. (Ch. iii)

More dramatically, this is the way Esther sees Chesney Wold:

> O, the solemn woods over which the light and shadow travelled swiftly, as if Heavenly wings were sweeping on benignant errands through the summer air; the smooth green slopes, the glittering water, the garden where the flowers were so symmetrically arranged in clusters of the richest colours, how beautiful they looked! . . . On everything, house, garden, terrace, green slopes, water, old oaks, fern, moss, woods again, and far away across the openings in the prospect, to the distance lying wide before us with a purple bloom upon it, there seemed to be such undisturbed repose. (Ch. xviii)

But perhaps the clearest indication that Esther's vision gets through the chaos seen by the third person narrator to some larger truth or meaning lying beyond it is her description of the storm she sees from the Dedlock's lodge:

> It was grand to see how the wind awoke, and bent the trees, and drove the rain before it like a cloud of smoke; and to hear the solemn thunder, and to see the lightning; and, while thinking with awe of the tremendous powers by which our little lives are encompassed, to consider how beneficent they are, and how upon the smallest flower and leaf there was already a freshness poured from all this seeming rage, which seemed to make creation new again. (Ch. xviii)

Esther's ability to see, as she puts it in another context, "the goodness of all about me" rises above the need for apology in that last sentence.

Esther is, however, a saint who fails, and the chief source of Dickens' failure with her, which becomes also the important source of the sentimentality in *Bleak House*, lies in his inability, within the limits of the conventions available to him (and indeed the larger difficulties of creating a "good" character), to convince us that his belief in the reality of Esther's view carries the same conviction and intensity as his belief in Tom-all-Alone's, Tulkinghorn, Krook's spontaneous combustion, even the Ghost's Walk. There seems to be no real awareness of how inadequate (except at her best, when, indeed, we are not always sure that the voice is entirely her own) Esther's consciousness is to oppose the mind and sensibility of the third person narrator. The split in Dickens' own mind is clear. The result is that Esther's private vision is based on a reality not convincingly grounded in the goodness from which she takes her strength, while Dickens succeeds in grounding the reality of the disintegrating phenomenal world in what we feel is a metaphysical as well as social evil. Put another way: Esther's will does not have a convincing source in some Principle of Good as does the terrible Will which pervades the novel's dark world in some Principle of Evil. The Devil is everywhere in *Bleak House;* since she makes claims which the novel does not render, we have to take Esther's word for God.

The nerve center of the Devil's kingdom (and ultimately the symbol of the kingdom itself) is Chancery, the deadly body of a stagnant and inhuman social will; and, again, to focus on the question of the will points up the perfect appropriateness of Chancery as the central symbol of the novel. Chancery does indeed spread its vicious and suffocating influence throughout society; and as R. A. Donovan, quoting Blackburn, recently pointed out, since the Chancellor had "the general superintendence of all charitable uses in the kingdom" Chancery practice presents us with a paradigm of the ways in which civilized men are responsible for one another, and fail in that responsibility. But Chancery's symbolic rightness goes even beyond these things. The important passage of striking Dickensian rhetoric at the end of the scene in which Guppy and Jobling discover Krook's ashes has often been noted without the full consequences being drawn from it:

> The Lord Chancellor of that Court, true to his title in his last act, has died the death of all Lord Chancellors in all Courts, and of all authorities in all places under all names soever, where false pretences are made, and where injustice is done. Call the death by any name Your Highness will, attribute it to whom you will, or say it might have been prevented how you will, it is the same death eternally—inborn, inbred, engendered in the corrupted humours of the vicious body itself, and that only—Spontaneous Combustion, and none other of all the deaths that can be died. (Ch. xxxii)

I think we may take Dickens altogether seriously here. "The death of all Lord Chancellors in all Courts where false pretences are made, and where injustice is done"—which is to say in all "courts." For the final radical insight in *Bleak House*, an insight which puts the novel at the heart of Dickens' work, is not that Chancery is symbolic of all large social institutions *gone wrong*, but, to a very considerable extent, of all large social institutions (and finally of all life from within the nightmare). Corporate society is what it is because the human will is what it is, and since the supreme achievement of the human will is law, the embodiment of human responsibility and justice and the law in *Bleak House* is Chancery, Chancery-as-symbol takes on a kind of inevitability. This perhaps becomes clearer if we reverse the sequence: What is rotten in Chancery points inevitably to what is ambiguous in the very nature of all corporate insitutions, and this in turn leads to what is ambivalent or destructive in what gives form to those institutions, the human will.

Bleak House would seem to make two statements here about Chancery. The first is clear and explicit, the second felt or inferred, and the second gives the first a special kind of resonance. Chancery, of which Jarndyce vs. Jarndyce is the test case, is life-destroying because its energies go into the perpetuation of itself rather than the protection of the human lives in its care. But this is possible because for the men who exercise power in Chancery the preservation of the self has usurped other ways of public self-expression, particularly the self-fulfillment which comes from the yielding of the will to the community good.

One of the most astonishing things about *Bleak House* is the way Dickens makes us feel the entanglement of the will in the physical and moral underworld of the novel, so that our judgment of the one involves our judgment, or at the very least our sense, of the other. But even more remarkable, especially in a novel whose characters have little or no psychology or inner life, is the way we come to feel the social will's entanglement in darker life-repressing forces not only outside the personality, but within it as well.

Such an idea might at first seem to make too large a claim for *Bleak House,* but once we surrender to the magical connection in Dickens between people and their environment, to his way (a way differing in both intensity and kind from what looks like similar ways in realistic novelists) of externalizing a character's inner life and moral reality, the idea calls up a series of images in its support. There is old Smallweed in his spider's den, "the dark little parlour certain feet below the level of the street," secretly clawing the air "with an impotent vindictiveness expressive of an intense desire to tear . . . the visage of Mr. George" and collapsing "into a shapeless bundle." Mr. Smallweed's relish in sucking the vigorous George's life-blood takes on added meaning when set against Smallweed's characteristic gesture of flinging the pillow at his imbecile wife's head, a gesture of frustrated rage at the limits of his power. There is the death-figure of the lawyer Vholes, buttoned to the chin and with "a red eruption" on his face, who "takes off his close black gloves as if he were skinning his hands" and fixes his eyes on Richard "as if he were looking at his prey and charming it." Or Tulkinghorn, hands clasped tight, closed in upon himself; or again the sick clutter of the Jellyby establishment and the thoroughly beaten Mr. Jellyby, and Mrs. Pardiggle, the oily Chadband in tow, coercing her children into "philanthropy" and out of their childhood; or poor mad Miss Flite waiting for judgment; or Sir Leicester atrophying in a dying Chesney Wold, his energy fixed on conserving the past; or the irresponsible Skimpole, betraying Jo for five pounds and peopling the landscape of his imagination, for his esthetic pleasure, with the black slaves of America.

These images have as their common denominator a disorder in the will, and they trace the general contours of the curve of the will which the novel plots. The point suggested by them is confirmed—indeed deepened—by testing it in an analysis of the "law," the condition of which is the measure of the community good, the community health (or the lack of these), in *Bleak House*.

The law exists on three rhetorical levels. The first of these is the Court of Chancery and its representative, the Lord Chancellor, who inhabits his throne like an ineffective and comic little god. Dickens takes an ironic stance towards the Chancellor and his court, presenting them from a distant view as puny figures caught in, yet perpetuating, the deadly confusion of the law:

> The Lord High Chancellor [sits] with a foggy glory round his head, softly fenced in with crimson cloth and curtains, addressed by a large advocate with great whiskers, a little voice, and an interminable brief. . . . Some score of members of the High Court of Chancery bar . . . are mistily engaged in one of the ten thousand stages of an endless cause. . . . Well may the court be dim, with wasting candles here and there; well may the fog hang heavy in it, as if it would never get out; well may the stained glass windows lose their colour, and admit no light of day into the place; well may the uninitiated from the streets, who peep in through the glass panes in the door, be deterred from entrance by its owlish aspect, and by the drawl languidly echoing to the roof from the padded dais where the Lord High Chancellor looks into the lantern that has no light in it, and where the attendant wigs are all stuck in a fog-bank! This is the Court of Chancery; which has its decaying houses and its blighted lands in every shire; which has its worn-out lunatic in every madhouse, and its dead in every churchyard . . . (Ch. i).

The Chancellor and the lawyers around him are two dimensional, and what goes on in the court itself as we watch it stimulates our risibilities more than our emotions. The High Lord seems less a focus of Dickens' anger than of his intuition that in a world gone so madly wrong the confusions of the political and social life tend to throw into positions of authority though not necessarily power people who have neither the inclination nor the strength to disturb the status quo.

But while Chancery, Parliament, and governmental bureaucracy—the whole matter of Boodle-Coodle-Doodle—remind us of the facts of our political lives, they are it seems to me inadequate even as play or metaphor for the numbing stupidities of our institutions. They are comic reductions without the kind of finality which Dickens sometimes achieves, and which prevents us from asking embarrassing questions. Further, since the Lord Chancellor is so flatly drawn he seems to be a shadow in the landscape of disorder rather than to cast the shadow of evil himself. But while it is quite true that we do not recall the Lord Chancellor very vividly or with very much animus, it is a mistake to allow the mild emotional response which is based on what we see of him in court to blur our moral judgment of him, which must come as the result of seeing him in a larger context. That is, the point of view is, I think, misguided which finds that the Lord Chancellor is "a harmless old gentleman" or that the Court of Chancery, "the main focus of evil in the novel and the mundane equivalent of hell, harbors no devil."[5] To say this is to misjudge the possibilities of the Dickens world, to read Dickens too much as realist, not enough as fantasist, forgetting, in Dorothy Van Ghent's words, that Dickens' world is "nervous throughout" and organized not according to laws "of physical mechanics but of moral dynamics."[6] For when we speak of hell and the devil we are talking surely of a moral reality, and the moral reality of the Lord Chancellor is inseparable from the moral reality of the lawyers in Chancery, above all, Tulkinghorn, and of Krook, who exemplify the second and third levels of the law.

The Lord Chancellor is one of the faces which evil wears, and a full moral vision of him would include, as in a montage, the specter of Krook, much as a full moral vision of Estella in *Great Expectations* includes the specter of Miss Havisham. (Recall the scene in which Pip, watching Estella walking on the barrels in the abandoned storehouse, suddenly finds the girl replaced by a nightmare image of a hanged Miss Havisham.)

At the end of Chapter Two we may leave an affable and sedate Lord Chancellor, but when we next meet him, in his moral aspect, this is how he appears: "He was short, cadaverous, and withered; with his head sunk sideways between his shoulders, and the breath issuing in visible smoke from his mouth, as if he were on fire within. His throat, chin, and eyebrows were so frosted with white hairs, and so gnarled with veins and puckered skin, that he looked from his breast upward, like some old root in a fall of snow." We are of course in the presence of Krook. But, as we are told, Krook is called among the neighbors the Lord Chancellor, his shop the Court of Chancery, and our first sight of him at once tinges Chancery with a new kind of evil: Krook is an image out of a fairy tale, the evil old man or woman who appears suddenly to endanger life and beauty.

Consider the brief scene which follows Miss Flite's announcement about the identity of Krook. Krook replies:

> "It's true enough . . . that they call me the Lord Chancellor, and call my shop Chancery. And why do you think they call me the Lord Chancellor, and my shop Chancery?"
>
> "I don't know, I am sure!" said Richard, rather carelessly.
>
> "You see," said the old man, stopping and turning round, "they—Hi! Here's lovely hair! I have got three sacks of ladies' hair below, but none so beautiful and fine as this. What colour, and what texture!"
>
> "That'll do, my good friend!" said Richard, strongly disapproving of his having drawn one of Ada's tresses through his yellow hand. (Ch. v)

It is curious that the answer to the question of why he is called the Lord Chancellor seems in effect first to be that he has sacks of ladies' tresses below: Krook's Rag-and-Bottle Shop is a place in which life and beauty are imprisoned, converted into commodities. And Krook's caressing Ada's tresses with his yellow hands speaks for itself, though its reverberations grow larger when we remember the dislocation in the sexual lives of the characters in *Bleak House* and the fact that the novel's melodramatic action stems from the sexual sin of Lady Dedlock and Captain Hawdon.

Krook then goes on to explain his reputation:

> "You see I have so many things here . . . of so many kinds, and all as
> the neighbours think (but *they* know nothing), wasting away and going to
> rack and ruin, that that's why they have given me and my place a christen-
> ing. And I have so many old parchmentses and papers in my stock. And I
> have a liking for rust and must and cobwebs. And all's fish that comes to my
> net. And I can't abear to part with anything I once lay hold of . . . or to
> alter anything, or to have any sweeping, nor scouring, nor cleaning, nor
> repairing going on about me. That's the way I've got the ill name of
> Chancery."

Then we find out that Krook has a cat, and no ordinary cat. Esther watches
her leap down from Krook's shoulder and rip "at a bundle of rags with her
tigerish claws"; and Miss Flite says that the cat, "sly, and full of malice," has
"her natural cruelty . . . sharpened by a jealous fear" that Miss Flite's birds
will regain their liberty.

By this time it must be clear that we are in a witch's cave or devil's lair,
and we are prepared for the striking effect Dickens achieves in the climactic
moment when the illiterate Krook "writes" for Esther, gleefully spelling out
the words BLEAK HOUSE and JARNDYCE, "beginning at the ends and
bottoms of the letters . . . without once leaving two letters on the wall
together."

The moment generates something of the atmosphere of black magic, of
the primitive idea that to control a man's name or his image is to control his
fate. And indeed the lives of Jarndyce, Richard, Ada, Gridley, Miss Flite
(and more or less directly those of everyone else of importance) are determined by the Chancery documents which possess their names. In the world
of *Bleak House* it is in fact true that to have one's name written down is to
find one's life cursed, delivered inevitably up to social evil. But Krook's shop
very early in the novel helps us to extend our sense of this evil, to see that it
goes deeper than the social. Krook's writing is to the lives of those connected
to Jarndyce vs. Jarndyce as the documents in the cellar of Chancery are to
the lives in Chancery. The old man's ominous spelling out of Jarndyce and
Bleak House and the relish he takes in the sense of power it gives him,
suggest a larger, more irrational doom than the selfish bumbling of mere
social man can be the cause of. And if, lacking Dickens' childlike vision, we
are willing to bring to the novel the kind of energy Dickens requires of us, so
that we see Krook's Shop not simply as exuberant "local color" or even as an
analogue or parody of Chancery, but in a magical way as Chancery itself, we
feel in Krook's writing as in his shop generally a malignant control over
events of the novel, a control rooted in an evil which becomes metaphysical.

The central importance of the Rag-and-Bottle Shop on both narrative
and symbolical levels reinforces the point I have been making here. A collection of dusty and useless things, the record of broken lives and lost youth,
beauty, and hope, Krook's Shop like the Court of Chancery symbolizes the

power for death of institutions. The emotional force as well as the moral meaning of the stacks of Court records in the cellars of Chancery, for example, is deepened not only by the piles of papers, but also by the sacks of ladies' hair downstairs at Krook's. Like Chancery again, Krook's Shop spreads tentacles that bring together all levels of society in their grasp; it is the diseased source from which much of the crucial action flows. From the shop's premises comes the affidavit copy which first puts Tulkinghorn on the track of Lady Dedlock's lover, Captain Hawdon; from the shop comes the collection of letters which ultimately brings that haughty Lady to the squalid cemetery where her lover lies; from the shop, finally, comes the will which fruitlessly ends Jarndyce vs. Jarndyce. And the climactic way in which Krook and his shop, as symbol, condition our response to Chancery and shape our feelings about it is brilliantly made clear in the famous scene of the spontaneous combustion.

The combustion has troubled some readers who, embarrassed both by the event and by Dickens' defense, tend to ignore or reduce it to "pure symbol." But, like all of Dickens' great symbols, the spontaneous combustion has a rich and independent life of its own before it functions as symbol. Coming to us from an imagination so powerful and so pressing in the demands it made on Dickens that it sometimes passed over into will, Krook's combustion is inescapable precisely because it gets to our senses before it gets to our minds. Here is Mr. Guppy, discovering Krook's oil on his hands:

> Mr. Guppy sitting on the window-sill . . . continues thoughtfully to tap it, and clasp it, and measure it with his hand, until he hastily draws his hand away.
>
> "What, in the Devil's name," he says, "is this! Look at my fingers!"
>
> A thick, yellow liquor defiles them, which is offensive to the touch and sight and more offensive to the smell. A stagnant, sickening oil, with some natural repulsion in it that makes them both shudder.
>
> "What have you been doing here? What have you been pouring out of window?"
>
> "I pouring out of window! Nothing, I swear! Never, since I have been here!" cries the lodger.
>
> And yet look here—and look here! When he brings the candle, here, from the corner of the window-sill, it slowly drips, and creeps away down the bricks; here, lies in a little thick nauseous pool.
>
> "This is a horrible house," says Mr. Guppy, shutting down the window. "Give me some water, or I shall cut my hand off."
>
> He so washes, and rubs, and scrubs, and smells and washes . . . (Ch. xxxii)

Krook's oil clings to our fingers as it does to Guppy's, and the impulse to wipe our hands on ours sides, to cleanse ourselves of the horrifying Krook-become-oil, forces the moment to take on moral overtones even before we remember that Krook is the Lord Chancellor, the representative of the law, and that the law is symbolic in *Bleak House* of all life-destroying institutions, in whose guilt we participate and whose evil we share. The symbolic work which Krook's death must do has been largely accomplished in our bones before it becomes abstract, before Dickens spells out Krook's symbolical meaning in the rhetorical flourish with which the chapter ends. Consequently, this passage, intended to arouse us not only to the point of the spontaneous combustion but also to the kind of moral anger Dickens expects us to feel, is to a considerable extent superfluous, however effective it may also be.

And yet, though Krook may arouse physical and moral disgust, he does not fully engage our feelings. He does not stimulate fear; he is himself too much a helpless victim, though a malignant one, and perhaps too easily a fairy-tale figure to seem really dangerous. Moreover, while we recognize that Krook is an image out of that profound but murky sea where archetypes find their form and take their power, we are forced, lacking the vision of the child or the primitive, and deeply distrustful of an event which violates scientific probability, to deal with him not on the level of intuitive feeling, where he more properly belongs, but on the level of intellect. The result is that Krook is inevitably made abstract and thus attenuated.

But between Krook and the Lord Chancellor in Chancery there stands a figure about whom we have no such difficulty. The lawyer Tulkinghorn's particular malevolence comes in forms only too familiar to us, and a closer examination of him will throw light on the kind of statement Dickens is making about the human will in *Bleak House*.

Among the first things one *feels* about Tulkinghorn is that, though he is at once the most vicious and familiar embodiment of the *human* evil at work in the novel, he is not sufficiently motivated. It is in fact only partially true that he is insufficiently motivated, but that he should seem to be so is fully consistent with Dickens' intention and his accomplishment. For when Tulkinghorn acts, we ask of him the same question we ask of Vholes or Smallweed: no so much what his motives are, but what he tells us of the nature of the world in which humans act as he does. We are interested less in the configuration of his character than in what he images of the social and metaphysical environment which gives birth to him. This is, in part, a way of saying again that Dickens, though he had considerable psychological sophistication, was often less interested in conveying the complex psychological reality of his characters than in conveying their moral reality. And like a fairy tale's, his morality is usually of a profoundly simple kind. To look for psychological motives, so that our adult sense of character may be satisfied, becomes as unnecessary in Tulkinghorn as in the witch of a fairy tale. A witch with human motivation would cease to be a witch; Tulkinghorn, neatly motivated, would add little to what we need to know about him and would become less ominous. The crucial thing to accept, despite our commitment by habit and choice to psychology and realism, is that an act by Tulkinghorn is intended to point less to a specific impulse within him than to a generalized evil of which he is but the sign. There cannot be a one-to-one correspondence between motive and act in him because he is the top of the iceberg, a point of viciousness thrown up by the vast weight of evil underlying the novel. In a world alive with this evil, the final answer to the question of why Tulkinghorn acts as he does would seem to be the same as the answer to the question asked about a witch: Evil exists.

Very much the same sort of thing may also be said about Krook, and that indeed helps us to understand Tulkinghorn. But I do not mean to suggest that they are the same kind of character or that they make similar impacts on our consciousness. Neither Krook, who conveys a sense of the demoniacal, nor the Lord Chancellor, who makes us feel the hopeless futility of Chancery, becomes a focus of our anger or our fear. Tulkinghorn does, and that he does seems to me very suggestive, for despite everything I have said of him, the main outlines of his psychological motivation are quite clear; and since he has a larger human reality than his colleagues, his personality yields some definition of one of the sources of human evil in the novel.

In a typically Dickensian way, Tulkinghorn's physical surroundings mirror his psychic reality. His office is among the most stifling of the many stifling interiors in *Bleak House:* "A thick and dingy Turkey-carpet muffles the floor where he sits, attended by two candles in old-fashioned silver candlesticks, that give a very insufficient light to his large room. The titles on the backs of his books have retired into the binding; everything that can have a lock has got one; no key is visible" (Ch.x). Here, like a "maggot in a nut," he lives, this "Oyster of the old school, whom nobody can open," as locked up and muffled as his surroundings. Like Chancery and Krook, he, too, has his papers (few collections of paper can be innocent in *Bleak House*): records and secrets in boxes "labelled with transcendent names" of "the great ones of the earth [who] are bored to death." These are the source of much of his sense of himself; they are signs of his power and a measure of his life hoard. "He is indifferent to everything but his calling," Lady Dedlock says of him. "His calling is the acquisition of secrets, and the holding possession of such power as they give him, with no sharer or opponent in it" (Ch. xxxvi). In a word, Tulkinghorn is a monstrous embodiment of the will to power: "The red bit, the black bit, the inkstand top, the other inkstand top, the little sand-box. So! You to the middle, you to the right, you to the left" (Ch. x). He maneuvers people as he maneuvers bits of wax. Always evident, his need to do so has a particular resonance in his relations with women: The special relish he takes in humbling Lady Dedlock is clear. Her pride and indifference—but also her beauty—enrage and stimulate him: "It may be that he pursues her doggedly and steadily, with no touch of compunction, remorse, or pity. It may be that her beauty, and all the state and brilliancy surrounding her, only gives him the greater zest for what he is set upon, and makes him the more inflexible in it" (Ch. xxix).

After obliquely informing Lady Dedlock that he knows her secret, he returns to his turret-room with "a rather increased sense of power upon him, as he loosely grasps one of his veinous wrists with his other hand" (Ch. xli); and in the scene which follows he makes his feelings about women explicit. "My experience teaches me," he says to Lady Dedlock, "that most of the people I know would do far better to leave marriage alone. It is at the bottom of three-fourths of their troubles" (Ch. xli). On two other occasions he reveals similar feelings: "There are women enough in the world, Mr. Tulkinghorn thinks—too many; they are at the bottom of all that goes wrong in it" (Ch. xvi); and again, "These women were created to give trouble, the whole earth over" (Ch. xlii). I am not suggesting that we try to explain Tulkinghorn in facile psychological terms, but I see no reason to refuse to recognize an insight which Dickens seems to have achieved here: Tulkinghorn's will to power has its roots in his denial of the sexual life.

As the relentless pursuer of Lady Dedlock and the instigator of the series of actions and discoveries which bring Esther and her dead mother together before Nemo's pauper grave, Tulkinghorn is the chief villain of the novel, and it is hardly surprising that he should act out of unhealthy motives. But my point is that his disease is in a general way the disease of the community, "inbred in the body itself." For Tulkinghorn is the man who most exactly understands the conditions of successful public or institutional life and who has made the most perfect adaptation to them, an adaptation which has dried up all human warmth, spontaneity, and feeling. By the time we meet him his place is so firmly established that we do not see him act from economic or social motives but only to satisfy his power lust, his self. Consequently we are made to connect public place with some terrible growth in the will and to recognize that the repression and the distortion of the personality we feel in Tulkinghorn is the necessary condition of his success in the world.

But what gives Tulkinghorn his power is also the thing that kills him. Just as Krook is spontaneously combusted by his inner corruption (and "Chancery" is in danger of blowing up from its internal tensions) so Tulkinghorn is destroyed by his own rottenness. I say this in full awareness that the lawyer is killed by a bullet fired by Hortense, Lady Dedlock's violent-tempered maid, and that the murder serves the melodramatic necessities of the plot. But it seems to me that Dickens invites us to find meaning and a warning in Tulkinghorn's death just as he does in Krook's. Hortense murders Tulkinghorn because, in the scene in which she flings the two guineas he pays her into the corner, he has crushed her will, violated her sense of herself. Tulkinghorn's will to power, that is, here connected with his attitude toward women, leads to his death. But we may go further. The figure of Allegory, with "cheeks like peaches, and knees like bunches of blossoms" seems too much insisted upon to be only a melodramatic device to keep up suspense by pointing the finger of doom at Tulkinghorn: it points as well to an "allegorical" meaning in the lawyer's death. As Tulkinghorn is all restraint, Hortense is all frustrated passion and unrestraint; she is the destructive dimension of what is repressed in Tulkinghorn's personality. "Alle-

gorically," Tulkinghorn is killed by what he represses, the emotional, instinc-
tual part of his nature.

The particular point need not be pressed, but what I am trying to
establish about Tulkinghorn is perhaps of enough significance for the novel
as a whole to justify briefly examining one further detail of the lawyer's
portrait. It is a commonplace of *Bleak House* criticism that Dickens has
surrounded the characters on the dark side of the novel with images of decay
and sterility. There is, however, one substantial exception to this, one lively
or life-bearing image associated with one of the dark figures—the precious
port which Tulkinghorn keeps in the cellar below his chambers. Like Allegory, the wine forces itself upon our attention. Tulkinghorn drinks it after
Hortense leaves his chambers; he is drinking it when he is murdered; he is
drinking it in the key scene in which he puts the detective on Lady
Dedlock's trail. In this scene the wine is given a striking introduction:

> In his lowering magazine of dust, the universal article into which his
> papers and himself, and all his clients, and all things of earth, animate and
> inanimate, are resolving, Mr. Tulkinghorn sits at one of the open windows,
> enjoying a bottle of old port. Though a hardgrained man, close, dry, and
> silent, he can enjoy old wine with the best. He has a priceless binn of port
> in some artful cellar under the Fields, which is one of his many secrets.
> When he dines alone in chambers, as he has dined to-day, and has his bit
> of fish and his steak or chicken brought in from the coffee-house, he
> descends with a candle to the echoing regions below the deserted mansion,
> and, heralded by a remote reverberation of thundering doors, comes
> gravely back, encircled by an earthy atmosphere, and carrying a bottle
> from which he pours a radiant nectar, two score and ten years old, that
> blushes in the glass to find itself so famous, and fills the whole room with
> the fragrance of southern grapes. (Ch. xxii)

The change in diction and rhythm in the last sentence would seem to confirm
the separation of the wine from the rest of Tulkinghorn's life: the port is the
lawyer's only indulgence in the life of the senses. And, this being true, I
should like to suggest that the nectar, "radiant," "blushing," "fragrant"—in a
word, feminine—is a surrogate for woman, and that the "binn" of port is
analogous to the sacks of ladies' tresses (recall, too, Krook's caressing of Ada's
beautiful hair) downstairs in Krook's Shop.

It is worth noting that in the paragraph which follows, we get a rare
glimpse of Tulkinghorn's inner life, and it is the port which gives us the
opening: Tulkinghorn sits pondering

> on all the mysteries he knows, associated with darkening woods in the
> country, and vast blank shut-up houses in town: and perhaps sparing a
> thought or two for himself, and his family history, and his money, and his
> will—all a mystery to every one—and that one bachelor friend of his, a
> man of the same mould and a lawyer too, who lived the same kind of life
> until he was seventy-five years old, and then, suddenly conceiving (as it is
> supposed) an impression that it was too monotonous, gave his gold watch to

his hairdresser one summer evening, and walked leisurely home to the
Temple, and hanged himself.

At the moment which comes closest to revealing something of the man
beneath the machine, the wine leads Tulkinghorn to an implicit analogy
between himself and the bachelor friend who hanged himself—a momentary
awareness of the fruitlessness of his life in which we sense another echo of
Tulkinghorn's "allegorical" meaning. Furthermore, in the rest of the scene
involving Tulkinghorn, Snagsby, and Bucket, the lawyer degrades the wine
by using it to maneuver and manipulate Snagsby. He plies his victim with
glasses of port, and the already weak stationer, further softened by Tulkinghorn's condescension, is then played upon by Bucket and, in a brilliant
Dickensian stroke, seems metaphorically transformed into the hat which
Bucket returns to him, "quite as intimate with it as if he had made it," as
indeed Bucket has made Snagsby into the puppet which Tulkinghorn and he
require. The lawyer and the detective are here committing (the whole scene
conveys this) the cardinal sin of the Dickens world—treating people as
things, that is, making the connection to fellow human beings not sympathy
or love, but will.

In so doing, Bucket, who—though in a less obvious way than, say,
Wemmick in *Great Expectations*—is split between his public and private
selves, confirms a corollary principle of *Bleak House,* which is to a considerable extent a principle of Dickens' novels generally: the strong male personality has few public outlets for its energy which do not distort it. Masculine
strength at the service of the will is usually evil, as in Tulkinghorn, or at best
ambiguous, as in Bucket ("angel and devil by turns," he says of himself); and
masculine strength at the service of the feelings, while admirable, has little
work that it seems able to do publicly. Private benevolence tends to become,
publicly, philanthropy, and philanthropy in *Bleak House* is the very type of
right human impulse become corrupt in public action. Like Chancery, Philanthropy thus takes on a kind of inevitability, becoming more than a part of
the theme of irresponsibility, more than a topical expression of Dickens' very
real anger at public charity. It is as if the novelist were saying, "Let us take
one of the most noble of human impulses, benevolence, and see what happens even to it when it expresses itself in public forms and institutions."

What happens is, of course, that philanthropy becomes Mrs. Jellyby
and Mr. Chadband, Caddy's maimed child, and the dead Jo—and gathers
around itself a host of evil connotations. It becomes a sign of the disease of
the society and, as it were, the context of a further sign of the disease: that
the good men in *Bleak House,* few of whom are strong, can do little public
good. Most of the good male characters, strong and weak, are in one way or
another ineffectual, not to say unmanned: Snagsby, Mr. Jellyby, Jarndyce,
Boythorn, George, Bagnet. They are unwilling victims of domineering
wives, like Snagsby, and Jellyby, or willing yielders-up of male authority like
Bagnet, or bachelor doers-of-good in a small way, like George, Boythorn,

and Jarndyce. Jellby leaves a mark on the wall where, broken-willed, he rests his head; Snagsby, caught in the Chancery works, fearfully sneaks shillings to Jo. George keeps a shooting gallery, his soldier friend Bagnet a music shop. Falling somewhere between art and entertainment, both activities are as little commercial and as little involved in the real life of the community as possible. Bagnet turns over to his wife whatever labor the "world" requires; George, sucked into the whirlpool, is saved from it through no efforts of his own, and wisely refuses to join his brother's factory, since the old soldier is as aware as we are that the larger world has no place for him. Significantly, he returns to Chesney Wold and the "family." Jarndyce's wisdom essentially consists of his knowledge that to ask questions of justice of the system, to join battle with Chancery, is to be destroyed by it. Accomplishing even his acts of private charity anonymously whenever possible, he moves always toward disengagement from the public realm, withdrawal to the family hearth. His final gesture, bestowing a new Bleak House on Esther and Woodcourt, is in some sense the symbolic expression of what the world has taught him.

Perhaps the points I am trying to establish about, first, the limited way in which masculine strength can express itself in *Bleak House,* which is finally a point about the giving up of the social will, and, second, the ambiguity involved in all forceful public action, can best be clarified by examining two characters who have an obvious vigor: Jarndyce's friend Boythorn and a man who would seem to be the exception to most of what I have been saying, the manufacturer Rouncewell.

Boythorn is paired with, and measured against, Jarndyce's other old friend, Skimpole. (That Dickens had Landor and Leigh Hunt in mind when drawing the two characters seems of little importance here.) It is a sign of Boythorn's rightness that he dislikes Skimpole so intensely; and he is very far from Skimpole in the scale of our feelings and in the scale of values of the novel. Morally, they are poles apart. But on the curve of the will, though they face in opposite directions, they are very close together, and it is this which makes the comparison enlightening.

Both are children, Boythorn, the thorny boy, and Skimpole, the child of May. Both measure their experience by and through their feelings. Neither has predatory instincts. But Skimpole's development has never got beyond the stage in which, in George Eliot's phrase, we take the world as "an udder to feed our supreme selves." As esthete and dilettante, he is without will only as a child who has not yet made a real distinction between self and other, who has not yet learned to make moral judgments, is without will, which is to say that he is full of will in the most primary sense, though his will does not take the adult forms of ambition and aggression. Still, his position begins in something to which, within the terms of the novel, we can give assent: The idea that if the world is as the third person narrator sees it, the sanest course for a man of sensibility is withdrawal, giving up the will to place and power in favor of the private feelings. Such a point of view is inadequate, but, given some of the alternatives in *Bleak House,* it is one with which we can find some sympathy. But what is charmingly irresponsible becomes morally corrupt. Our final judgment of Skimpole must be shaped by his betrayal of Jo and by his relentless feeding upon Richard Carstone, even though Richard is being consumed by Jarndyce vs. Jarndyce. Skimpole thus points up more than the inadequacy of the esthetic point of view. In a world which requires moral commitment Skimpole shows us *how not to do it;* he becomes a despicable parody of the negation of the social will.

Boythorn, on the other hand, is generous, morally responsible, and sensitive to every kind of injustice, to which he reacts with violence. He is in fact so full of energy in his reactions that we are apt to forget to ask whether he really acts. Is not his violence verbal, his reaction a kind of ritualistic game? Boythorn's boisterousness and bluster, his damning all the trivial uses of the world equally to everlasting hell, reduces everything to a kind of high-spirited play which draws off the energy for which the will finds no fit object in the world. His elaborate feud with Sir Leicester is, ironically, as sure a sign of his denial of the social will as the canary on his arm is of his softheart-edness. Though Boythorn has brought actions against Sir Leicester, the real feud is conducted on their private preserve, where the form of the battle can establish the principle involved. The feud becomes a kind of metaphor, existing in some sense on the same level as Boythorn's angry words. It does not get beyond the control of individual action, so that when Sir Leicester has fallen under the blow of Lady Dedlock's guilt and death, Boythorn can suspend the abstract principle of right as he sees it in favor of concrete human sympathy for a fellow sufferer.

Boythorn withdraws originally because of a personal injury for which Lady Dedlock is indirectly responsible; but, as his constant anger suggests, the cause of his retirement comes finally to exist not only in the events of his private life but in the conditions in the world around him. In an eccentric way, he defines the limits of the possibilities for action of the good man.

What, then, about the ironmonger, Rouncewell, the "heroic self-made industrialist," as he has been called? Clearly we are intended to admire him;[7] he is a man of manifest virtues. But from the beginning we are not permitted to like him very much, and the reason for this becomes apparent in the scene in which the manufacturer and the Dedlocks discuss the possible marriage of Rouncewell's son and Lady Dedlock's maid, Rosa. In a "modest clear way" (Dickens always gives him his due) Rouncewell develops his argument:

> "A son will sometimes make it known to his father that he has fallen in love, say with a young woman in the factory. The father, who once worked in a factory himself, will be a little disappointed at first, very possibly. It may be that he had other views for his son. However, the chances are, that having ascertained the young woman to be of unblemished character, he will say to his son, 'I must be quite sure you are in earnest here. This is a serious matter for both of you. Therefore I shall have this girl educated for two years'—or, it may be—'I shall place this girl at the same school with

your sisters for such a time, during which you will give me your word and honour to see her only so often. If, at the expiration of that time, when she has so far profited by her advantages as that you may be upon a fair equality, you are both in the same mind, I will do my part to make you happy.' I know of several cases such as I describe, my Lady, and I think they indicate to me my own course now." (Ch. xxviii)

The speech severely qualifies our admiration for the liberal good sense which in part inspires it. It is too calculating for a matter of love, the girl too much like some worthwhile but flawed raw material that the manufacturer's skill may yet refine into something profitable. The virtues that Rouncewell sees are too few in the maid, too many in the manufacturing process.

And when, at the end of the novel, Trooper George goes to the iron country and we see Rouncewell in the world he has helped to make, it is impossible not to feel uneasy about him. For George, "journeying . . . north to look about him," discovers a country which has no room for a man of soft ambitions who loves birds, a country which bears everywhere the cost of "steel and iron": "coalpits and ashes, high chimneys and red bricks, blighted verdure, scorching fires, and a heavy never-lightening cloud of smoke, become the features of the scenery." Having asked directions of a workman along the way, George (his journey seems naturally to fall into the rhythms of the quest)

> comes to a gateway in the brick wall, looks in, and sees a great perplexity of iron lying about, in every stage, and in a vast variety of shapes; in bars, in wedges, in sheets; in tanks, in boilers, in axles, in wheels, in cogs, in cranks, in rails; twisted and wrenched into eccentric and perverse forms, as separate parts of machinery; mountains of it broken-up, and rusty in its age; distant furnaces of it glowing and bubbling in its youth; bright fireworks of it showering about, under the blows of the steam hammer; redhot iron, white-hot iron, cold-black iron; an iron taste, an iron smell, and a Babel of iron sounds. (Ch. lxiii)

From here George is conducted by young Rouncewell to his father's office, bare and full of iron dust, and, when the manufacturer enters, takes "a rusty chair."

Rouncewell then gives George a generous welcome, "more than brotherly" and full of feeling. But by that time, much as we may approve of the private man and his conduct, Rouncewell cannot escape his context, the consequences of his public function as manufacturer. Behind George's journey through the iron country lies the larger wasteland of the novel with the full force of its imagery, rhythm, and social fact.

The blighted landscape of London hovers in the ruined countryside, whose smoke must bear for us some of the moral smell of London's smoke and fog. The list of metal shapes, the "great perplexity of iron" echoes like the restatement of a theme, calling up again Krook's Rag-and-Bottle Shop with its "blacking bottles, medicine bottles, ginger-beer and soda-water bottles, pickle bottles, wine bottles, ink bottles"; and Snagsby, the Law-stationer's: "all sorts of blank forms of legal process; in skins and rolls of parchment; in paper—foolscap, brief, draft, brown, white, whitey-brown, and blotting; in stamps; in office-quills, pens, ink, India-rubber, pounce, pins, pencils, sealing-wax, and wafers; in red tape and green ferret" (Ch. x). And the Jellybys': "bits of mouldy pie, sour bottles, Mrs. Jellyby's caps, letters, tea, forks, odd boots and shoes of children, firewood, wafers, saucepan-lids, damp sugar in odds and ends of paper bags, foot-stools, blacklead brushes, bread" (Ch. xxx). Rouncewell's iron cannot escape the implications of other accumulations of dead or life-destroying things.

So that when George chooses to return to the moribund Sir Leicester's service, our sympathies must be on his side; and his brother, though disappointed, must acquiesce, even expressing some doubt about himself: "You know youself, George, and perhaps you know me better than I know myself." It is a doubt which Dickens seems to have shared, for Rouncewell never fulfills the promise that somehow clings to his name as the one potentially effective force for social order in *Bleak House*. He is, indeed, Dickens' "good" industrialist, but he is so almost in spite of his public function (he has—wisely—refused to stand for Parliament). He is admirable as a man of character; he does nothing particularly admirable as a manufacturer; he was not born to set these times right. It is not only that there must be some suspicion that to run a successful factory the ironmonger must maneuver and coerce men as well things, not only that Rouncewell, unlike him as he may be, must share some of Bounderby's values. It goes deeper than that. The man of will who by strength, energy, and intelligence shapes his environment into a productive and progressive order: the world of *Bleak House* would seem to await some such redeemer of the chaos. But by the disclosures it makes about its essential nature, by the very terms of its existence, that world makes such a hero impossible. Even offscene, in the iron country where none of the significant action takes place, Rouncewell remains an uncertain value in the novel. For belief in the efficacy of heroic social action requires faith in the capacity of the human will to challenge and defeat evil, in such a way that the defeat will bring about not only individual salvation but also the restoration, or at least the possibility, of moral renewal, of the society as a whole. But as we have seen, there is no faith in *Bleak House* in the capacity of the will for redemptive public action. The novel everywhere demonstrates that the world must destroy or spoil the man who pits his will against the maddening and inhuman forces which oppose him.

Hence Esther Summerson; and since what I am insisting upon is that her mode of action (as distinct from the way she talks about her actions—her manner) is determined not merely by her character but by requirements which the novel itself otherwise generates, it might be appropriate to note again that she is called "summer-sun," that she is in fact keeper of the keys and a bringer of order, warmth, and life. Wherever Esther is, Jarndyce remarks, there is "sunshine and summer air"; and Ada says of her friend's activities at the Jellybys' that it "rained Esther." That is, *Bleak House* implies a contrast between Esther—the irony is not at her expense—and the archetypal hero who, succeeding in his quest, confirms his own masculine valor and will and frees the land of the death which is upon it. (I find it suggestive that *Bleak House* has the dialectical structure of archetypal romance, in which, in Northrop Frye's words, "the enemy is associated with winter, darkness, confusion, sterility, moribund life, and old age, and the hero with spring, dawn, order, fertility, vigor, and youth";[8] though Dickens' novel is of course a parody of romance.) But, unlike the hero, Esther can do no more than brighten the corner where she is. Her actions are all individual encounters between her goodness and others' need; perfect in being selfless and self-contained, they carry no larger hope in them, no hope that Esther or anyone else can restore the sun to the blighted landscape or halt the drift toward fragmentation.

Though there will be no moral or political renewal of the community, Esther herself does change—not in purpose or action but in the extent and quality of her awareness. Discovering the nature of her involvement in guilt, she learns to act not merely out of an instinctive goodness, but with knowledge, which is to choose to act. In a word, she undergoes a ritual journey during which she reaffirms in experience her natural impulse to act out of love.

Esther's psychological journey is not satisfactorily rendered, but one can quickly sense Dickens' impulse to render it[9] by recalling Esther's dreams, moments when her manner is least likely to blur her deeper consciousness. The first (not fully a dream) comes early in the novel, at the Jellybys', when Esther begins to fall asleep with Caddy's head in her lap. "I began to lose the identity of the sleeper resting on me. Now it was Ada; now, one of my old Reading friends from whom I could not believe I had so recently parted. Now it was the little mad woman worn out with curtseying and smiling; now, some one in authority at Bleak House. Lastly, it was no one, and I was no one" (Ch. iv). Torn from her childhood, and encountering the first of the world's victims, Caddy and Miss Flite, Esther confirms her need to define her relationship to herself and to the community, to establish her identity.

What this self-identification involves in the inner landscape is rendered by two perfect nightmare images at the nadir of Esther's journey, when she is blind and stricken with fever. "I laboured up colossal staircases," she writes, "ever striving to reach the top, and ever turned, as I have seen a worm in a garden path, by some obstruction, and labouring again":

> Dare I hint at the worse time when, strung together somewhere in great black space, there was a flaming necklace, or ring, or starry circle of some kind, of which *I* was one of the beads! And when my only prayer was to be taken off from the rest, and when it was such inexplicable agony and misery to be a part of the dreadful thing? (Ch. xxxv)

These are Esther's dark night of the soul, from which she emerges to labor up the staircases of her real life. Recovering from her illness in Lincolnshire, she learns who her mother is and, knowing this, must renew her sense of her own innocence and of some larger purpose working through her ("I saw very well how many things had worked together, for my welfare. . . . I knew I was as innocent of my birth as a queen of hers . . . I renewed my resolutions . . . feeling that the darkness of the morning was passing away" [Ch. xxxvi]). She must again conquer her impulse to hide her scars, to withdraw, weakly symbolized by her fear of being seen by Ada; and in embracing and uncovering the face of her dead mother before her father's grave, she must at once embrace her birth and leave it behind her.

This is the end of Esther's psychological journey, and in the confused and dreamlike pursuit of Lady Dedlock ("I was far from sure that I was not in a dream," Esther writes [Ch. lvii]) with its thawing snow and the rushing energy of the horses, one feels an analogue of the final release in Esther's personality, a release which, once she has recovered from the illness that follows (absorbed the effects of that release?), prepares her for her proper marriage.

The degree to which Woodcourt is indeed the right mate for Esther is, I think, worth noting. He is a doctor, which means, since he is a good man, that his function as citizen and his responsibility as a feeling human being can express themselves identically in the act of healing which is at once the measure of what he does professionally and what he is morally. Like Esther's, his duty and his benevolence are one. Moreover, as a doctor he can—as he must—do a man's work in the world without committing himself to the world's deadly institutions. He remains very much a private actor, his commitment to his fellowmen being always individual and personal. Like Esther's, again, his acts of charity are one-to-one encounters between his skill and kindness and others' suffering; like her, he has no will to place or power.

Though Woodcourt does not commit himself to the affairs of the world, Dickens by a happy instinct seems to have sensed the necessity of Esther's husband's having to win his spurs, and it is significant that he does so off stage. While Esther is recovering from her illness, her initiation, she learns from Miss Flite that Woodcourt has undergone a baptism at sea in a "terrible shipwreck." In "fire, storm, and darkness," Miss Flite says, "my dear physician was a hero" (Ch. xxxv). What begins in the requirements of the plot, since Woodcourt must be temporarily gotten off scene, becomes symbolically appropriate.

What is at stake here is Dickens' awareness of the struggles within the self in its initiation into the realities of our public and private lives—a not very extravagant claim, it seems to me, when we set Esther's in the context of other symbolic moments of death and rebirth in the novels which follow *Bleak House*. In *Little Dorrit*, for example, Arthur Clennam, dying in prison under the weight of the guilt of the House of Clennam, is nursed back to life by Little Dorrit; in *Great Expectations*, Pip is burned in saving the life of

Miss Havisham (he and Miss Havisham having first forgiven and blessed each other) and later suffers a long fever, during which he often loses his reason and has nightmares like Esther's: "I was a steel beam of a vast engine, clashing and whirling over a gulf, and yet . . . I implored in my own person to have the engine stopped, and my part in it hammered off" (Ch. lvii); in *Our Mutual Friend*, the dandy Eugene Wrayburn, nearly drowned in his struggle with Bradley Headstone, in many ways Wrayburn's double, is brought back from death by the girl of the lower classes, Lizzie Hexam, whom he marries. In each of these, both the psychic meaning and the social consequences are clearer than in Esther's case; in none of them is the movement toward the radical separation of individual salvation and social destiny so dramatic as it is in *Bleak House*.

It would be ludicrous to neglect the solid basis of *Bleak House* in traditional "social criticism." Tom-All-Alone's, Chancery suits, crossing sweeps hounded to death, bricklayers' babies dying of starvation, politicians stupidly perpetuating themselves in power at whatever cost to the community, gentlemen aristocrats decaying and letting the land decay with them—and a poisonous fog connecting all: surely Dickens' imagination was stimulated by social fact. But to do justice to Dickens' vision one must see that what *Bleak House* is finally about transcends social criticism. For while the novel may call for social action, it at the same time everywhere denies the possibility that any action arising from corporate society will better man's condition. And that denial comes about in part because Dickens profoundly distrusts institutions, inevitably corrupt because the social will is always corruptible, and in part because in his most intense daylight vision Dickens must have seen man as Esther sees herself in her nightmare: as an agonized link on a chain of suffering and guilt blazing in a black void. By an act of private vision, by the denial of the social will, we may save ourselves; by individual acts of responsibility and love we may sometimes save others. Such would seem to be the "message" of *Bleak House*. It is a familiar enough message, and its poignancy lies in its very familiarity; for it is a message which the twentieth century, without Esther's faith and her sure knowledge of where duty lies, is still painfully struggling to redefine in its own terms.

Notes

1. Lionel Trilling, "*Little Dorrit*," in *The Opposing Self* (New York, 1955), pp. 50–65.

2. For some balancing views see Leonard W. Deen, "Style and Unity in *Bleak House*," *Criticism*, III (1961), 206–218; Robert A. Donovan, "Structure and Idea in *Bleak House*," *ELH*, XXIX (1962), 175–201; W. J. Harvey, "Chance and Design in *Bleak House*," in *Dickens and the Twentieth Century*, ed. Gross and Pearson (Toronto, 1962), 145–157; J. Hillis Miller, *Charles Dickens, The World of His Novels* (Cambridge, Mass., 1958), and Morton Dauwen Zabel, Introduction to the Riverside Edition of *Bleak House* (1956).

3. Mark Spilka develops interesting parallels and connections between Kafka and Dickens in his *Dickens and Kafka* (Bloomington, Ind., 1963).

4. But see John Butt, "*Bleak House* in the Context of 1851," *NCF*, x (1955), 1–21; and Humphrey House, *The Dickens World* (New York, 1942).

5. Donovan, pp. 177–178.

6. Dorothy Van Ghent, *The English Novel, Form and Function* (New York, 1961), p. 132.

7. For a possible source of Dickens' own admiration ("the behavior of a group of manufacturers"), see Butt.

8. Northrop Frye, *Anatomy of Criticism* (Princeton, N.J., 1957), pp. 187–188.

9. For a fuller description and analysis of Esther's journey, see James H. Broderick and John E. Grant, "The Identity of Esther Summerson," *MP*, LV (1957–58), 252–258; and Norman Friedman, "The Shadow and the Sun: Notes Toward a Reading of *Bleak House*," *BUSE*, III (1957), 147–166.

"Through a Glass Darkly": Esther Summerson and *Bleak House*   Lawrence Frank*

"You are further to reflect, Mr. Woodcourt . . . that on the numerous difficulties, contingencies, masterly fictions, and forms of procedure in this great cause, there has been expended study, ability, eloquence, knowledge, intellect, Mr. Woodcourt, high intellect. For many years, the—a—I would say the flower of the Bar, and the —a—I would presume to add, the matured autumnal fruits of the Woolsack—have been lavished upon Jarndyce and Jarndyce."—Conversation Kenge

Bleak House has attained the status of a classic in the sense in which Frank Kermode speaks of the classic nature of *King Lear*. This is not to equate the two works, but to confront the fact that *Bleak House* asserts a pressure upon the modern imagination which cannot be ignored. The novel, like Shakespeare's play, *survives* through those readings of it which make it comply with what Kermode calls those "paradigmatic requirements for a classic" in our time.[1] Recent changes in the attitudes of modern readers toward Esther Summerson reflect both the pressure the novel asserts and the paradigms we find satisfying. For these reasons Esther's "case" remains, like those of so many others in the novel, in Chancery. The legacy of her written progress has yet to be exhausted by the critics, with all their "study, ability, eloquence, knowledge, intellect." The current, and I think the legitimate, emphasis on Esther's story as a complex psychological study reveals not only the needs of the modern reader, forever in search of such tales to engross his attention, but that element of Dickens' art, his psychological awareness, which seems still to be the least readily accepted part of his achievement. And in a time of sexual politics, we can perceive, in retrospect, the audacity, if not the sheer masculine arrogance, of Dickens' decision to

*Reprinted from *Dickens Studies Annual* 4 (1975): 91–112, by permission of AMS Press, Inc., New York.

have an illegitimate child, now a woman, tell her own story in her own words. We can agonize over Jane Austen's Fanny Price or Charlotte Brontë's Jane Eyre without feeling the need to deal with this other fact, a male writer trying to imagine himself into the consciousness of an Esther. These concerns become increasingly important as Esther's responses to the world she encounters, the fictive world of *Bleak House*, grow more inadequate, evasive, faintly self-righteous in their persistent humility and self-negation.

The existence of the double narrative in the novel complicates matters. Esther may be seen to exist as a foil played off against the verbal and imaginative virtuosity of the present-tense narrator. The presence in the novel of a consciousness so different from Esther's, whether we call this consciousness Dickens' or the narrator's, serves to emphasize the limitations of Esther's perspective, and the inevitability of such limitation for every character in the novel. Neither Mr. Bucket nor Esther, in mounting the high towers of their minds, can imagine the full complexity of the murky world in which they live. But Esther's "silent way of noticing what [passes] before" her is peculiarly her own. The silence which so often accompanies the retelling of her story suggests, not simply a coyness bordering on the vacuous, but a failure to understand, a failure not fortuitous, but, in some way, willed. As early as her first visit to Krook's rag and bottle warehouse, it becomes clear that Esther's silences create an aura of mystery as important as any of the mysteries in *Bleak House*. As Krook ticks off the names of the families involved in Jarndyce and Jarndyce, "the great suit," he mentions the name Barbary—and nothing happens. Esther remains discreetly silent. There is no shock of recognition on her part at the mention of the surname of her aunt, the woman who has perhaps done more to define her being than even the mother whose "disgrace" she is. Like the letters which the illiterate Krook chalks upon the wall and then rubs out, leaving each one in a state of isolation and meaninglessness, until someone joins them to form the name, Jarndyce, "Barbary" is left in suspension, unintelligible by itself until some consciousness is brought to bear on it to give it meaning. Krook's eccentric gesture is one emblem for the novel as a whole: only at the end will all the mysteries be brought together to reveal a meaning inherent in apparent chaos. If Esther ignores, consciously or not, the signs which might provide a clue to her identity, she will remain a mystery to herself, and radically incomplete.

Dickens, as always, understands fully what it means to deny the past. Lady Dedlock, "bored to death" behind the mask of her acquired self, undergoes a process of disintegration, of internal combustion, as fatal as that experienced by any other figure in the novel, including Captain Hawdon, who has chosen to acknowledge his own annihilation through the pseudonym, Nemo. Lady Dedlock believes in the story of the Ghost's Walk because she knows the past inevitably asserts itself. Like the Lady of Sir Morbury Dedlock whose history she relives, she never speaks "to any one of being crippled, or of being in pain," but she is as deeply maimed psychically as her ghostly predecessor was physically.[2] In part, Esther's silence about the name, Barbary, is her attempt to deny the past, to shut out memories of her aunt's denunciations and bitter resentment. She seeks to bury the past as she buried the doll which was her only real companion in her childhood. But the past cannot be buried, as her aunt's unexpected stroke reveals. With a rather curious innocence, Esther implicitly challenges and condemns her aunt by reading from St. John, "He that is without sin among you, let him first case a stone at her!" (iii). Miss Barbary's response is her desperate attempt to justify herself, and to warn Esther: "Watch ye therefore! lest coming suddenly he find you sleeping. And what I say unto you, I say unto all, Watch!" (iii). The lines from St. Mark remain forever ambiguous. Perhaps Miss Barbara has been found "sleeping," culpable, in her treatment of Esther. But Esther herself may one day be found "sleeping," under far different circumstances. The ambiguity must be unresolved because Miss Barbary's paralysis becomes her refuge. The years of oppression take their toll; she chooses, or she is reduced to, immobility, and silence.

Dickens is working here, as in other novels, with a full awareness of the psychological predicaments of his characters. Miss Barbary's stroke is rooted in her own response to Esther's muted accusation. It is Dickens' knowledge of such experiences, reinforced by the objectivity potentially inherent in the double narrative, which permits him to maintain, through much of *Bleak House*, a remarkable detachment toward Esther. On that first night in London, as Ada sleeps and Caddy Jellyby rests her head in her lap, Esther's situation becomes clearly defined:

> At length, by slow degrees, they [Ada and Caddy] became indistinct and mingled. I began to lose the identity of the sleeper resting on me. Now it was Ada; now, one of my old Reading friends from whom I could not believe I had so recently parted. Now, it was the little mad woman worn out with curtseying and smiling; now, some one in authority at Bleak House. Lastly, it was no one, and I was no one. (iv)

Esther is not only a social "no one" because of her illegitimacy. She tends to perceive herself as a "no one," and her dilemma is, in part, to become a *some one*, to say, with some kind of confidence and authenticity, either I or Me, as she apparently does in the final pages of the novel. If she fails to define, or redefine, herself in some viable way, she will run the risk of following in the steps of her father, Captain Hawdon, whose sign she encounters in the window of Krook's shop on the morning after her premonitory dream.

John Jarndyce and Bleak House provide Esther with an opportunity to define herself, to create an identity. She accepts the housekeeping keys and the names conferred upon her: Old Woman, Little Old Woman, Cobweb, Mrs. Shipton, Mother Hubbard, Dame Durden.[3] In the process, her "own name soon [becomes] quite lost among them" (viii). She participates in a communal fantasy which, in part, alienates her from herself, from her own name. She is submissive and eager to earn the love of others, on their terms.

And she finds comfort in thinking of herself as "a methodical, old-maidish sort of foolish little person" (viii). She seeks to deny or to evade the consequences of her illegitimacy. She fixes herself psychologically in a "time" safely beyond that in which her own mother dealt, unsuccessfully, with the fact of her sexuality. For a Dame Durden, a Little Old Woman, a Mother Hubbard, there seems no threat of another dashing captain's appearing to set in motion a painful reenactment of her mother's fate.[4]

Esther is also trying, however inadequately, to reconcile herself to her own humanity in a more general sense. All people inevitably feel, as Esther feels in her childhood, both "guilty and yet innocent." This has nothing to do with illegitimacy or original sin. In Dickens' greatest novels, there is a full recognition of the ways in which we incur guilt and lose forever our precious innocence. In *David Copperfield*, the young David begins to perceive Annie Strong through the jealous, suspicious eyes of Mr. Wickfield, without at the time being aware that he is doing so. David becomes, however unwittingly, responsible for his misunderstanding of Annie. He is guilty *and* innocent. He has been unknowingly deceived by an adult. But when he becomes aware, later, of what has happened, he must feel that his miscomprehension of Annie Strong has been a subtle violation of her integrity. This is not melodramatic in the way of Esther's illegitimacy, which tends to obscure the fact that, in *Bleak House,* Dickens is always getting at something more than Victorian sexual mores and their inadequacies.

Esther's dilemma is always both psychological and moral. Her "progress" involves Dickens,' if not Esther's, emerging recognition that, sinned against as she may be, Esther is not fully the innocent, the victim. Her attempts to cope with herself may involve her, like David, in the violation of others. She must learn to see herself and her situation as clearly as she can in a world permeated by fog, dust, drizzle, and all that obscures one's vision. It is in this context that the verse from I Corinthians becomes so central to the novel: "For now we see through a glass darkly; but then face to face: now I know in part; but then shall I know even as also I am known." Within this novel we rarely know other than in part; we "know," at best, detached, isolated letters which seem to form no intelligible word. We read newspapers in the midst of a "London particular," without understanding what the words mean. We may not know even our own names, our own selves: for "now we see through a glass darkly." There is no assurance we shall ever see "face to face," to know even as one is, presumably, known by God—if there is a God in *Bleak House*.[5]

Dickens suggests the inadequacy of the ways in which Esther chooses to know herself, and to be known by others, through her relationships with Ada and Caddy. She presides over, and is enchanted by, Richard's courtship of Ada. She is at least indirectly responsible for Caddy's marriage to Prince Turveydrop, for the two have met at Miss Flite's, and it is through Esther that Caddy first encounters the mad old woman. She becomes involved, inevitably, in the sufferings of others, especially in those of Ada through whom she tries to realize what she has denied herself. But these developments exist upon the periphery of Esther's story. It is through Esther's relationships to Jo, the illiterate crossing-sweeper, and to Lady Dedlock that Dickens explores more fully her situation and her response to it. The visit to Boythorn's estate, in the company of Ada, Jarndyce, and Skimpole, leads to the inevitable meeting between Esther and Lady Dedlock, and to a series of events culminating in her exposure to the diseased Jo and in her physical disfigurement.

The meeting occurs in the church near Chesney Wold and is introduced as the service begins, " 'Enter not into judgment with thy servant, O Lord, for in thy sight [shall no man living be justified]' " (xviii). The verse from Psalm 143, the explicit reference to "judgment," returns us to the question of innocence and guilt and to that moment when Esther, however unconsciously, had challenged her godmother and precipitated the fatal stroke. As the priest reads, Esther encounters the eyes of the woman who will prove to be her mother:

> Shall I ever forget the rapid beating at my heart, occasioned by the look I met, as I stood up! Shall I ever forget the manner in which those handsome proud eyes seemed to spring out of their languor, and to hold mine! It was only a moment before I cast mine down—released again, if I may say so—on my book, but I knew the beautiful face quite well, in that short space of time.
> And, very strangely, there was something quickened within me, associated with the lonely days at my godmother's; yes, away even to the days when I had stood on tiptoe to dress myself at my little glass, after dressing my doll. And this, although I had never seen this lady's face before in all my life—I was quite sure of it—absolutely certain. (xviii)

What Esther sees, of course, is a version of her own face. She "knows" the beautiful face as Guppy knew the portrait of Lady Dedlock: " 'I'm dashed!' adds Mr. Guppy . . . , 'if I don't think I must have had a dream of that picture, you know!' " (vii). Esther is thrust back into the past, to her godmother's house, to her doll and to herself on tiptoe before her "little glass." It is a moment in time when she first sees herself in a mirror and becomes self-conscious. What Esther has seen in the mirror is not just a reflection of herself; rather, it is a vision of herself deeply rooted in her godmother's conception of her. Her vision of herself, even the reflection, is mediated by Miss Barbary's perception of the child. And Esther wills to be something quite different: good, industrious, contented. It is the image of herself by which she tries to live, in order to make life possible. But it is an image, however "good," conditioned by the inescapable shadow of her illegitimacy. Hers is a self founded upon a twisted definition of innocence and guilt, and as such it is false.

In Lady Dedlock she sees a reflection of her own face quite different from the face of one set apart by a nameless disgrace (she cannot know that

Lady Dedlock is, in fact, secretly set apart as much as she). Esther encounters a potentiality quite beyond that she has imagined for herself. That beautiful face becomes, "in a confused way, like a broken glass" to Esther in which she sees "scraps of old remembrances." She thinks, appropriately, of the broken glass. The fragments of her unintegrated past are assembling themselves mysteriously before her. The impact of Lady Dedlock's appearance is so disorienting that Esther ceases to hear the reader's voice: instead, she hears "the well-remembered voice of [her] godmother." And she links Lady Dedlock's face to that of the dead woman whom Esther thinks of, throughout this sequence, not as her aunt, but as her godmother, as if to deny any real relationship to her. But the broken glass refers to the present, as well as to the past: Esther's image of herself has failed her as it has once before in the dream in which she became "no one."

As she dwells upon the way in which Lady Dedlock has magically evoked her childhood self "before [her] own eyes," Esther gradually becomes aware of the gaze of the French maid, Hortense. Dickens reveals in a stroke that curious triad for which he has already prepared. Hortense has been introduced as "a very neat She-Wolf imperfectly tamed," with "something indefinably keen and wan about her anatomy" (xii). And, through the imagery of the glass, a special relationship between Hortense and Lady Dedlock emerges, a relationship Lady Dedlock tries to deny:

> One night, while having her hair undressed, my Lady loses herself in deep thought. . . , until she sees her own brooding face in the opposite glass, and a pair of black eyes curiously observing her.
> "Be so good as to attend," says my Lady then, addressing the reflection of Hortense, "to your business. You can contemplate your beauty at another time." "Pardon! It was your Ladyship's beauty!" "That," says my Lady, "you needn't contemplate at all." (xii)

The juxtaposition of Lady Dedlock's brooding face and Hortense's black eyes connects the two by contiguity alone. But Lady Dedlock has already disguised herself in her maid's cloak to visit Captain Hawdon's grave. The fusion of the two women is more or less complete. Whatever Lady Dedlock has suppressed by falling into a "freezing mood," as her sister fell into the frozen immobility of paralysis, still exists within her, projected, however melodramatically, in the form of Hortense. The scene anticipates that in *A Tale of Two Cities* when Charles Darnay glances up at the "glass" fixed above the prisoner's box in the Old Bailey: it is like gazing into the ocean which is "one day to give up its dead" (II, ii). The mirror does not simply reflect; it offers a glimpse into the self's depths. What Lady Dedlock sees are those eyes which always lurk within the depths of her habitually languid gaze. She characteristically rebuffs the Provence-bred Hortense and that teeming, fecund world for which Provence traditionally stands in British fiction.

The triangular configuration Dickens has so deftly forged continues to haunt Esther during this visit to Boythorn's and through other episodes in

Bleak House. For when she, with Ada and Jarndyce, takes refuge from the sudden storm in the keeper's lodge on the edge of Chesney Wold, Esther undergoes a further reconfirmation of all the possibilities which the appearance of Lady Dedlock has already raised. The voice which warns the girls not to sit near the window, "in so exposed a place," is Lady Dedlock's, not Esther's. But Ada, responding not only to the concern in the words, but to a familiar tone, turns to Esther, and the "beating of [Esther's] heart [comes] back again": "I had never heard the voice, as I had never seen the face, but it affected me in the same strange way. Again, in a moment, there arose before my mind innumerable pictures of myself" (xviii). Esther confronts, if not the intuition that this stern and beautiful woman is her mother, at least the sense that they are not so unlike. The "innumerable pictures" of herself which occur in her imagination suggest a world of possibilities as well as the swirl of remembered moments. And to initiate her further into the ambiguous energies and potentialities within herself and others, Esther is left, as the episode ends, with an unforgettable sight: the enraged Hortense, spurned by Lady Dedlock, removes her shoes and walks toward Chesney Wold, "through the wettest of the wet grass"; which, someone speculates, she fancies is blood:

> We passed not far from the House, a few minutes afterwards. Peaceful as it had looked when we first saw it, it looked even more so now, with a diamond spray glittering all about it, a light wind blowing, the birds no longer hushed but singing strongly, everything refreshed by the late rain, and the little carriage shining at the doorway like a fairy carriage made of silver. Still, very steadfastly and quietly walking towards it, a peaceful figure too in the landscape, went Mademoiselle Hortense, shoeless, through the wet grass. (xviii)

Chesney Wold, its enchanted world and the people fortunate enough to inhabit it become fragile, delicate artifacts totally vulnerable to the implacable juggernaut moving toward them. Esther has been introduced to forces which have no place in *her* world, or so she thinks. Soon, she will, however mistakenly, become identified with these forces. She will have to deal with their implications for her own life.

Hortense's attempt to offer her services to Esther as her "domestic" is, in part, a suggestion that the energies Hortense possesses either exist in some form within Esther or that they may be conferred upon her magically through some proximity to the Frenchwoman. But Esther, true to her version of herself, recoils, especially from the ardor which Hortense so clearly possesses. Madame Defarge already exists within Esther's response to the maid: she "seemed to bring visibly before me some woman from the streets of Paris in the reign of terror" (xxiii). Esther's response to Lady Dedlock remains more ambiguous and complex: it involves admiration, fear and yearning, a yearning based on the "fancy . . . that what this lady so curiously was to me, I was to her—I mean that I disturbed her thoughts as she influenced mine, though in some different way" (xxiii).

The three women become inextricably joined, in Esther's imagination and in the shape of the novel itself, when Jo and Esther finally meet at St. Albans. Jo has come from London in search of Jenny, the other woman in whose clothes Lady Dedlock will finally disguise herself. What happens in this meeting involves more than the inescapable taint of the disease which emanates from Tom-all-Alone's and the cemetery where Nemo is buried. The night is stormy, toward London "a lurid glare [overhangs] the whole dark waste"; and as she proceeds toward the brickmaker's cottage, Esther has, "for a moment an undefinable impression of [herself] as being something different from what [she] then was" (xxxi). Her impression, her vague sense of her inauthentic condition, is only confirmed by Jo's apparently delirious response to her. The boy has already seen both Lady Dedlock, disguised in her maid's cloak, and later Hortense herself in Tulkinghorn's chambers. He at first mistakes the veiled Esther for the "t'other lady" he has led to the "berryin ground." Even after Esther raises her veil and Jenny seeks to assure him that this is *her* lady standing before them, Jo remains unconvinced: "She looks to me the t'other one. It ain't the bonnet, nor yet it ain't the gownd, but she looks to me the t'other one." Jo's doubt, in the face of the assurances of Jenny and Charley, simply cannot be dispelled. At last, he makes the connection which is the most disturbing of all: "Then he hoarsely whispered Charley. 'If she ain't the t'other one, she ain't the forrenner. Is there *three* of 'em then?' Charley looked at me a little frightened. I felt half frightened at myself when the boy glared on me so" (xxxi). The connection between Lady Dedlock, Hortense, and Esther has become inescapable.

Jo's confusion only mirrors Esther's own sense of her being different from what she has, until now, thought herself to be. To be mistaken for a Lady Dedlock or a Hortense is to be seen in some way as like them. It is not a question of how much Esther "knows" at this point in the novel, the extent to which she associates herself, in her own consciousness, with these two women. Dickens has asserted, through plot and language, a relationship. Its full meaning may at best be working within Esther in an inarticulable way. But the moorings of her old self have been cut loose upon this stormy, disorienting night. Esther must begin to live with the possibility that, metaphorically, Jo is right: there are "*three* of 'em then," floating somewhere behind the veil of Esther's public self.

The illness which follows is the natural consequence of the dilemma Esther now faces. The identity of Dame Durden no longer protects her from the complexities into which she has been pushed. She is responsible for Jo without having known him. On one level the responsibility is clearly social: no one can legitimately claim to be innocent of the horrors of Tom-all-Alone's which touch every one. But social guilt is only one element of the illness which follows. As Esther herself remarks, "It may be that if we knew more of such strange afflictions, we might be the better able to alleviate their intensity" (xxxv)—curious words to use in speaking of smallpox, but not at all inappropriate for the spiritual and psychological affliction which is Esther's.

The first stage of her travail is marked by blindness. In a novel obsessed with the interpretation of signs, blindness, like the illiteracy of Krook and Jo, is hardly the result of pure contingency.[6] Jo shuffles through the streets of London "in utter darkness as to the meaning, of those mysterious symbols, so abundant over the shops, and at the corners of streets, and on the doors, and in the windows!" (xvi). He is "stone blind and dumb" to the language of the written word. But Esther, too, has been accosted by "mysterious symbols"; she sinks into blindness through her inability, or her unwillingness, to "see": to decipher and give meaning to the signs which threaten her.

Esther's blindness is a prelude to a sense of disorientation and her attempt to deal with everything she has so recently experienced. She has, in the broadest terms, been confronted with the terrible complexities of being human, complexities which transcend the fact of her illegitimacy. Her sexuality and her relatedness to others are involved. In her delirium, the "stages of [her] life" become confused and mingled "on the healthy shore," while she is separated from them by "a dark lake":

> At once a child, an elder girl, and the little woman I had been so happy as,
> I was not only oppressed by cares and difficulties adapted to each station,
> but by the great perplexity of endlessly trying to reconcile them. I suppose
> that few who have not been in such a condition can quite understand what
> I mean, or what painful unrest arose from this source. (xxxv)

Esther has lost a sense of unified being, and with it her usual relation to time.[7] She perceives herself in fragments. Like the pieces of a shattered glass, each fragment mirrors back to her disparate and incompatible images of herself. She is in pieces. The fragile self she has created, with the help of Jarndyce, Ada, and Richard, has momentarily ceased to be, broken by its contact with the very realities it was designed to evade. If she accepts the shattering of herself and the need to forge a new identity, Esther risks immersion in the world of sexuality, social injustice, and victimization inhabited by Lady Dedlock, Hortense, and Jo. This is both dangerous and frightening. It would also involve an act of disloyalty. To cease to be Dame Durden is a betrayal, implicitly, of the community which has sustained that identity through a mutual effort. And the community of Bleak House is comprised of all those for whom she most deeply cares. If the re-creation of herself in new terms seems impossible, her present state of disunity offers no viable alternative: it is non-being.

Esther's impasse is at the center of her "disorder"; it is revealed in the frustrated yearnings for rebirth: "it seemed one long night. . . . I laboured up colossal staircases, ever striving to reach the top, and ever turned, as I have seen a worm in a garden path, by some obstruction, and labouring again." This almost De Quinceian "labour" which does not fulfill itself in birth leads Esther to that "worse time when, strung together somewhere in great black space, there was a flaming necklace, or ring, or starry circle of some kind, of which *I* was one of the beads! And when my only prayer was to be taken off from the rest, and when it was such inexplicable agony and misery to be a part of the dreadful thing" (xxxv). The passage is unique in Dickens' novels. There is no other place in which Dickens so completely expresses what we would call both religious and existential despair. Esther's prayer "to be taken off from the rest" is her denial of herself and the chain of interconnectedness which comprises the human condition. She wishes to escape from the incongruities inherent in her own humanity. There is the injustice of her illegitimate birth. There is the inevitable loss of innocence which occurs as one moves from childhood to adulthood. There is the unbearable fact that one's fate is joined, however mysteriously, with the fates of others. Esther is incapable of experiencing, at this point in the novel, the kind of acceptance of herself embodied in this account of a woman, also illegitimate, which appears in *Existence:*

> I remember walking that day under the elevated tracks in a slum area, feeling the thought, "I am an illegitimate child." I recall the sweat pouring forth in my anguish in trying to accept that fact. Then I understood what it must feel like to accept, "I am a Negro in the midst of privileged whites," or "I am blind in the midst of people who see." Later on that night I woke up and it came to me this way, "I accept the fact that I am an illegitimate child." *But* "I am not a child anymore." So it is, "I am illegitimate." That is not so either: "I was born illegitimate." Then what is left? What is left is this, *"I Am."* This *act* of contact and acceptance with "I am," once gotten hold of, gave me (what I think was for me the first time) the experience "Since I Am, I have the right to be."[8]

In the case of this woman, as in Esther's, the fact of illegitimacy is fundamentally metaphorical: it poses the question of every one's "right to be." The woman whose story appears in *Existence* unravels the contradictions in her conception of herself and comes to a moment of affirmation. Esther only wants to escape the contradictions which plague her. When she awakens from *her* long night, she has failed to change significantly her idea of herself. She has been unable to accept the "flaming necklace" or "starry circle" of which she is a part.

Esther seeks, in short, a simplification of the human condition. She accepts what she calls her "altered self" because it seems to offer the security she knew as Dame Durden. The absent mirrors do not go unnoticed. But when Esther speaks to Charley there is a curious ambiguity in her question: " 'Yet, Charley," said I, looking round, 'I miss something, surely, that I am accustomed to?' " (xxxv). She can live without the "old face" which has marked her resemblance to Lady Dedlock, or so she thinks. Perhaps she can even live without her love for Allan Woodcourt. But to do this she must think of the past, of the "childish prayer of that old birthday, when [she] had aspired to be industrious, contented, and true-hearted, and to do good to some one, and win some love to [herself] if [she] could" (xxv). She repeats the prayer in an effort to fix herself, once again, in a state beyond temptation, a state which in some way will reconcile "the various stages of [her] life" and protect her from the shame of her unknown mother and from the ambiguous power embodied both in Lady Dedlock and Hortense. She acquiesces to the "old conspiracy to make [her] happy."

Esther knows that she has undergone some physical change. But it is only when she arrives at Boythorn's in Lincolnshire that she has the courage, finally, to look into the glass and face her altered self:

> My hair had not been cut off, though it had been in danger more than once. It was long and thick. I let it down, and shook it out, and went up to the glass upon the dressing-table. There was a little muslin curtain drawn across it. I drew it back: and stood for a moment looking through such a veil of my own hair, that I could see nothing else. Then I put my hair aside, and looked at the reflection in the mirror; encouraged by seeing how placidly it looked at me. I was very much changed—O very, very much. At first, my face was so strange to me, that I think I should have put my hands before it and started back, but for the encouragement [of Jarndyce and the others] I have mentioned. (xxvi)

Esther moves through a number of veils, that of the muslin curtain and the veil of her own hair, toward a view of her "self" in the glass, a self which seems to look autonomously back at her. It is a moment of discovery echoing moments in the past, foreshadowing others in the future. It repeats her childhood emergence into self-consciousness when she first saw her face in her "little glass . . . after dressing." It calls up that moment in the church when Esther first sees Lady Dedlock and Hortense. Even poor Jo's surprise and terror at the sight of the veiled, and unveiled, Esther are evoked as Esther sees herself, however darkly, in the glass. All the characters in *Bleak House* are veiled, to some extent, to others and themselves. The muslin curtain and the dark hair through which Esther moves suggest levels of ignorance. The image she sees may be but another veil, another reflection floating upon the surface of the depths which Esther chooses not to plumb. She has not yet seen herself face to face: perhaps she only does so later in the novel when she pulls aside the "long dank hair" which veils the features of her dead mother.

Gradually the face before Esther ceases to be strange: "very soon it became more familiar." Esther pieces herself together by accepting the face from which she originally recoils. She submits to her godmother's notion of her as someone tainted, to Jarndyce's notion of her as the "little housewife." She chooses to diminish herself through this "new" identity, altered, scarred, desexualized. She feels a sense of loss. Her muted, "I had never been a beauty, and had never thought myself one; but I had been very different from this," and her allusion to Allan Woodcourt's flowers reveal, in Esther's perhaps too quiet way, the protest rising within her. But disfigurement, real or imagined, offers a sanctuary, even if an illusory one, from the agonies of the flaming necklace. Esther ceases to be a "perfect likeness" of

Lady Dedlock, as her visit to Guppy will prove. No one will be able, apparently, to connect the two of them. When Lady Dedlock acknowledges her and fulfills something the girl has "pined for and dreamed of . . . [as] a little child," Esther feels "a burst of gratitude to the providence of God that I was so changed as that I never could disgrace her by any trace of likeness; as that nobody could ever now look at me, and look at her [as Hortense has done], and remotely think of any near tie between us" (xxxvi). Esther's gratitude is double-edged, to say the least. The tie binding the two, and seemingly sundered by Esther's illness, reaches beyond that between mother and daughter. The relinquished likeness is a relinquished potentiality. Esther will never encounter the situation which led to her mother's love for Captain Hawdon and her own birth. *She* will never be humbled, as Lady Dedlock so gratifyingly is, before the living embodiment of a past indiscretion.

Esther's "strange affliction" becomes a denial both of her mother and herself. Her forgiveness of her mother is a terrible rebuke: "I told her that my heart overflowed with love for her, . . . [that] it was not for me, then resting for the first time on my mother's bosom, to take her to account for having given me life; but that my duty was to bless her and receive her, though the whole world turned from her" (xxxvi). How deftly the knife is turned in the wound! Esther's words to Lady Dedlock are full of Victorian rectitude. They are as suspect as the hauteur in Lady Dedlock's denial to Jo's innocent query, " 'You didn't know him [Nemo], did you?' " (xvi). Dickens has captured the mother, and the daughter, in situations which expose the radical dishonesty of their lives. Lady Dedlock denies that she has known the dead law-writer. Esther implicitly denies her mother. Each response is morally and psychologically untenable. And Esther's sense of worthlessness and fear reveals how difficult it will be for her to live with the knowledge she now possesses. Lady Dedlock's letter to Esther undermines completely whatever "right to be" Esther has ever possessed: "I had never, to my own mother's knowledge, breathed—had been buried—had never been endowed with life—had never borne a name" (xxxvi). Had never *been*. Esther is once again momentarily nameless, a no one, like Nemo; she weeps "afresh to think [she is] back in the world, with [her] load of trouble for others." No wonder that, as she walks near Chesney Wold and the Ghost's Walk, she imagines her echoing footsteps are those of the legendary ghost and that she runs, in terror, from herself and "everything."

Esther runs, of course, to Bleak House and to Jarndyce and Ada. She returns to her former role as Dame Durden and to her curious relationship with Ada, through whom she seems willing to live. But none of this is ever really satisfactory, for us, for Dickens, even for Esther, who remains far more knowing than even she is willing to admit.

> It matters little now, how much I thought of my living mother who had told
> me evermore to consider her dead. I could not venture to approach her, or
> to communicate with her in writing, for my sense of the peril in which her

> life was passed was only to be equalled by my fears of increasing it. Know-
> ing that my mere existence as a living creature was an unforeseen danger
> in her way, I could not always conquer that terror of myself which had
> seized me when I first knew the secret. At no time did I dare to utter her
> name. I felt as if I did not even dare to hear it. If the conversation any-
> where, when I was present, took that direction, as it sometimes naturally
> did, I tried not to hear—I mentally counted, repeated something that I
> knew, or went out of the room. I am conscious, now, that I often did these
> things when there can have been no danger of her being spoken of. (xliii)

In retrospect it may matter little. But *then* it mattered a great deal. Nor is it
simply the melodramatic plight of Lady Dedlock which is central. Rather, it
is that Esther dares not to utter her mother's name, dares not even to hear it.
And if it were possible, she would perhaps choose not even to think it. She
resorts to a device which will drive "Lady Dedlock" out of her very consciousness. Perhaps the "something" that she knew which she repeats is Dame
Durden, Dame Durden, Dame Durden. She remains in full flight from her
mother and herself. To make the flight complete, to consolidate her loss into
something permanent and irreversible, for the loss involves, really, a state of
mind or being, she accepts John Jarndyce's proposal, knowing that in this act
she is being untrue to herself.

Esther commits herself to John Jarndyce not out of love, or passion, but
out of gratitude; she is aware that she will "become the dear companion of his
remaining life" (xliv). She chooses to acquiesce once more to that "conspiracy" to make her happy which has in it the element of coercion which even
Esther can detect. But her decision to marry Jarndyce is, finally, her own
doing. She is repeating her mother's fateful, and fatal, decision to marry Sir
Leicester Dedlock. Esther will fall into her own version of a "freezing mood,"
a condition of stasis only apparently beyond the realities of time and change,
innocence and guilt. As she reads Jarndyce's letter of proposal, Esther girds
herself for the "one thing to do":

> Still, I cried very much; not only in the fulness of my heart after reading
> the letter, not only in the strangeness of the prospect—for it was strange
> though I had expected the contents—but as if something for which there
> was no name or distinct idea were indefinitely lost to me. I was very
> happy, very thankful, very hopeful; but I cried very much. (xliv)

This is quintessential Esther. But it reveals not just the enduring, self-
negating touchstone of goodness, but a woman who is relinquishing something, however threatening to her, of real value, the opportunity for passion
in her life. Esther's choice leads to the almost ghoulish act in which she
kisses the sleeping Ada and presses Allan Woodcourt's withered flowers to
Ada's lips before she burns them and they turn to dust: the same kind of
"dust" existing within the combusting selves of so many in the novel. She will
sacrifice her own legitimate desire for self-fulfillment and live vicariously
through Ada and Richard. But even this morbid act of self-sacrifice occurs

only after Esther has conducted a curious dialogue with herself in her "old glass." She talks to her reflected face, even holds up her finger at it, in her determination to reestablish that "composed look you [the face in the glass] comforted me with, my dear, when you showed me such a change!" (xliv). She gazes at a Medusa's head, her own scarred face, and turns herself to stone, as her mother and her dead aunt have done before her.

Dickens knows very well that this will not do, for a number of reasons. Apart from that Victorian commitment to the satisfying happy ending, there is in Dickens' imagination a streak of integrity which modern readers continue to underestimate or to ignore. It is this integrity and the equally fierce will to overcome the very paradoxes he has posed which generate the fixated structures in so many of Dickens' novels, both early and late. Time and again we see a hero or heroine reenacting the same experience or a slightly transmuted version of it. This is true of the early *Oliver Twist*, of *David Copperfield*, even of the last completed novel, *Our Mutual Friend*. The novels begin with a paradox, recurrently involving someone burdened with that confused sense of innocence and guilt, inextricably combined. The novels proceed to unravel the very Gordian knot which, by definition, seems impervious even to the sword of Dickens' imagination. *Oliver Twist* deals obsessively with the fact that Oliver's birth is inseparably connected with his mother's death, and that Oliver's genteel aspirations, however legitimate, entail the destruction of Nancy, Sikes, and Fagin who preside over Oliver's final resurrection into the Brownlow world of unassailable bourgeois respectability. This almost naïve persistence in grappling with the unresolvable lies at the center of *David Copperfield* as David returns again and again to the experiences of his childhood, finally to emerge successful, famous, and married to Agnes. The sea changes which John Harmon chooses to undergo in *Our Mutual Friend* are designed to free him from the temptation posed by his father's will, a temptation to become forever implicated in, and compromised by, the Harmon fortune, built upon the dust mounds. Much of *Our Mutual Friend* deals with Harmon's earning, however dubiously, both Bella Wilfer and his father's money through a series of rebirths modeled on the paradigmatic rebirths of Oliver Twist and David Copperfield.

In *Bleak House* Esther's acceptance of John Jarndyce's proposal is her attempt to deal with the old Dickensian paradox. But her meeting with the returned Allan Woodcourt illustrates how intolerable her situation has become. By now Esther is all too clearly in dialogue, not with herself, but with a "self" conjured up by her own imagination and designed to obliterate the traces of the past. But, however earnestly she may address the Esther in the mirror, the old longings return: "I saw that he was very sorry for me. I was glad to see it. I felt for my old self as the dead may feel if they ever revisit these scenes. I was glad to be tenderly remembered, to be gently pitied, not to be quite forgotten" (xlv). Esther sees, in part, what she wishes to see in Allan Woodcourt's manner; she reads the signs and tokens he presents to confirm the wiseness of her decision and to keep her "old self" down. But that self is not dead: it exists beyond the face she sees in her glass, and even in the eyes of others who are equally mirrors of herself. Like the ghost of the Ghost's Walk, its footsteps can be heard in Esther's consciousness and the consciousness of others. The willed "deadness" which Esther as Dame Durden feels must be confronted and dispelled. If not, it will become a permanent condition: she will be no less a "sleeping beauty" than her mother, Lady Dedlock.

The concluding episodes of the novel represent Dickens' efforts to resolve the impasse, to sever the Gordian knot he has himself so deftly tied. Through Sir Leicester Dedlock's stroke and the pursuit of Lady Dedlock by Esther and Inspector Bucket, Dickens seeks to resolve Esther's situation. Sir Leicester's continued loyalty to his wife, even after he has been felled by the news of her past and reduced to almost total silence, plays off revealingly against Esther's response to her mother. For he accepts and acknowledges his wife, as she is, in the presence of witnesses: " 'in case I should not recover, in case I should lose both my speech and the power of writing, . . . I desire to say, and to call you all to witness . . . that I am on unaltered terms with Lady Dedlock. That I assert no cause whatever of complaint against her. . . . Say this to herself, and to every one' " (lviii). It is a noble gesture, and a sincere one. There is no note of reproach as there has been in Esther's response to her mother. Sir Leicester's compassion reminds us of Esther's failure to accept her mother and herself.

So Esther and Bucket move through the snow into which the stricken Sir Leicester stares, "the giddy whirl of white flakes and icy blots," which suggests the ultimate inscrutability of the world in which these characters find themselves. Her previous illness, an abortive Carlylean "Baphometic Fire-baptism," has not produced a "Spiritual New-birth." The earlier experiences are reenacted: but this time the process of rebirth involves the more traditional baptismal process of immersion. The disorientation through which Esther passed during her "fever-paroxysms" returns. As she rides with Bucket, she feels that she is in a dream, that she is entering the labyrinthine world of streets, bridges, and serpentining river which is as much internal as external. She is losing herself once more, descending into a world in which she may again encounter the ambiguous self she has relinquished or finally succeed in exorcising its presence forever.

The "something wet" which Bucket and another man, "dark and muddy, in long swollen sodden boots and a hat like them" (lvii), inspect proves not to be the body of a drowned Lady Dedlock. But Esther continues to fear, and perhaps to hope, that the tide in its rush toward her will "cast [her] mother at the horses' feet." In her dreamlike state Esther's identification with her mother is now so complete that even the "shadowy female figure" which flits past the carriage is as much herself as Lady Dedlock:

> The river had a fearful look, so overcast and secret, creeping away so fast between the low flat lines of shore: so heavy with indistinct and awful

shapes, both of substance and shadow: so deathlike and mysterious. . . .
In my memory, the lights upon the bridge are always burning dim; the
cutting wind is eddying round the homeless woman whom we pass; the
monotonous wheels are whirling on; and the light of the carriage-lamps
reflected back, looks palely in upon me—a face, rising out of the dreaded
water. (lvii)

But whose face rises out of the water? The entire sequence is constructed
upon the logic of dreams. Esther, Lady Dedlock, and the homeless prosti-
tute are one. In this phantasmagoric setting, Esther gazes into the night, the
water, or both, and looks into a watery mirror out of which rises not her
mother's face, but her own: the face of that unquiet ghost which has not been
charmed by the spell Esther has tried so vainly to cast upon it.

Dickens has transported Esther back into the past, to earlier events
with which she has not come to terms. She is returned to the brickmaker's
cottage and Jo's unnerving query: "If she ain't the t'other one, she ain't the
forrenner. Is there *three* of 'em then?" (xxxi). Verbal parallels to Jo's words
occur throughout the events following Tulkinghorn's murder. The arrested
George Rouncewell recalls that on the night of the murder "[he] saw a shape
so like Miss Summerson's go by [him] in the dark, that [he] had half a mind
to speak to it" (lii). Esther shudders at George's words: she thinks at once of
Lady Dedlock. Within the larger structure of the novel, beyond Esther's
consciousness, we see that, metaphorically, all three women—Esther, Lady
Dedlock, and Hortense—are placed at the scene of the crime. George's
observation becomes but another sign or token to be understood before the
mysteries of Tulkinghorn's murder and Esther's identity can be fully resolved. When Esther and Bucket arrive at the brickmaker's cottage, they
learn, in the words of Jenny's husband, that "one went right to Lunnun, and
t'other went right from it." Once again words are spoken which echo those of
Jo. The former confusion of identities is reinforced. Esther is back at the
moment when she first *must* have perceived, however darkly, the implications of her similarity to Lady Dedlock and Hortense. The old triad reasserts
itself once more, as it did when Esther gazed from the carriage window at
the "homeless woman" in the dark. Esther and Lady Dedlock are fixed into
an apparently eternal configuration, of which they are the two constants; only
the third term alters: first Hortense, then the homeless woman of the streets,
now Jenny.

Under the pressure of these most recent events, Esther retraces more
and more closely the course of her earlier illness. She is blind to the signs at
which Bucket so eagerly grasps. She begins to lose her sense of time and
feels, "in a strange way, never to have been free from the anxiety under
which [she] then [labours]" (lvii). But on this occasion the psychic laboring is
designed to bring forth a more legitimate offspring. Esther has begun to be
able to think of her mother, even if in death, and to speak of her, even if only
in a whisper to Inspector Bucket. She is moving toward a gesture of loyalty

and acceptance like that Sir Leicester Dedlock has made, in the presence of witnesses. Esther's moment of what should be authentic rebirth approaches. As it does, the falling snow continues to melt and find its way into the moving carriage: the wetness penetrates her dress. Esther and Bucket descend further into "a deeper complication" of the "narrowest and worst streets in London" (lix), moving inexorably toward Nemo's grave and Lady Dedlock.

The rhythms of Esther's previous suffering have come finally to dominate Dickens' imaginative conception of the search for Lady Dedlock. Once the parallels between these two critical episodes in Esther's life become established. Bucket's lecture to the near-maddened Mrs. Snagsby becomes curiously inevitable: "And Toughey—him as you call Jo—was mixed up in the same business, and no other; and the lawwriter that you know of, was mixed up in the same business, and no other; and your husband, with no more knowledge of it than your great-grandfather, was mixed up (by Mr. Tulkinghorn, deceased, his best customer) in the same business, and no other; and the whole bileing up of people was mixed up in the same business, and no other" (lix). Bucket's prosaic litany, with its persistent refrain, "the same business, and no other," takes us, and Esther, back to that "flaming necklace, or ring, or starry circle of some kind, of which [she] was one of the beads!" Bucket's matter-of-factness, his wry acceptance of the unthinkable, makes it all too clear that no one can cease to be "a part of the dreadful thing." No process of physical or psychic disfigurement can free an individual, even an Esther, from her participation, "with no more knowledge of it than [her] great-grandfather," in this same business, and no other. The only viable response to this predicament, though it need not be like Bucket's too easy professional acceptance, is one's immersion into the world of *Bleak House*.

As she approaches the figure of the woman lying before the gate to the burial ground, in which her father's body has been placed. Esther experiences not just the melting, and dissolution, which her mother has undergone since the disclosure of the great secret. Esther melts within herself. She remembers "that the stained house fronts put on human shapes and looked at [her]; that great water-gates seemed to be opening and closing in [her] head, or in the air; and that the unreal things were more substantial than the real" (lix). The unreal *is* more substantial than the real. The "clogged and bursting gutters and water-spouts" are within: her state of mind, associated with the breaking of the waters, is the real truth of this moment. The fixed and frozen waters of the self break apart, melt: the waters within her flow once more. The tide of the river rushes at her, to deliver the body of her mother at her feet: "I passed on to the gate, and stooped down. I lifted the heavy head, put the long dank hair aside, and turned the face. And it was my mother cold and dead" (lix).

The death of Lady Dedlock is, of course, unsatisfactory in many ways. Esther's inability to understand that it is *not* "Jenny, the mother of the dead child," before the graveyard gate pushes the irony almost too far, though it may accurately reflect Esther's unwillingness to know and to experience the truth fully. The death seems also to reflect too readily the Victorian notion that this is the only satisfactory punishment for the sin that Lady Dedlock has committed. But Dickens, through Nemo, Krook, Tulkinghorn, Miss Barbary, and others, has asserted throughout the novel that certain ways of being constitute a corrosive death-in-life which can lead to literal death. Lady Dedlock has lived too long with her secret, with her bored and emptied self, to survive. But what is most disquieting is that Esther comes face to face with her mother only in death: she sees her, in the presence of witnesses, only after her mother is no longer the kind of threat a living Lady Dedlock poses. When Esther pulls aside the veil of hair, as she once pulled aside her own hair before the mirror, to see that the heavy head is *not* Jenny's, the moment seems emptied of its full meaning. Cold and dead, no longer passionate, haughty, and alive, Lady Dedlock offers nothing really dangerous to encounter. And, in dying for her own sins, she seems also to atone for those which have accrued to Esther as an essentially innocent participant in the "dreadful thing" that is the human condition.

The endings of Dickens' novels are rarely satisfactory. Inseparable from that imaginative integrity which I have mentioned there is in Dickens that equally powerful desire to eradicate much that his novels so effectively dramatize. No honest reader can be really comfortable with the concluding pages of *Bleak House*. Esther's marriage to Allan Woodcourt, their retreat to a virtual reproduction of the original Bleak House are, I think, discordant notes in the novel. But there is evidence that Dickens himself is aware of the falseness of the ending and works to emphasize the arbitrariness of it. For Esther's happiness is achieved in the midst of general misery. Richard Carstone dies. Ada becomes the captive of Jarndyce's coercive benevolence. Caddy Jellyby's [*sic*] baby is deaf and dumb, her husband an invalid. Even Mrs. Snagsby's jealousy reminds us that marriage is no final answer to the human capacity for the irrational: there will always be Mrs. Snagsbys convinced of their husbands' infidelities—and there will always be, in fact, unfaithful husbands and unfaithful lovers.

The double narrative itself helps us to retain a complex awareness of things. A final description of Chesney Wold precedes Esther's final words about herself and her felicity:

> Thus Chesney Wold. With so much of itself abandoned to darkness and vacancy; with so little change under the summer shining or the wintry lowering: so sombre and motionless always—no flag flying now by day, no rows of lights sparkling by night; with no family to come and go, no visitors to be the souls of pale cold shapes of rooms, no stir of life about it;—passion and pride, even to the stranger's eyes, have died away from the place in Lincolnshire, and yielded it to dull repose. (lxvi)

It is a place inhabited by invalids with blighted dreams, an asylum for those who cannot deal with the new hell that Mr. Rouncewell, the ironmaster, is now creating to replace the hell of the dying aristocracy. "Thus Chesney Wold." Thus Bleak House in Yorkshire. Perhaps Allan Woodcourt and Esther, surrounded by the blighted lives of their friends, are no less refugees from an alien world than are Volumnia, Mrs. Rouncewell, George, and Sir Leicester.

Bleak House ends, as it begins, in ambiguity. Esther seems to have gained the "right to be." She observes, "the people even praise Me as the doctor's wife. The people even like Me as I go about, and make so much of me that I am quite abashed" (lxvii). Esther seems at last to possess an identity, even if it is primarily that of "the doctor's wife." And, yet, this gentle affirmation is not the conclusion of Esther's narrative. Rather, Esther finds herself before her "glass," puzzling over the image that is reflected there:

> "My dear Dame Durden," said Allan, drawing my arm through his, "do you ever look in the glass?"
> "You know I do; you see me do it."
> "And don't you know that you are prettier than you ever were?"
> I did not know that. I am not certain that I know it now. (lxvii)

This is not simply Esther at her self-abasing worst. There is no reason to assume that the face she sees "now" in her glass is any more herself than the altered face which met her eyes after her illness. She lives in a relationship to that image of herself which she perceives in her glass, in her imagination, in the eyes of others. But that the image is truly herself can never be known. Even the words of others cannot be fully trusted. Allan Woodcourt has never known Esther completely. She has been quite forthright when she tells him, however quietly, that during and following her illness she has had "many selfish thoughts." Woodcourt's response resonates throughout the final exchange of the novel: " 'You do not know what all around you see in Esther Summerson' " (lxi). But what others choose to see in Esther may be no more than their own conception of her. Ultimately, neither Woodcourt nor others can affirm the absolute validity of that face they see. Esther, after all, has found herself at the conclusion of her progress in but another conspiracy to make her, and others, happy. To be known as Dame Durden is not, finally, to be Dame Durden. This version of Esther may not be consonant with what she truly is. We are left, with Esther, not seeing face to face, but looking through a glass darkly, seeking the forever elusive self floating within the mirror's depths beyond the reflection on its surface. The veil between the self and self-knowledge is never fully raised.

"It is too often forgotten that man is impossible without imagination, without the capacity to invent for himself a conception of life, to 'ideate' the character his is going to be. Whether he be original or a plagiarist, man is the novelist of himself."[9] There is no end, no period, to *Bleak House* or to the novel which is Esther's unfolding self: there is a dash, a hiatus, and no more. We encounter another mystery. Esther remains as enigmatic as the Roman figure of Allegory floating upon the ceiling of Tulkinghorn's chambers, a silent witness whose pointing hand is subject to the arbitrary suppositions of the "excited imagination," and to endless interpretation.

Notes

1. Frank Kermode, "Survival of the Classic," in *Shakespeare, Spenser, Donne: Renaissance Essays* (New York: Viking Press, 1971), p. 170.

2. Charles Dickens, *Bleak House* (London: Oxford University Press, 1962), vii. References to Dickens' novels are all to the Oxford Illustrated Dickens; subsequent quotations are identified by chapter number in parentheses.

3. See William Axton, "Esther's Nicknames: A Study in Relevance," *Dickensian* 62 (1966), 158–63, for a discussion of the implications of Esther's nicknames.

4. See Alex Zwerdling, "Esther Summerson Rehabilitated," *PMLA* 88 (1973), 429–39. Mr. Zwerdling's essay appeared when my essay was in the final stages of revision. There are obvious parallels between our views of Esther. However, I believe my own concern with certain patterns of language in *Bleak House* and my effort to make Esther a part of the novel as a whole, in a manner different from Mr. Zwerdling's, will become clear.

5. See J. Hillis Miller, "*Bleak House*," in *Charles Dickens: The World of His Novels* (Cambridge: Harvard University Press, 1958), pp. 160–224.

6. See J. Hillis Miller, "Introduction," in *Bleak House*, ed. Norman Page (Baltimore: Penguin Books, 1971), pp. 11–34.

7. See Rollo May, "Contributions of Existential Psychotherapy," in *Existence*, ed. Rollo May, Ernest Angel and Henri F. Ellenberger (New York: Simon and Schuster, 1958), p. 68.

8. Ibid., p. 43.

9. José Ortega y Gasset, "History as a System," in *History As A System and other Essays Toward a Philosophy of History*, trans. Helene Weyl (New York: W. W. Norton, 1961), p. 203.

The High Tower of His Mind: Psychoanalysis and the Reader of *Bleak House*

Albert D. Hutter*

I want to propose a psychoanalytic method which will analyze both an individual reader's response to a text and the common text that many readers share. Two extreme positions define the boundaries of contemporary psychoanalytic criticism: an old school ignores differences among readers and explores only the text's latent content (primal scene, oedipus complex, oral fixation); other critics refuse to analyze the text alone and, like Norman Holland, insist instead that text and individual reader, object and subject, cannot be separated.[1] The first group's reductionism counters the spirit and practice of modern psychoanalysis; the second group overemphasizes the

*Reprinted by permission from *Criticism* 19, no. 4 (Fall 1977); 296–316.

individual reader's reaction and thereby forfeits the freedom to generalize about the *products* of human activity (text) apart from the *experience* of reading.

Reductionistic psychoanalytic criticism often transforms the text into a pretext for extraliterary argument. Frederick Crews, however, suggests that the psychoanalytic method may itself block "the path of a critic who would avoid reductionism." Dismissing most of the recent developments in analytic theory as "complications," Crews wonders whether psychoanalysis can alter its overvaluation of the infantile.[2] I shall later argue that even such sophisticated psychoanalytic critics of Dickens as Gordon Hirsch perpetuate this kind of overvaluation—but not because it is inherent in analytic theory. Two important trends in modern psychoanalysis correct such reductionism. One is a movement away from content analysis toward structural analysis, a position characterized clinically, for example, by Erikson's paper on "The Dream Specimen in Psychoanalysis."[3] A second movement, clear in the widely different approaches of Erikson, Blos, Mahler, the British "object relational" psychoanalysts, and, most recently, Galenson and Horowitz,[4] favors a developmental view which amends an exclusively infant-centered theory. Both movements help free applied psychoanalysis to treat adult concerns as something more than a disguise for earlier conflicts.

In *Five Readers Reading* Norman Holland expands his earlier theory into a valuable affective model. "Processes like the transformation of fantasy materials through defenses and adaptations take place in people," writes Holland, "not in texts. They require a mind, either the writer's or the reader's" (19). The statement is irrefutable, and talking about a text as if it possessed a mind is indeed misleading. But Holland rejects any other way of generalizing about a text apart from its author or readers; he rejects absolutely his own earlier attempt to talk about a common text shared by many readers. Holland writes:

> At first, I believed that the text contained a psychological process of transformation—the fantasy-defense model of *The Dynamics of Literary Response*. The text embodied the transformation fully, and each reader participated in it partially, filtering it through his personality structure, subtracting from the textual totality what he could accept. . . . Alas, responses proved far too idiosyncratic for this subtractive explanation. Then I reluctantly tried the opposite explanation, *never separating the reader from the text* but asking instead how he added it to himself, how he re-created it in his own experience. (my italics, 289)

This is too limiting. We need the freedom to talk about readers and texts both in combination *and* separately, to generalize about shared responses, and to expand our psychoanalytic approach to the text itself as the best correction for what Holland calls "subtractive explanation."

I offer here one way of talking about the structure of a text—not simply this individual reader's structuring of a text—and then relate that structure to a shared pattern of reader response. By analyzing Dickens' double narrative in *Bleak House* and his creation of a synthesizing detective figure, I try to answer specific questions of latent content and reader response.

Inspector Bucket enters *Bleak House*—suddenly—in chapter xxii:

> Mr. Snagsby is dismayed to see, standing with an attentive face between himself and the lawyer, at a little distance from the table, a person with a hat and stick in his hand, who was not there when he himself came in, and has not since entered by the door or by either of the windows. There is a press in the room, but its hinges have not creaked, nor has a step been audible upon the floor. Yet this third person stands there, with his attentive face, and his hat and stick in his hands, and his hands behind him, a composed and quiet listener. He is a stoutly built, steady-looking, sharp-eyed man in black, of about the middle-age. Except that he looks at Mr. Snagsby as if he were going to take his portrait, there is nothing remarkable about him at first sight but his ghostly manner of appearing.
>
> "Don't mind this gentleman," says Mr. Tulkinghorn, in his quiet way. "This is only Mr. Bucket."[5]

The opening sentence interposes a series of phrases between grammatical subject and object and defines that object before it is identifed: his attentive face, his position in the room. Our curiosity is aroused—what is the object of "dismayed to see"?—and then intensified by the delay in completing the main clause. When we finally reach Bucket, he still eludes us, appearing simply as "a person" before he gives way to the hat and stick and to the mysterious circumstances of this first appearance. The second sentence compounds the mystery. It consists of three separate clauses linked by "but" and "nor," and it provides us with three facts, superficially unrelated. As in the first sentence, we focus sharply here on objects—press, hinges, floor—and their capacity to reveal hidden meanings or hidden people. But the more we focus, the more confused we become, as sentence three makes clear: nothing has moved, nothing has been heard, *yet* there this person stands—attentive, listening, composed, the same hat and stick in his hands. This sentence obliges the reader to return to its predecessor to understand its full meaning. Indeed, the entire paragraph builds a series of separate and isolated facts and then implies their interdependence. "But," "nor," "yet," "except" define the gradual emergence of Bucket.

These connectives create the deeper disconnection of Bucket's appearance. For Snagsby, as for the reader, Bucket cannot be explained: he is himself a piece of magic. When reading Dickens we come to expect that all details, all circumstances, will be accounted for. The more bizarre an event, the more disconnected or trivial or apparently accidental, the more important is its ultimate relationship to the plot. The reader is encouraged to believe in a universe which is both knowable and complete. But long after the other mysteries of *Bleak House* have been explained, the explainer himself remains a mystery, and we are never told how he achieved that miraculous first appearance. Dickens' language encourages us to look, to discover, only to be disappointed: a phrase like "there is a press" urges us to look for something substantive, a positive clue, only to find the press empty. The word "there" is again used non-referentially to introduce the phrase "there is nothing," and for a brief moment that is the way we read the noun phrase of the last sentence in the paragraph. The sentence, at least momentarily, implies a nothingness at its subject's core, an emptiness which ends in the comparison of Bucket to a ghost.

The mysteriousness of Bucket is developed throughout by the substitution of part objects for the whole person—"face," "hand," "face," "hand," "hands," and even "step"—or by the repetition of other objects, the hat and stick, which come to stand for the person himself. The "press" in sentence two also stands for Bucket, not only because as a closet it is—like a bucket—a container or receptacle, but because it may also mean something that squeezes: an apparatus for extracting juice (or information).[6] The repeated references to a "person" and a "third person" emphasize Bucket's role as "other," as listener and interpreter. Externally he looks like a tradesman—stout, steady, middle-aged, subdued in dress—but he is in fact compared to an artist-photographer, looking at Snagsby as if he were going to take his portrait. And Dickens develops this parallel between Bucket and the artist, ultimately between the detective and the novelist, throughout *Bleak House*.

Skilled in disguise and dissimulation, Bucket is naturally linked to a great variety of professions in the course of the novel. He is not only an artist (liii, 720) but a student (liv, 724), a gambler (liv, 724), a very early psychoanalyst (liv, 725–26), an angel and a devil by turns (liv, 743), a mind reader (lvi, 762–63), a magician (xxiv, 332), even a god ("a homely Jupiter"—liv, 743). "He is," remarks Dickens, "like man in the abstract. . . . here to-day and gone to-morrow—but, very unlike man indeed, he is here again the next day" (liii, 712). At one point, Bucket adopts the profession of Alan Woodcourt, the novel's ostensible hero. When George returns to his shooting gallery, he finds "a very respectable old gentleman, with grey hair, wearing spectacles and dressed in a black spencer and gaiters and a broad-brimmed hat, and carrying a large gold-headed cane," who reveals himself to be a physician "requested—five minutes ago—to come and visit a sick man, at George's Shooting Gallery." But once they are inside

> the physician stopped, and, taking off his hat, appeared to vanish by magic, and to leave another and quite a different man in his place.
> "Now look'ee here, George," said the man, turning quickly round upon him, and tapping him on the breast with a large forefinger. "You know me, and I know you. You're a man of the world, and I'm a man of the world. My name's Bucket, as you are aware, and I have got a peace-warrant against Gridley." (xxiv, 349)

This passage identifies Bucket with the heroic role of doctor, ready to cure the ills of society; it also identifies detective work with science. Two years before the first appearance of *Bleak House*, Dickens had published an article in *Household Words* entitled "The Modern Science of Thief-taking," which extolled the new "science" of detective work as a deterrent to the "art" of crime.[7] Later in the century it would be claimed that "chemistry, the microscope and the spectroscope," were "unerring detectives," the strongest allies of the police.[8] Bucket is very much the scientist in his objectivity, his coolness, and a rationality so effective that, like science itself, it appears magical to the layman. But Bucket combines scientific objectivity with a peculiar aesthetic of his own. Addressing Sir Leicester and Volumnia Dedlock, Bucket repeatedly describes his "beautiful case—a beautiful case—," but it is beautiful in a special way: "When I depict it as a beautiful case, you see . . . I mean from my point of view. As considered from other points of view, such cases will always involve more or less unpleasantness" (liii, 719). A page later, Dickens is still amusing himself and the reader by having Bucket play the artist as he extracts information from Mercury, Lady Dedlock's footman:

> "Why, you're six foot two, I suppose?" says Mr. Bucket.
> "Three," says Mercury.
> "Are you so much? But then, you see, you're broad in proportion, and don't look it. You're not one of the weak-legged ones, you ain't. Was you ever modelled now?" Mr. Bucket asks, conveying the expression of an artist into the turn of his eye and head.
> Mercury never was modelled.
> "Then you ought to be, you know," says Mr. Bucket; "and a friend of mine that you'll hear of one day as a Royal Academy Sculptor, would stand something handsome to make a drawing of your proportions for the marble. My Lady's out, ain't she?"
> "Out to dinner."
> "Goes out pretty well every day, don't she?"
> "Yes."
> "Not to be wondered at!" says Mr. Bucket. "Such a fine woman as her, so handsome and so graceful and so elegant, is like a fresh lemon on a dinner-table, ornamental wherever she goes."   (liii, 720–21)

Soon after, Bucket is clearly identified with the other artist of this novel, the omniscient narrator.[9] Bucket has been empowered to trace Lady Dedlock and to prevent her suicide. He has, in good detective fashion, wandered about her room, looked into her mirror and cupboards, sniffed at her possessions like a bloodhound. He emerges with a handkerchief belonging to Esther Summerson. As he waits for Esther to join him, his imagination is already at work trying to locate Lady Dedlock:

> There, he mounts a high tower in his mind, and looks out far and wide. Many solitary figures he perceives, creeping through the streets; many solitary figures out on heaths, and roads, and lying under haystacks. But the figure that he seeks is not among them. Other solitaries he perceives, in nooks of bridges, looking over; and in shadowed places down by

the river's level; and a dark, dark, shapeless object drifting with the tide, more solitary than all, clings with a drowning hold on his attention.

Where is she? Living or dead, where is she? If, as he folds the handkerchief and carefully puts it up, it were able, with an enchanted power, to bring before him the place where she found it, and the night landscape near the cottage where it covered the little child, would he descry her there? On the waste, where the brick-kilns are burning with a pale blue flare; where the straw-roofs of the wretched huts in which the bricks are made, are being scattered by the wind; where the clay and water are hard frozen, and the mill in which the gaunt blind horse goes round all day, looks like an instrument of human torture;—traversing this deserted blighted spot, there is a lonely figure with the sad world to itself, pelted by the snow and driven by the wind, and cast out, it would seem, from all companionship. It is the figure of a woman, too; but it is miserably dressed, and no such clothes ever came through the hall, and out at the great door, of the Dedlock mansion.   (lvi,767)

In the solitary figures and the shapeless object drifting with the tide, Bucket accurately perceives Lady Dedlock's flight toward self-destruction. But he does not yet perceive Lady Dedlock herself—not until the second paragraph. Then, through a series of rhetorical questions and answers, we actually observe what the narrative, several chapters later, will confirm: the Lady Dedlock changed clothes with the brick-maker's woman. The point of view of the detective here merges with that of the omniscient narrator. Poor Jo's belief that Bucket is "in all manner of places all at wunst" is here fulfilled.

The subject matter of this selection is far more complex and difficult than the passage introducing Bucket, and several of the sentences, such as the one beginning "On the waste, where the brick-kilns are burning," are particularly demanding. The reader must fight his way through the prose of this sentence to reach its rapidly disappearing subject: the lonely figure of Lady Dedlock, concealed behind some seventy words of description and circumstantiality. The technique is like that used in sentence one of the initial description of Bucket, but it is more exaggerated and difficult. Yet, the later passage offers us a sense of knowledge and understanding notably lacking in our first meeting with Bucket. We were initially asked to respond to an exposition of isolated facts which could not be fit together. The sentences in the later passage are more markedly cumulative, and their repetitive structure offers a feeling of reassurance. In the second and third sentences of the first paragraph the inversion of subject and object places the sought-for figure immediately before us, and does so over and over again. Although the repetition of "dark, dark" does not bode well for that object, it does, by its very rhythms, convey a certainty of knowledge which was absent before. The second paragraph opens with questions, but they are quickly answered by the third sentence, where the subjunctive mood helps to merge the perspectives of Bucket and the omniscient narrator. That mood, which grows out of the wish to see Lady Dedlock, moves to more explicit—even miraculous—detail. Bucket, the artist, builds a vision from a single material object, the handkerchief, and finds magic in the web of it; through the accretion of compelling images his speculation becomes narrative truth.

In the passage introducing Bucket the word "there" was repeated as a pronoun, a function word; the later selection begins with "there" used as an adverb meaning "in that place," and the same word is used in the same way in the second paragraph; "would he descry her *there?*" The word now points toward something more definite; it has become referential and adds to our sense of discovering something, rather than, as in the initial selection, uncovering "nothing." When, toward the close of the first paragraph, "there" is used as a function word in the primary clause ("there is a lonely figure"), the word now also seems to be referential as well, pointing out the place where the figure is. I feel the thrust of these paragraphs to be toward the identification and solution of a mystery, whereas the language of the first selection helped me to build a mystery out of its syntax and its focus on isolated objects.

Dickens' sleight of word connects his sentences, so that the end of one becomes the apparent subject or object of the next. Such a connection is made with the "dark, dark, shapeless object" of the first paragraph, which initially appears to be the object of the earlier "perceives" but becomes the subject of the later verb "clings." Similarly, in the second paragraph, the phrase "would he descry her there?" appears to have an immediate answer— there, "on the waste." Syntax thus creates the illusion of intimate connection between separate facts and observations, and the very complexity of the writing gives the reader a sense of meaning and knowledge which was so remarkably absent when Bucket first appeared. By the time Bucket has "mounted the high tower of his mind," reader, omniscient narrator, and detective all seem to share a common perspective and, for the moment at least, a common identity.

The two Bucket passages demonstrate two stylistic polarities that Dickens frequently exploited: the splitting of figures and objects leading toward mystification and their ultimate reunification through syntax, through vocabulary and image, through the temporal movement of phrases as they register upon a reader. This broad manipulation of language is certainly not restricted to descriptions of detectives, although detectives assume a particularly important role in Dickens' fiction and the fiction of the later nineteenth century by reuniting a chaotic world through knowledge and through language. But the specific qualities of style I have identified here are inherent in all language, as Richard Ohmann suggests when he speaks of a subverbal demand for completion:

> To state something is first to create imbalance, curiosity, where previously there was nothing, and then to bring about a new balance. . . . prose builds on the emotional force of coming to know . . . resolving the tensions which exist between the human organism and unstructured experience.[10]

Norman Holland extends this argument to the experience of reading: "The reader, by means of his ego's ability to organize and synthesize reality, creates a unity from his positive relations to the story. Each act of reading is constructive."[11]

Dickens' readers constantly retrace, from the simplest level of phrase and sentence to the broadest experience of plot, a process of mystification and solution—or resolution. Even in his comic passages, Dickens manipulates linguistic suspense:

> There was an innocent piece of dinner-furniture that went upon easy castors and was kept over a livery stable-yard in Duke Street, Saint James's, when not in use, to whom the Veneerings were a source of blind confusion. The name of this article was Twemlow. Being first cousin to Lord Snigsworth, he was in frequent requisition, and at many houses might be said to represent the dining-table in its normal state. (*Our Mutual Friend*, ii, 6)

The humor of making Twemlow, the quintessential poor relation, into a piece of furniture turns on Dickens' continued ability to surprise us in moving from phrase to phrase, manipulating our expectations of agreement and appropriate language. Here he again exploits the non-referential "there was" form noted earlier, using its vagueness to push the reader too quickly into answering the question "What was?" The first answer ("It was") momentarily forces us to treat Twemlow in the way he is treated by virtually everyone in the novel—as an object. Twemlow's famous relation dominates the quotation's last sentence, but the quotation closes without either Twemlow's name or even a representative pronoun where we would normally expect it ("and at many houses [he] might be said . . ."). The very qualities which, at the level of plot, determine Dickens' handling of crime, suspense, and detection here contribute to his comic language. Twemlow appears and disappears before our eyes, and such conjuring tricks mystify and disturb. As the reader moves from phrase to phrase, he must solve apparent verbal contradictions and consequently reexamine his own perceptions. Bucket helps the reader to explore and resolve these central mysteries in *Bleak House*. And as Bucket solves the restricted "mystery story" of Lady Dedlock, he also guides the reader's emotional development.[12]

When we first saw him, Bucket was a cipher, almost invisible, "nothing." We saw him through Snagsby, a sympathetic character throughout the novel, and in Snagsby's impressionable mind Bucket was inextricably linked with the powerful and secretive lawyer, Tulkinghorn. Snagsby is not alone. "Bucket," writes John Lucas, "is like Tulkinghorn. He takes possession of people in a way that denies any deep sense of human responsibility."[13] Lucas dismisses the change which will occur later in Bucket as "a simplifying and sentimentalizing of his earlier image. . . . Bucket emerges as a man whose unpleasantness and human inadequacies are intimately bound into his social role. He is incurious and complacent." J. Hillis Miller also connects Bucket and Tulkinghorn, but he distinguishes between Tulkinghorn's retrospective detection, acting only on the past, and Bucket's "superb logic" which acts on both past and present. However, Bucket still fails because "he is always a moment or two behind the event itself. . . . However superhuman his prodigies of deduction, he can only reconstruct the past, even though it may be a past which has just happened. He is unable to anticipate the future, and he is thus, in the end, immensely inferior to the divine Providence."[14]

He may well be inferior to divine Providence, but as we have seen in the "high tower" passage, Bucket attains a godlike stature of his own; he does anticipate the future. Miller's point, however, is part of a widely accepted moral view of Bucket. Michael Steig calls Bucket "a monster whitewashed . . . who begins as a fittingly grotesque representative of law and order but ends as a kind of hero."[15] Citing Philip Collins,[16] Steig notes the apparently heartless way in which Bucket proceeds against poor Jo, Gridley, and even Mr. George, whom Bucket arrests and leaves in jail when he knows George to be innocent; yet later, complains Steig, as Bucket becomes an increasingly important character, he also seems more humane. But this change is prepared for and is consistent with other character transformations in the novel;[17] the transformation appears contrived only when we expect Bucket's character to develop realistically and when we ignore the thematic significance of his behavior and its impact on the reader. From the "high tower of his mind" Bucket identifies imaginatively with Lady Dedlock. His action and the language in which it is described enlarge the reader's empathic understanding.

Bucket's progress guides our progress until Bucket eventually bridges the narrative gulf of the novel. Linked from the beginning to the omniscient perspective, knowing, observant, cool to the point of apparent heartlessness, Bucket's alliance with Esther in the final chase symbolically connects him with the emotional subjectivity of the first person narration, and the plot now ties the various strands of the novel together. Dickens' outline for this chapter begins as follows:

chapter LVI.
Pursuit.

Sir Leicester ill. To him, Mr. Bucket. "Save her"—
Hurry, in pursuit. Handkerchief. *Takes Esther
    with him.* Hurry, Hurry!
All Esther's Narrative? No.
Pursuit interest sustained throughout.
Ending with the churchyard gate, and Lady Dedlock
lying dead upon the step.

Mr. Bucket and Esther.[18]

In this outline, Bucket first appears as part of the mystery plot. Dickens then wonders about the narrator: Esther alone will not do, since the detective theme ("pursuit interest") must be continued. Eventually, with a separate note, "Mr. B. and Esther," Dickens uses detection and pursuit to blend the two narratives. As the completed number shows, the detective's fascination

with detail ("Handkerchief") will link two very different narrative perspectives and two very different emotional points of view.

Bucket's ability, however, is not absolute. He is godlike but not God, as
Mlle. Hortense makes clear:

> "Listen then, my angel," says she, after several sarcastic nods. "You
> are very spiritual. But can you restore him [Sir Leicester] back to live?"
> Mr. Bucket answers "Not exactly."
> "That is droll. Listen yet one time. You are very spiritual. Can you
> make a honourable lady of Her?"
> "Don't be so malicious," says Mr. Bucket. (liv, 743)

This passage articulates the limitations of knowledge and empathy, and
Bucket's experience at the close of the novel governs our own experience of
the text. Like Bucket, we may become involved in human affairs, we may
learn about them and try to "solve" them, we may at times (and especially in
the experience of reading fiction) attain a temporary, godlike perspective
where we not only integrate the past and the present but look accurately into
the future. But we cannot absolutely control the universe we observe.
Bucket, as detective, is not a notably flawed human being; on the contrary,
the detective in *Bleak House* is a particularly representative figure with
characteristic human limitations.[19] The failures of detection, like its triumphs, mirror the activity of reading itself, that search for connection, explanation, and motive which must remain, at best, partially complete.[20]

The achievement of *Bleak House* rests with its particularly complex view
of human and social behavior, and the reader is encouraged to share that
view by trying to make sense out of it, by trying to complete its puzzling
disconnections, by "solving" its plot. If it is to remain believable, the plot
cannot be solved in any final sense. Dickens' greatest aesthetic problem in
this novel was to achieve a balance between complexity and solution, between the stretching of narrative and emotional perspective and the reader's
desire for unification and reconciliation.[21] Bucket moves between the two
narrations and brings them together, but he does not, and cannot, make
them perfect. The problems raised by *Bleak House* dominate the remainder
of Dickens' career. He would increasingly challenge his readers to reinte-
grate a fictional world intentionally split or fragmented. Even his sense of
history, as rendered in *A Tale of Two Cities*, is subordinated to the dominant
double vision of that novel, to a process of splitting and reintegration which
is particularly striking in its double plot, doubled characters, and dual setting. And his final novel builds its story from the beginning out of a mind that
is itself fragmented, so that the split consciousness of John Jasper seems to
determine the structure of *Edwin Drood*.

Dickens' style often exploits a process of splitting and reintegration. This
process controls the structure of individual phrases and sentences and the
larger structures of plot and theme. Splitting lends itself to Dickens' social

interests, reproducing for the reader the isolation and fragmentation which inform *Bleak House* and the author's satire. Fragmentation creates caricature, and the caricatures themselves—like the Jellybys or Mrs. Snagsby—recall the novel's preoccupation with parental care and parental loss. Splitting and reintegration define both a dominant technique and a dominant theme in this text.

These two processes have a universal psychological function which transcends any single historical period or social context. As a defense, splitting allows us to cope with and conceptualize the world, and it develops very early in all children; a normal part of individual growth, splitting helps to determine our first relationship. In these early years of life we begin to establish an individual identity while maintaining a necessary dependence on others, especially the mother. Psychoanalytic theory has increasingly attributed significance to this developmental period, which both predates and to a large extent determines the outcome of the oedipal struggle. We are, at birth, absolutely dependent, but we always remain "relatively dependent on a mother," or on some nurturing relationship:

> "Growing up" entails a gradual growing away from the normal state of human symbiosis, of "one-ness" with the mother. . . . This growing away process is . . . a lifelong mourning process. *Inherent in every new step of independent functioning is a minimal threat of object loss* [loss of the internal image of a significant individual]. . . . Consciousness of self and absorption without awareness of self are the two polarities between which we move, with varying ease and with varying degrees of alteration or simultaneity . . . this development takes place in relation to (*a*) one's own body, and (*b*) the principal representative of the world, as the infant experiences it, namely the primary love object. *As is the case with any intrapsychic process, this one reverberates throughout the life cycle.* It is never finished; it can always become reactivated; new phases of the life cycle witness new derivatives of the earliest process still at work.[22]

The theory of individuation is relevant to *Bleak House* in two ways: it accounts for the thematic core of Dickens' story, the relationship between Esther and Lady Dedlock, between mother and child, which derives its dramatic impact from a traumatic separation, a subsequent reintegration which cannot be maintained, and the ultimate loss of the mother. Dickens referred to the discovery of the relationship between Esther and Lady Dedlock as "the great turning idea of the Bleak House."[23] The second and more pervasive relevance of separation and individuation in *Bleak House* is to the structure of the novel: the double narration and double plot, reconnected, in large part through Bucket, at the close; the splitting of emotional perpectives implicit in the double narration, that separation of objective and emotional attitudes which come to be equated with intellectual clarity, coolness, and isolation on the one hand and emotional involvement, empthy, and a narrowed subjective vision on the other; and the time split, which carries additional significance if it is related to the psychological trauma of separation itself. Nostalgia, for example, arises from precisely such an attempt to recapture an earlier unity by introducing past experience and emotion into present time.

In practice, the various echoes of separation and individuation—in content and through formal structure—are merged in our experience of the story as we read. Through our identification with Esther we may well experience the novel's central action as a "splitting of the object," in this case, a division of the mother into an unloving godmother and an idealized parent (Jarndyce). The novel may thus stimulate a specific fantasy involving the recovery and attempted reintegration of a lost or divided image of a parent, but this fantasy is in turn governed by the more formal splitting of narrative, plot, affect. Insofar as we experience Esther's story as a recapitulation of the separation-individuation process, the novel's structure will govern our response to that, or any other, fantasy. Put another way, no isolated psychoanalytic analysis of content can be convincing, in part because such an analysis always asks us to read through the *apparent* content to latent meaning, and if we focus exclusively on psychosexual content, we must assume that every reader creates an identical "deep" fantasy in reaction to the novel. Some readers may have had a normal experience of separation-individuation at this earliest phase but have suffered at later moments when the same crisis is most likely to re-emerge (i. e., adolescence); other readers may have had a good developing relationship with their mothers but an extremely difficult relationship with their fathers; still others will have suffered critical losses of one or both parents at varying times in their lives. How can psychoanalysis account for readers' various backgrounds, assuming a reasonable ability and sensitivity to the text on the part of different readers? The answer, I think, must be that it cannot account for response if it equates response with a single statement about latent *content*, but that it can account for a wide range of response if it analyzes psychological *structure*. The combination of Esther's story with the complex plot and narration should evoke in the reader of *Bleak House* a response to a psychological problem (separation) which continues through life, and to a universal adaptive process (splitting). Different readers are bound to respond in different ways, but it is possible to describe broadly the nature of their psychological response and to relate it to the structure of the text.

A thorough psychoanalytic reading of a novel must incorporate, and even transcend, the specific limitations of content or psychological subject matter. A stage like separation-individuation or a process like splitting-reintegration originates in infancy, but because these issues continue to operate unconsciously in adult life their appearance in a literary work does not oblige us to contradict the obvious: that the text is an adult product read by adults with adult concerns, and these concerns are not simply a disguise or bribe for something "earlier," "deeper," or somehow "more fundamental."

According to Anton Ehrenzweig, splitting and reintegration are essential in the creation of any work of art:

Fragmentation, to a certain extent, is an unavoidable first stage in shaping the work and mirrors the artist's own unavoidably fragmented personality. The artist must be capable of tolerating this fragmented state without undue persecutory anxiety, and bring his powers of unconscious scanning to bear in order to integrate the total structure through the countless unconscious cross-ties that bind every element of the work to any other element. This final integrated structure is then taken back (re-introjected) into the artist's ego and contributes to the better integration of the previously split-off parts of the self.[24]

This analysis of artistic creation also applies to reader response, and specifically to reader response in *Bleak House*. The initial sense of fragmentation, the need to tolerate that fragmentation, and finally to integrate it will structure our responses to the novel. The entire process is considerably aided by the detective story form, with its movement toward order and completion which the reader then takes back (re-introjects) into his own consciousness. *Bleak House* creates a particularly clear structure for stimulating in its readers a process of fragmentation, integration, and re-introjection of a "whole object." And its final integration is achieved in large measure through the "syncretistic"[25] or synthetic figure of the detective. The very form of serial fiction, read in weekly or monthly numbers for a year or more, must have further stimulated in its readers a similar integrative process. The reading audience "takes in" the monthly parts, ponders events, projects into the future and rereads the past, living with the story until it becomes connected and whole.

Most psychoanalytic criticism of this novel has concerned itself with isolated psycho-sexual symbolism or with a psychoanalysis of the characters—as if they were real—rather than with the effects of character, style, narrative form on the reader. The sexual "crime" of Lady Dedlock and Captain Hawdon has been a central subject of psychological speculation. "The action of this novel," claims one recent critic, "generates from a disguised fantasy of sexual guilt. . . . sexual energy becomes displaced and colored with guilt because it threatens to subvert the orderly outside world."[26] Esther turns out to be the primary victim of such guilt and must, according to Alex Zwerdling, be "rehabilitated" from an early psychic "trauma," a childhood "wound that never fully heals."[27] Gordon Hirsch claims more broadly that "the mysteries of *Bleak House* are connected at root with the child's curiosity about parental sexuality and his struggle to manage his own complex and ambivalent feelings about that sexuality."[28] The complex actions of the novel, and particularly the detective plot, are here reduced to infantile content, to a hidden "primal scene," or to a vague "sexual guilt."

I believe that all of these interpretations have psychological accuracy and teach us something important about the text, but they are not central to any balanced critical analysis of the novel. The "primal scene" thesis is a good example, since the appearance of the primal scene here and in other detective stories has been analyzed at length.[29] Yet what does it mean to postulate, as Hirsch does, that *Bleak House's* success as a formal mystery is built from its successful working through of "its latent content, its concern with the investigation of the mysteries associated with parental sexuality" (152)? We are being asked to accept that our response is derived from our own actual or fantasized primal scene experience, our own individual memories of, or speculations about, our parents' sexuality.

The broader psychological patterns I have suggested seem far more appropriate than any specific fantasy derived solely from the content of the novel. By definition, the process of splitting and the stage of separation-individuation predate and determine more specific events, such as the trauma of witnessing a primal scene. These processes are universal, which is not the case for the literal primal scene nor even for the generalized guilt and psycho-sexual disturbances cited by other psychoanalytic critics. Most important, such processes or stages develop through an entire life, and conflicts derived from them are appropriate to the adult readers of a novel. Later developmental conflicts incorporate traces of early experiences, but they are not reducible to them. If we recognize the range and significance of developmental issues in the adult reader of a novel, we are not obliged to attribute the "true" power of a text to its infantile determinants, even if we can prove, through an analysis of imagery or through biographical interpolations, the relationship of events within the text to an early childhood trauma outside that text.

Dickens manipulates the inherent suspense of language and exploits crime, mystery, and its ultimate solution to intensify a more general quality of reading prose—indeed of human development—and to connect language with a dominant fictional theme, the recovery of the lost parent. Dickens' "detective style" thus builds on every reader's experience of transforming, from infancy, a mysterious and alien world into something integrated, whole, and ultimately, internalized. *Bleak House* enables us to reexperience a basic and pervasive pattern of psychological growth.

Notes

1. See particularly *Poems In Persons* (New York: Norton, 1973) and *Five Readers Reading* (New Haven: Yale University Press, 1975).

2. "Reductionism and Its Discontents," *Out Of My System: Psychoanalysis, Ideology, and Critical Method* (New York: Oxford University Press, 1975), p. 176.

3. *Journal of the American Psychoanalytic Association*, 2 (1954), 5–56.

4. Mahler works almost exclusively with infant and early child observation, Galenson extends the range of such observation, Blos, following Erikson, studies adolescence and its relationship to earlier behavior, while Horowitz attempts to analyze adult problems in cognitive terms. All of these writers recognize the influence of later behavior on earlier constructs and all of them attempt to enlarge the psychoanalytic model of development. See Margaret Mahler, *On Human Symbiosis and the Vicissitudes of Individuation* (New York: International Universities Press, 1968) and "On the First Three Subphases of the Separation-Individuation Process," *The*

International Journal of Psychoanalysis, 53 (1972), 333–38; Eleanor Galenson, "A Consideration of the Nature of Thought in Childhood Play," *Separation-Individuation: Essays in Honor of Margaret S. Mahler,* eds. J. B. McDevitt and C. F. Settlage (New York: International Universities Press, 1971), pp. 41–49; Galenson and Herman Roiphe, "The Impact of Early Sexual Discovery on Mood Defensive Organization and Symbolization," *The Psychoanalytic Study of the Child* (New York: Quadrangle Books, 1971), pp. 195–216; Galenson, Roiphe, and Robert Miller, "The Choice of Symbols," *The Journal of The American Academy of Child Psychiatry,* 15 (1976), 83–96; Galeson and Roiphe, "Some Suggested Revisions Concerning Early Female Development," *Journal of the American Psychoanalytic Association,* 24 (1976), 29–57; Peter Blos, *On Adolescence* (New York: The Free Press, 1962); Mardi J. Horowitz, *Stress Response Syndromes* (New York: Jason Aronson, 1976). I shall use object relations theory, particularly the work of Anton Ehrenzweig, later in this paper.

5. Charles Dickens, *Bleak House* (London: Oxford University Press, 1949), xxii, 307–8. All citations of Dickens' works are to the Oxford Illustrated Edition; they include chapter and page and appear parenthetically following the quotation.

6. J. Hillis Miller notes that the name "Bucket" suggests both a repository (for evidence) and something hollow (*Charles Dickens: The World of His Novels* [Bloomington: Indiana University Press, 1958], p. 176).

7. William Henry Wills, "The Modern Science of Thief-taking," *Household Words,* 1 (13 July 1850), 368–72.

8. Allan McL. Hamilton, M. D., "The Scientific Detection of Crime," *Appleton's Journal,* 15 (24 June 1876), 825–27.

9. When Bucket is first introduced he is referred to as both a "person" and a "third person" (xxii, 307). It is tempting to see this as a reference to Bucket's ultimate identification with the third person narrator, but it is not very likely that Dickens was here anticipating a Jamesian concern with narrative point of view. Dickens is not making a self-conscious narrative innovation, but he does treat Bucket as a kind of god *and* a kind of author. John Forster called Dickens' detective "the immortal Bucket," thus elevating Bucket to heaven—or even beyond—to join "the Inimitable" (*The Life of Charles Dickens* [London: J. M. Dent and Sons, 1966], 2, p. 116.).

Dickens was certainly aware of the meaning of first and third person narration. "He often speaks of himself in the third person," Dickens writes of Durdles, in *The Mystery of Edwin Drood,* "perhaps, being a little misty as to his own identity, when he narrates" (iv, 37). In *Nicholas Nickleby* Wackford Squeers has his own identity problems which are also reflected in his grammar: "It's me," he says, greeting Peg Sliderskew, "and me's the first person singular, nominative case, agreeing with the verb 'it's,' and governed by Squeers understood" (lvii, 750).

10. "Prolegomena to the Analysis of Prose Style," in *The Theory of the Novel,* ed. Philip Stevick (New York: The Free Press, 1967), p. 207.

11. *Five Readers Reading,* p. 122.

12. Several critics, beginning with Edmund Wilson, have noted the particular importance of the detective and the detective story in *Bleak House.* See: Edmund Wilson, "Dickens: The Two Scrooges," *The Wound and the Bow* (1941; rpt. London: Methuen, 1961), p. 32; Morton D. Zabel, *Craft and Character* (New York: Viking, 1957), pp. 40–41; Robert A. Donovan, "Structure and Idea in *Bleak House,*" *ELH,* 29 (1962), 190; Albert J. Guerard, "Bleak House: Structure and Style," *Southern Review,* 5 (1969), 334. More recently, Ian Ousby has suggested that Bucket guides Esther not only in the literal chase after Lady Dedlock but toward greater knowledge, and that such guidance also directs the reader of the novel. See particularly "The Broken Glass: Vision and Comprehension in *Bleak House,*" *Nineteenth-Century Fiction,* 29 (1974–75), 391–92; and *Bloodhounds of Heaven: The Detective in English Fiction from Godwin to Doyle* (Cambridge: Harvard University Press, 1976), pp. 105–10.

13. *The Melancholy Man: A Study of Dickens's Novels* (London: Methuen and Co., 1970), p. 215.

14. *Charles Dickens,* pp. 174–76.

15. "The Whitewashing of Inspector Bucket: Origins and Parallels," *Papers of the Michigan Academy of Science, Arts, and Letters,* 50 (1965), 575.

16. Philip Collins had written: "One of the greatest compliments a novelist can pay to his characters is to let them harm the 'good' characters with impunity. In *Bleak House,* Inspector Bucket also proceeds against Jo, and against Gridley and George Rouncewell as well, without ever being meant to forfeit our approval" (*Dickens and Crime* [1962, rpt. London: Macmillan and Co., 1965], p. 204). Steig notes the word "meant" and questions "the consistency of Dickens' intentions" (576).

17. See, for example, Alex Zwerdling, "Esther Summerson Rehabilitated," *PMLA,* 88 (1973), 429–39. Zwerdling's argument concentrates on the importance of character transformations in *Bleak House,* and particularly on the transformation which takes place in Esther: "The blossoming of Esther's working intelligence is a continuous and uninterrupted process in the book" (433).

18. The number plans for the novel are reprinted in Duane DeVries' edition of *Bleak House* (New York: Thomas Y. Crowell, 1971), pp. 837–75.

19. Ellen Serlen writes that "it is precisely Bucket's function to detect the objective reality masking the appearance. He has the ability to cut through the fog to the light. Bucket is 'a man of the world,' a good man not despite his profession, but because of it" ("The Two Worlds of *Bleak House,*" *ELH,* 43 [1976], 556).

20. The peculiar transparency of Esther's narration complements Bucket's partial vision. She must portray others—like her "god-mother," or Mrs. Jellyby or Skimpole—so that we may make a more realistic judgment than she is inclined, or even able, to do. Different perspectives in the novel thus balance and correct one another, giving the reader an omniscient perspective as he connects the limited visions within the novel, but also reminding the reader of the inevitable subjectivity of all narrative accounts. Dickens here anticipates Wilkie Collins' more complex experiments with narrative point of view—and detection.

21. Serlen argues that the two worlds of *Bleak House* "are intended to be two totally separate entities rather than two halves of a whole fictional world" (551). H. M. Daleski maintains that the double narrative is not a double story, but one plot arbitrarily split in two (*Dickens and the Art of Analogy* [London: Faber, 1970], pp. 156–90). Most helpful and persuasive is Ralph W. Rader's unpublished essay delivered to the English Conference, University of California, Berkeley, Spring 1975, "The Comparative Anatomy of Three 'Baggy Monsters': *Bleak House, Vanity Fair, Middlemarch.*" Rader "emphasizes how much Dickens was driven to fragment his novel in the service of giving it general significance." The final section of my own paper attempts to explain the psychological significance of the double narration and the broader structural problems of fragmentation and reintegration.

22. Mahler, "On the First Three Subphases of the Separation-Individuation Process," 333. Mahler's concepts develop directly from Freud's writings on object relations and object libido (334), but her thinking complements British object relations theory. For Melanie Klein and her followers, the mechanism of splitting plays a particularly important role because it "allows the ego to emerge out of chaos and to order its experiences." It "orders the universe of the child's emotional and sensory impressions and is a precondition of later integration" (Hanna Segal, *Introduction to the Work of Melanie Klein,* [New York: Basic Books, 1973], p. 35). Splitting and reintegration refer to a developmental *process,* although there is still a debate over its origins; separation-individuation refers to a *stage* of human development which continues to affect later stages of crisis and transition, such as adolescence.

23. Dickens to Burdett-Coutts, 19 November 1852, *The Heart of Charles Dickens, As Revealed in His Letters to Angela Burdett-Coutts,* ed. Edgar Johnson (New York: Duell, Sloane, and Pearce, 1952), p. 215.

24. Anton Ehrenzweig, *The Hidden Order of Art: A Study in the Psychology of Artistic Imagination* (Berkeley and Los Angeles: University of California Press, 1967), p. 102. For much of my thinking about the literary applications of object relations theory, and particularly the work of

Ehrenzweig, I am indebted to Arthur F. Marotti, "Countertransference, the Communication Process and the Dimensions of Psychoanalytic Criticism," forthcoming in *Critical Inquiry*.

25. This term is used extensively by Ehrenzweig, who borrows in turn from Piaget. For both men, "syncretism" refers to more than simply putting together or synthesizing: it refers to a mode of early thinking in which we do not break down visual objects into component parts but rather we see whole and inclusively. The concept has obvious relevance to art and an often overlooked relevance to the detective in nineteenth-century fiction, because these detectives, beginning with Poe's Dupin, characteristically combine analysis with a broader, intuitive thinking. They are more than logicians and rational problem solvers.

26. Steven Cohan, " 'They Are All Secret': The Fantasy Content of *Bleak House*," *Literature and Psychology*, 26 (1976), 79.

27. "Esther Summerson Rehabilitated," 430.

28. "The Mysteries in *Bleak House:* A Psychoanalytic Study," *The Dickens Studies Annual*, 4 (1975), 133.

29. See particularly Geraldine Pederson-Krag, "Detective Stories and the Primal Scene," *Psychoanalytic Quarterly*, 18 (1949), 207–14, and Charles Rycroft, "A Detective Story: Psychoanalytic Observations," *Psychoanalytic Quarterly*, 26 (1957), 229–45. I detail the inevitable reductionism of these and related essays in "Dreams, Transformations, and Literature: The Implications of Detective Fiction," *Victorian Studies*, 19 (1975), 181–209.

The Battle of Biblical Books in Esther's Narrative

Janet L. Larson*

Dickens alludes to the Bible and *The Book of Common Prayer* more often than to any other texts. Yet weighing the heterogeneous, even antithetical allusions to Scripture in his protean later fiction is a more delicate task than is commonly assumed. These acts of alluding are usually seen as unproblematic performances in Dickens's Victorian "repertoire of the familiar" (to borrow Wolfgang Iser's phrase)[1]—pious gestures toward his culture's most cherished treasury of sacred stories, archetypal images, stable moral values, and privileged inspirational language nineteenth-century readers recognized and required. What has not been examined by some is the assumption that the Bible according to Boz is an unbroken book, like Carlyle's Scripture "before all things *true*, as no other Book ever was or will be."[2] Even without this premise, the Word in Dickens is read as a univocal presence providing interpretive stability within the welter of human voices that strain the limits of orderly discourse in the major novels. Thus biblical allusions and underpatterns are thought to clarify the "religious centre" of fictional works that are "about ends," as Alexander Welsh has argued in *The City of Dickens;* "whatever sense of direction or purpose can be salvaged from experience."[3]

*Reprinted by permission from *Nineteenth-Century Fiction* 38, no. 2 (September 1983):131–60.
© 1983 by the Regents of the University of California.

Certainly Dickens does attempt to use the Bible in these ways. His Esther Summerson, for example, reaches for consolation in the resurrection miracle of Luke 7 in chapter 31 of *Bleak House* ("that young man carried out to be buried, who was the only son of his mother and she was a widow";[4] cf. Luke 7:12) and assumes the reader will immediately recognize this story of the widow of the city of Nain, which also has a prominent place in Dickens's *Life of Our Lord*. But as I will suggest, there are other resurrection miracles in *Bleak House* that jar these Gospel pieties. Such antithetical allusions suggest that it is a broken Scripture which lies behind Dickens's later fiction. As Carlyle very well knew, and taught Dickens to observe, in their times of religious uncertainty and babble of doctrines, the Bible, like nineteenth-century religion, had been "smote at . . . needfully and needlessly" until it was "quite rent into shreds."[5] Certainly Dickens deplored the acrimonious religious debates of his day—what he called in 1856 "those unseemly squabbles about the letter which drive the spirit out of hundreds of thousands";[6] and from the intellectual circles in which the Bible's authority was being debated he was excluded by temperament and education. Nonetheless, Dickens's whole procedure with Scripture, even his harmony of the gospels written for his children (an 1846–49 manuscript suppressed until 1934),[7] presupposed developments in biblical interpretation that had divided the sacred book and jeopardized its claim to absolute authority.

Thus, while rationalist critics were treating Scripture as a book of myths, Dickens was drawing upon some of its stories as divine fairy tales—the Book of Esther on the level of Cinderella. While orthodox typological interpretation was being discredited, with its elaborate readings of Old Testament characters as types or prefiguring shadows of Christ, Dickens's David, Esther, and Job types, even his Christ figures, are wholly humanized; they represent only religious and moral ideals severed from the fuller implications of the typologists' sacred text.[8] Like other Victorian writers Dickens secularized sacred plots; Adam and Eve leave the Garden of Eden at the close of both *Great Expectations* and *Little Dorrit*. More important for the concerns of this essay, the Bible's contradictions that were given such alarming attention in nineteenth-century intellectual circles turn up in the popular novelist's work, as he invites rival subtexts from quite different parts of Scripture to coexist uneasily in the same fictional world.

In the multivocal works of Dickens's maturity, we discover a welter of biblical allusions, echoes, and subtexts which are not altogether concordant: they are capable of being harmonized (as "archetypal patterns" or "the social gospel") only selectively, and more often arrange themselves in patterns of contradiction and dissonance. Like other Victorian novelists described by George Levine in *The Realistic Imagination*, Dickens could not totally "acquiesce in the conventions of order" he had inherited, not even with the Authorized Version; yet he struggled as they did "to reconstruct a world out of a world deconstructing, like modernist texts, all around him."[9] Although Levine excludes Dickens from his survey of Victorian realists, these conflicting aims, I would argue, govern the form of Dickens's mature fictions and direct his manipulations of biblical texts. The hypothesis to be tested through this reading of Esther's Narrative in *Bleak House* is that in Dickens's mature fictional reconstructions the Bible becomes a paradoxical book: it is at once a source of stability, with its familiar conventions of order, and a locus of hermeneutical instability reflecting the times of Victorian religious anxiety in which Dickens wrote.

I

With a deep sense of my great responsibility always upon me when I exercise my art, one of my most constant and most earnest endeavours has been to exhibit in all my good people some faint reflections of the teachings of our great Master. . . . all my good people are humble, charitable, faithful, and forgiving. Over and over again, I claim them in express words as disciples of the Founder of our religion.[10]

Why is all art to be restricted to the uniform level of quiet domesticity? . . . Whenever humanity wrestles with the gods of passion and pain, there, of necessity, is that departure from our diurnal platitudes which the cant of existing criticism denounces. . . . The mystery of evil is as interesting to us now as it was in the time of SHAKESPEARE; and it is downright affectation or effeminacy to say that we are never to glance into that abyss, but are perpetually to construct our novels out of the amenities of respectable, easy-going men and women.[11]

Up to its fairy-tale-like conclusion, Esther Summerson's Narrative is a pious but conflicted approximation of the *Bildungsroman*. In the play of meanings to which the language of this text gives access, Esther's biblical allusions and the subtexts for her account provide points of intelligibility, locating her authorial voice and characterization sub specie aeternitatis, but they are also problematic, occasioning interpretive dissonances that register her unresolved tensions. But to make this claim is to make another assumption not universal among Dickens critics: that Esther as inscribed in her language is more complex than the lineaments of the Christian "ideal" she does embody, as Dennis Walder says, in the "humble, charitable, faithful, and forgiving" actions so important to Dickens.[12] This complexity of characterization is reflected in her allusions because Esther Summerson is one of Dickens's "good people" who are not merely opposed to "the mystery of evil" but are inducted into its depths.

With its task of achieving a more mature self from which to write her spiritual autobiography, Esther's *Bildung* is "A Progress" more subtly elaborated and less shapely than Little Nell's version of the pilgrim journey to which this Bunyanesque chapter title alludes: Esther's is a provisional forward movement toward deeper understanding through many setbacks, descents into false guilt, and authentic encounters with evil, mitigated and redeemed by guardian-angel rescues as well as by Esther's gradual discoveries about herself and about this wicked world which, she believes, the other world "sets . . . right" (p. 763).[13] Up to her final chapter, which begins the fairy-tale resolution with Jarndyce's gift of two hundred pounds, Esther grows toward modest maturity through a narrative pattern that bears partial resemblance to a familiar process in Victorian fiction: myths of identity and society are shattered by disruptions—by Esther's encounters with the incongruous, with what does not fit her picture of herself and the world—as she is gradually and most unevenly educated through her trials.[14] Because Dickens makes her explicitly a religious woman, it might be expected that Esther's biblical texts simply secure her struggles in a reassuring framework, bringing a stability of outlook to the ordering of her narrative and thus to the whole of *Bleak House*. But while her religious mythos generally counters the fury and despair of the other narrator's chaos, Esther's Bible quotations, allusions, echoes, and subtexts also reflect the tensions of her provisional "progress." Granting this character a complexity beyond that of a religious icon.[15] I will argue that in three different senses a battle of biblical books underlies Esther's Narrative.

First and least problematic is the conflict between Law and Gospel. Esther is a "[disciple] of the Founder of our religion" not only in her good deeds but explicitly in some of her sincere biblical citations. Bearing witness to the "broad spirit" of the New Testament in which Dickens professed belief,[16] she repeatedly rewrites in this spirit the narrow letter of Old Testament texts associated with her Calvinist aunt and her self-doomed mother. We see this process of revision most strikingly in the verbal combat of Esther's generating chapter. As though to correct her aunt's vengeful application of Exodus 20:5 in chapter 3 ("pray daily that the sins of others be not visited upon your head, according to what is written"; p. 19), which also omits the Lord's promise of "mercy unto thousands of them that love me, and keep my commandments" (Ex. 20:6),[17] Esther reads to her aunt Jesus' words in John 8:7 reversing the Law for the adulterous woman ("He that is without sin among you, let him first cast a stone at her!"). In an exchange of Scripture texts reminiscent of fundamentalist debates, the aunt interrupts Esther's reading at a place in the Scripture where words of mercy follow ("Neither do I condemn thee: go, and sin no more"; John 8:11) by "crying out, in an awful voice," another Scripture "from quite another part" of the Bible: "Watch ye therefore! lest coming suddenly he find you sleeping. And what I say unto you, I say unto all, Watch!" (p. 21). At this apocalyptic moment, when the aunt hurls Mark 13:35–37 like an Old Testament prophet's warning, she is stricken like a shattered idol, and the visitation upon her self-serving bibliolatry comes down.

Esther is thus melodramatically vindicated early in the novel, but the Law-Gospel debate is not over. As I shall show in my last section, it continues, internalized, in Esther's own dialogues with herself as she strives to unlearn the psychically damaging story about her original guilt for having been born illegitimate—the Law myth which "has utterly nothing to do with God or with justice" and cannot save.[18] This internal battle of the books is the least problematic in the novel because the New Testament values of forgiveness and charity are stable, there for Esther to realize if only she can. Still, the persistent difficulty she has in believing the Gospel for herself subtly puts in question its power to cast out the demons of legalistic modes of thought and feeling. Thus, until her happy resolution, the very persistence of this tension within the religious voice lends some corroboration to the far more profound skepticism of the other narrator, whose bleak account of a populace hopelessly entangled in English legal practice, with its false promises to save, is further darkened by his vision of humanity mired "in a general infection of ill-temper . . . slipping and sliding since the day broke" (p. 5) as though they were created fallen (illegitimate) and remain unredeemed.[19]

To ennoble her Christian character and adumbrate certain plot developments, Dickens also associates his heroine with an Old Testament type of Christ or the Church, the self-sacrificial Queen Esther, who risked death to save her people. More attention will be paid to this parallel shortly; let it be said here that Esther Summerson is not just a "pattern young lady" (p. 747) modeled after an ideal human type, nor is she only a clearly readable sign of the "summer Son,"[20] neatly opposed to the other narrator of Chaos and Old Night. While Dickens associates Esther Summerson with New Testament texts and a Christological queen, he also challenges these identifications in two important ways—the second and third senses in which battles of the books underlie her narrative.

The second is the way that Dickens inducts Esther into the novel's problems by involving her with another type of Christ: the longsuffering and godforsaken Job, whose extensive importance for *Bleak House* is established in the opening chapter,[21] and whose curse upon "the day . . . wherein I was born" (Job 3:3) is invoked upon Esther's birthday in chapter 3. While the Book of Esther, as I shall discuss in the next section, forms a reassuring biblical subtext for this Victorian heroine's autobiography, the parallels also reveal important limits; and these limits are marked by the corrective presence of a Joban subtext qualifying and deepening the meaning of Esther's queenly "progress" through a novel of much *de profundis* poetry. Both the books of Esther and Job are necessary to the general movement of *Bleak House* from curse to blessing amid suffering, but they coexist in tension as though a struggle between their differing perspectives were going on beneath the surface of Esther's story. The Joban subtext also links her account with that of the other narrator: for however carefully Dickens separates his religious and skeptical voices, these two narrators "from opposite sides of great gulfs, have, nevertheless, been very curiously brought together" (ch. 16, p. 197) to form *Bleak House* out of common nineteenth-century experiences, experiences for which many Victorians found the Book of Job an appropriate interpretive paradigm.[22]

Third, Dickens permits alternative interpretations of those Bible passages Esther quotes naïvely as if their hermeneutic stability were absolute, thereby creating the tension not precisely of "books" but of readings (with muted irony at Esther's expense). Because her New Testament passages are frequently used as means of inspirational repression, they often perform a double function: they may speak a gospel that needs to be heard, yet they can also serve unconsciously to "cover a multitude of sins" (I Pet. 4:8) by perpetuating some crucial evasion that makes it easier for Esther to seem to forgive what has not in fact been fully brought to mind. In chapter 8, "Covering a Multitude of Sins," Esther's acts of charity alternate with or double as acts of evasion; even with her pious attempt to comfort the brickmaker's wife (whose baby has died) by "whisper[ing] to her what Our Savior said of children" (p. 100; cf. Mark 10:14), Esther in pointedly making one biblical allusion unconsciously avoids "alluding" to other, unpleasant things.[23] (The unconsoled mother "answered nothing, but sat weeping—weeping very much.") On other occasions of comforting herself, when Esther's own internal struggles culminate in a hopeful text, the Bible becomes an aid to her unstable recoveries from those "glance[s] into that abyss" of evil which periodically draw her attention beyond its "uniform level of quiet domesticity" associated with God's providential care. Because her recoveries *are* only temporary, these moments of biblically sponsored repression become a distinctive note of her narrative; behind them is the Joban existential anxiety she strives faithfully—and vainly—to overcome. Discerning the psychological dynamics of Esther's New Testament usages, the reader enters into Dickens's Victorian understanding of the psychic needs religion serves. That kind of understanding is, of course, mingled with forgiveness for weak Esther, although it is laced with cynicism for the novel's satiric religionists such as Mrs. Pardiggle, whose piety is a "rapacious benevolence" forced upon the poor in order to satisfy her own need to be a "prominent . . . character" (pp. 93, 96).

In arguing for some ironic instability in Esther's New Testament usages, I aim to show that an ambivalence toward conventional religious resolutions is detectable in the self-revealing text produced by this fictional author. Dickens's actual literary intentions and personal state of religious belief as discerned from Esther's voice are impossible to prove definitively from the novel alone, particularly given his use of the uninterpreted first-person point of view for her story.[24] Indeed, what may seem his mimetic use of quotation to reflect Esther's pious but evasive character may more simply indicate his own need to impose religious interpretations on crisis experiences (just as his other narrator imposes divine justice following Krook's death in chapter 32). If that is the case, the irony lies entirely in the skeptical reader's reconstruction of the text and exists at Dickens's as well as Esther's expense. Whatever the author's intentions, the larger point of my reconstruction, in which three battles of biblical books mark Esther's points of tension, is that the whole of *Bleak House*, not just the skeptical narrative, reads as a work written amidst Victorian religious anxieties and discords. What has been called its "radical dilemma . . . between denial and affirmation"[25] is not simply embodied in the existence of two entirely distinct narratives, as many critics assume, but is a tension the reader experiences as well in the fluctuations of Esther's progress.

II

With its similarities to other Persian tales such as *A Thousand and One Nights*, its Cinderella motif, its melodramatic suspense and folkloristic plotting, its "satiric invention" and "comic art,"[26] the Book of Esther is just the sort of Old Testament tale Dickens would have relished. This underpattern for Esther's narrative operates within a moral framework for human action as a fairy story of God's deliverance. To adapt Northrop Frye's terminology in *The Great Code* for the "divine comedy" of other Bible narratives, this book's double U-shaped pattern projects its heroine prophetically upward, takes her through a fall into danger, and propels a second, more glorious rise that identifies her personal victory with the redemption of her race.[27] Commentaries popular in Dickens's day, like Matthew Henry's, emphasized Esther's "[wonderful] concurrence of providences,"[28] the apocalyptic motif elaborately built into the multiple polar reversals of this tale. While the legal and political evils of *Bleak House* are not redeemed like those in the Book of Esther,[29] the novel's theme of the "renewal of faith in divine providence" amid "the apparent hopelessness of a human history dominated by secular power"[30] is the redeeming substance of Esther Summerson's testimony.

Both Esthers begin their stories in bondage followed by Cinderella-like rises in social station and comfort that show how "God . . . rais[es] up friends for the fatherless and motherless."[31] An orphan and, like Esther, "no one" socially (p. 45), the Jewish slave girl earns the people's favor and King Xerxes' notice through her winsome, natural qualities, living up to the name given by her Babylonian captors and derived from Ishtar, goddess of love.[32] Her benefactor Mordecai is a "cousin" who proves so loyal a friend that according to one tradition he generously yields to her "better preferment" as Xerxes' chosen queen even though he desires her (as Jarndyce does Esther) for his own wife.[33] Dickens's "orphan" heroine is born into a peculiarly Victorian captivity: she is captive not to pagans but to biblical texts barbarously applied in an unchristian spirit, and the slave name bestowed is a euphemism to cover the shame of Esther Summerson's fallen woman associations. On her chaste Victorian terms, she too obtains "favour in the sight of all them that looked upon her" (Est. 2:15; cf. Woodcourt's "what sacred admiration and what love she wins"; ch. 61, p. 731). In chapter 3, hints of royalty already attend her childhood "at Windsor" where she says she was "brought up . . . like some of the princesses in the fairy stories, only I was not charming" (p. 17), a way of suggesting noble kinship while denying the sexual charms of her biblical counterpart. As the stories continue, this sexual denial forms the most striking of several important contrasts between these parallel characters.[34]

Both are raised from their "desolate" positions to do their "duty" (as Kenge proses) "in that station in life unto which it has pleased—shall I say Providence?—to call" them (p. 23).[35] The rise of both heroines is tainted by guilt, however, and complicated by hidden identities. To keep her new social positiion as the Persian king's concubine, Queen Esther must conceal the Jewish identity that makes her association with a Gentile unclean. When the plot thickens with the king's edict against Jews and Mordecai's secret appeal that Esther intervene, she delays, fearing for her life if she reveals her Jewish kinship. But the queen cannot escape the pogrom just because she lives in the king's palace any more than Esther Summerson can avoid the general contagion, or conceal forever her connections because she lives in snug Bleak House, or in her illness escape the fiery ring of the human condition.

Forced to difficult choices in their relation to wider communities, both heroines decide to risk self-sacrifice for others, illustrating how "the lives of God's people are so intertwined that none of them can ever find salvation without seeking it for his brothers also."[36] After mourning in solidarity with her people—putting ashes and dung on her head and covering herself "with her tangled hair" (Apoc. Est. 14:2)—the queen appears before the king as a splendid actress ("her countenance was cheerful and very amiable: but her heart was in anguish for fear"; Apoc. Est. 15:5), gradually discloses her kinship, and succeeds in her plea for mercy. Through her mediation, the "*appointed* time" of death to Jews is transmuted into the appointment of a celebration for life, the festival of Purim (Est. 9:27).

Esther Summerson's sacrificial consideration for others and widening circle of charity cause her to be "held in remembrance above all other people" (ch. 13, p. 163), like the "memorable" queen.[37] But even as Dickens's heroine fulfills her biblical commissions, she is enmeshed in complexities of her own: even after she learns her identity, she strives to maintain her social and moral position by acquiescing in the suppression of her true identity and its "unclean" association with Lady Dedlock. While the biblical queen has political reasons for disguise and uses her physical charms for high national purpose, Esther Summerson tries to serve in only a domestic way, and by desexualizing herself. She is not vindicated by playacting but victimized by her subterfuges and incompatible roles, all part of a "communal fantasy"[38] that encourages destructive deceptions. In contrast to the queen who opposes those "placed in authority unworthily" (Apoc. Est. 16:7), Summerson's worst enemies are the demons within that prevent her from establishing her own authority as a coherent person.

Because it lacks this complexity, the Book of Esther is finally an inadequate subtext for Esther's "progress": its characters are Wisdom literature stereotypes,[39] its evils are nominalized in villain figures providentially converted or destroyed, and it does not deal with the psychological and moral dilemmas that Esther Summerson must face in herself, notably the anomaly of guilty innocence. For the Victorian woman who matures to become a "river of good" for others, though much more modestly than the heroine of Mordecai's dream,[40] limited growth comes not through the stark transformations of fairy-tale logic that empower the Book of Esther's forward movement and that prevail only at the happy conclusion of Esther's Narrative but through the more psychologically credible means typical of realist fiction, as her daily trials instruct her progressively in the common human problems of *Bleak House*.

For these maturing experiences, the appropriate subtext is the Book of Job, which offers what Matthew Henry calls "more manly meat" for exercising the spiritual senses than the books (including Esther) preceding it in the Authorized Version. [41] While the Book of Job is framed by a folktale embodying a doctrine of poetic justice similar to Esther's apocalyptic design, the unmerited sufferings in the middle chapters challenge that doctrine. Job's lamentations and his circular, Chancery-like debates pose problems of faith and evil that preoccupy both narrators of *Bleak House:* both in their distinctive ways reveal the limits of worldly wisdom, the failure of the patriarchs to provide trustworthy moral guidance, the prevalence of hermeneutic uncertainty in a world of mysterious signs, and the folly of unrealistic expectation (false apocalyptic and fairy-tale thinking) as well as impious despair. Again and again in this novel's valley of "the shadow of death" (Job 10:22)—and "of the law" (p. 391)—Dickens returns to the *de profundis* poetry of Job that links the two narratives, while in both he portrays a range of Joban character types, from patient sufferers and rebellious victims to miserable false comforters. As I shall show, at different times Esther Summerson embodies all of these types.

The relevance of the Joban subtext for her story is complicated by its introduction in an act of misguided religious zeal; Esther is persecuted by a puritanical society as Job is by God. Treating this living child as "an hidden untimely birth" (Job 3:16), Miss Barbary cruelly transmutes Job's "let the day perish wherein I was born" (3:3) into the social curse upon this nobody's child who should "never [have] been born!" (p. 19). Much of Esther's inner warfare is her confused wrestling with the opprobrium of this misapplied text. Like Job she strives to maintain her belief that God loves her and to assert her honesty and virtue, for both Esther and Job are God's elect, acknowledged for practical acts of charity ("I was eyes to the blind . . . a father to the poor," Job 29:15, 16, a text Dean Stanley used in his funeral sermon on Dickens). Yet in the face of her unmerited calamity of being "born unto trouble" (Job 5:7) in a society that condemns illegitimacy as a crime, Esther feels "confusedly . . . guilty and yet innocent" (p. 20). It is this complex state of soul—caught between a "psalm of innocence" and a "psalm of penitence" as in the Book of Job[42]—that generates internal debate and a shifting style of ambivalent utterance from the third chapter of both narratives.

Esther's ambivalences are nearly ended, as Job's are definitively, only at the end of the book when the hero of faith is rewarded after many trials; but hers comes in a peculiarly Victorian way. Job's debates with a silent God are ended by his admission of utter humbling: "I abhor *myself*, and repent in dust and ashes" (42:6). Esther, in contrast, must recover from self-abhorrence in her pilgrimage toward wholeness of self,[43] moving successfully away from the injustice of the curse upon her birth. In implicitly associating the child with such as Job, Esther's "godmother" had perverted the role of baptismal name-giver, for the Order of Baptism is meant to expel the devil, not bring demonic forces down on the infant's head. But even as Esther is on the way to rejecting a false Job-identification, she encounters in later life her own authentic experiences of the depths, which I will discuss in my final section. Through two major trials that intensify the struggles with the anomalousness she continues to experience in adult life, Dickens's heroine of faith matures in understanding with the hopeful motto for Job-reading which Matthew Henry appended to his exposition of this book, "*Plus ultra—Onward.*"[44] Dickens wanted to ennoble as well as reward Esther through these experiences; as he reminded himself in the memoranda for Number x in his outline for *Bleak House* (where she is stricken blind), "Esther's love must be kept in view, to make the coming trial the greater . . . and the victory the more meritorious."[45] More significant than her suffering is Esther's interpretation of it, her imposition of a progressive pattern, following the Victorian view of Job (as James Anthony Froude wrote) that one might "[tread] his temptations under his feet, and [find] in them a ladder on which his spirit rises.[46] A heroine governed by the conventions of the renunciation story Dickens so admired,[47] Esther, too, is to prove that one can rise on the stepping-stones of one's dead selves to higher things.

Despite this religious pattern, Dickens also shows through Esther's story the self-deceptions and other moral dangers that attend such dyings to self when burial is premature; again, upon the biblical subtext he works his psychological modifications. Esther's modest "progress" labors in fact under double jeopardy, courting the distinctive dangers the two major underpatterns for her story epitomize. With the Book of Esther she risks the simplifications of magical scheming that effect a world of desire: thus she succumbs at times to the temptation to reduce the ways of Providence to simple patterns that confuse her wishes with the Divine Will (see ch. 50, p. 606) and to believe in a fairy-tale logic incongruous with her adult experience—the illogic of her advice to herself after Jarndyce's proposal, "You are happy for life" (ch. 44, p. 538), or the nonsense of the nursery-rhyme vocation of sweeping "the cobwebs out of the sky" when she cannot cleanse Lady Dedlock's guilt nor rightly order Richard Carstone's life. Dickens's Esther learns at length that some things (like Chancery promises) are "too good to be true" in this world (ch. 65, p. 758). If Joban realism qualifies the Book of Esther fantasy, the Joban poetry invading her narrative poses its own perils. Esther risks being consumed by self-pitying passivity and the submerged anger, deflected typically toward herself, of one victimized by "a combination on the part of mankind against an amiable child" (as Skimpole puts the Joban injustice; ch. 61, p. 729). It is because she so narrowly misses embracing the limited views represented in both biblical subtexts, the easy affirmation and the debilitating despair that are both on trial in *Bleak House*, that her development becomes neither "a constantly triumphant progression"[48] nor a downward journey but a more provisional, uncertain Victorian pilgrimage. In its quality of fluctuation, it bears more affinity to *In Memoriam*, which appeared just two years before *Bleak House*, than anything Dickens wrote. Esther's Narrative is his "way of a soul."

III

The biblical allusions associated with Esther's major crises in the second half of the novel (chs. 35, 36, 57, 59) mark her alternations between Joban confusion and despair, Joban patience, and queenly hope; the allusions also mirror her internal stresses between Law and Gospel, showing the reader the moral importance of the endangered New Testament values in which Esther struggles to believe, if also, ironically, the emotional attractiveness of religious language to authorize her mechanisms of evasion. Her resolutions of major conflicts, often culminating in a biblical allusion or echo, are for most of the novel unstable and temporary; compulsively, the familiar battles of texts continue to surface in chapter after chapter.

Esther's first "little trial" (p. 437) of major importance takes up scarcely more than a page in chapter 35. Even more effectively containing the experience than the forced brevity of the account is the familiar biblical pattern in which Dickens encapsulates her dark night of the soul. Suffering Job's "wearisome nights" (Job 7:3) of guilty complaint and diseased imaginings of mortality ("My flesh is clothed with worms and clods of dust"; 7:5), "full of tossings to and fro unto the dawning of the day" (7:4), she nearly meets the "appointed time" of death for which he longs (7:1); and of this she "speak[s] in the anguish of [her] spirit" (7:11). Unlike the bitter complaints of Gridley or the querulous unease of Jobling (a little Job) in chapter 32, Esther reports her "one long night" with tremulous apology as though her "painful unrest" were a bitter blasphemy her Christian reader can scarcely understand or forgive:

> I am almost afraid to hint at that time in my disorder—it seemed one long night, but I believe there were both nights and days in it—when I laboured up collossal staircases, ever striving to reach the top, and ever turned, as I have seen a worm in a garden path, by some obstruction, and labouring again. . . . I would find myself complaining, "O more of these never-ending stairs, Charley,—more and more—piled up to the sky, I think!" and labouring on again. (p. 431)

When the terrors of a godforsaken cosmos come upon her, she is "scare[d] . . . with dreams, and terrifie[d] . . . through visions" (Job 7:14); appalled by the condition she shares with all mortals, like Job she "long[s] for death, but it *cometh* not" (3:21). "Dare I hint," Esther asks timidly,

> at that worse time when, strung together somewhere in great black space, there was a flaming necklace, or ring, or starry circle of some kind, of which *I* was one of the beads! And when my only prayer was to be taken off from the rest, and when it was such inexplicable agony and misery to be a part of the dreadful thing? (p. 432)

Job's "days are swifter than a weaver's shuttle," and he declares his "eye shall no more see good" (7:6, 7). Blind Esther becomes aware of "how short life really was, and into how small a space the mind could put it." "Oppressed . . . by the great perplexity of endlessly trying to reconcile" the disparate images of her life (p. 431), she is "full of confusion" (Job 10:15) about guilt and innocence, for unmerited calamity has challenged the very legitimacy of her existence. Esther has always been oppressed by the sense of an ending—intensified in the apocalyptic images of her fever-nightmare, lingering after her recovery in her consciousness of the lost face, the self she tries to bury. That this loss represents not just a blow to vanity but her new intolerable knowledge of a kind of death she has *chosen* is hinted in Esther's internal questioning as she later waits for Ada's return: "Might she not look for her old Esther, and not find her?" she asks (ch. 36, p. 455), echoing Job's bolder suicidal addresses to God in 7:21, "thou shalt seek me in the morning, but I *shall* not *be*."[49]

Although love is as strong as death, conquering even the death wish, in Esther's victories she has not simply been purified by this "little trial"; it has exacerbated the battle of Law and Gospel within. As all the old "pet" names for her "guardian" and his "dear, dear girl" return in full force after her illness (see ch. 35, pp. 434–37), Esther embraces not the wisdom of greater maturity but "the childish prayer of that old birthday" in which one finds these two forces of judgment and mercy contending still; in her resolve "to be industrious, contented, and true-hearted, and to do some good to some one, and win some love to myself if I could" (p. 437), vestiges of her aunt's Law-sermon on the "submission, self-denial, diligent work" (p. 19) through which Esther might atone for the guilt of having been born linger in her mind.

Capping this regression is the "appointed day" of Miss Flite's arrival, leading to Esther's coy admission that she has won Woodcourt's love and to her immediate retreat from it. Esther is glad to learn the "gentle lesson" of the "poor afflicted creature['s]" greater affliction and "to soothe her under her calamity" (p. 438). But she cannot learn from Flite's literally maddening use of Bible promises—cannot observe, as the reader does ironically, that while she sensibly advises Flite to abandon the old inappropriate apocalyptic expectations of Chancery, Esther deflects her yearning for earthly union with Woodcourt through her own inappropriate expressions of Christian hope, "aspir[ing] to meet him, unselfishly, innocently, better far . . . at the journey's end" (see pp. 437–443). The secret community of feeling between these two patient Joban sufferers—"the little mad woman worn out with curtseying and smiling" and the Little Woman who makes herself "no one" in her deferential cheeriness (ch. 4, p. 45)—is their common anguish, "the sickness of hope deferred" (ch. 24, p. 307; cf. Prov. 13:12). (Esther recognizes this sickness in Chancery suitors and makes the allusion to Proverbs but does not apply it to herself.)[50]

When chapter 36 opens, the recovering Esther is prematurely blessed with a folktale restitution at Boythorn's lovely country house, as though she were "a princess" favored by "a good fairy" after all (p. 444). But the cheerful attempt to produce a "happily ever after" ending breaks down, just as her resolutions to deny the flesh fail because she does love the created world;

again and again Esther returns to the "loss" of the old face while striving in conventional ways to count some "gain" from her illness (see p. 443). After the deeply troubling encounter with Lady Dedlock in this chapter, Esther's ambivalent response is characteristically reflected in two rival sets of scriptural allusions. Lady Dedlock's remorseful confessional letter prompts Esther to recall the first set of (Old Testament) texts, climaxing with the savage return of her repressed Joban death wish. Later, Ada's and Jarndyce's loving letters inspire Esther to rewrite the legalism that has nearly crushed her; reversing the Joban curse, she takes heart with a New Testament allusion and makes a birth announcement of kinship with the innocent Queen Esther. But for reasons that will appear, these resolutions are unstable and allow the reader to make some ironic observations about Esther's use of religious texts.

To understand how the Law and Gospel, Job and Esther texts remain in tension in chapter 36, we must recall the first time Esther had encountered her mother in Chesney Wold chapel. This truncated recognition scene had been framed by a fragment of penitential psalm used to open Morning Prayer in the Anglican liturgy: "Enter not into judgment with thy servant, O Lord, for in thy sight————" (ch. 18, p. 224).[51] In her narrative Esther breaks off the verse from Psalm 143:2 to record her mother's "look"—not God's, for the words of judgment that follow are omitted ("in thy sight shall no man living be justified"). Although Esther does not know it, Lady Dedlock cannot pray David's prayer, for she is another "official representative of all the pomps and vanities" who has not renounced them as the Catechism bids in "this wicked world" (p. 224; see also n. 6). The Joban fate feared by the psalmist will become the dark end of Lady Dedlock's history in the desolate pit of a pauper graveyard:

> For the enemy hath persecuted my soul; he hath smitten my life down to
>   the ground; he hath made me to dwell in darkness, as those that have
>   been long dead.
> Therefore is my spirit overwhelmed within me; my heart within me is
>   desolate.
> I remember the days of old; I meditate on all thy works; I muse on the
>   work of thy hands.
> I stretch forth my hands unto thee: my soul *thirsteth* after thee, as a thirsty
>   land. Sĕ'lah.
> Hear me speedily, O Lord: my spirit faileth: hide not thy face from me, lest
>   I be like unto them that go down into the pit.   (Psalm 143:3–7)

What follows Psalm 143:2 in the liturgy is the priest's exhortation to the Confession of Sins ("we should not dissemble nor cloke them before the face of Almighty God") and the Absolution. But the rite in progress falls to the background as Esther's partial memories of "the days of old" surface and the "reader's voice" becomes the stern "voice of my grandmother" (p. 225). Just as the psalmist's plea for mercy is left unfinished and the words of Absolution remain unheard in the service. Esther and her mother miss the promises of forgiveness. Nor have they confessed: just as the half-verse brings only partly into the open a statement of guilt, so Esther's "scraps of old remembrances" produce only partial confession of kinship. With only haughty evasion for Lady Dedlock and evasive self-subdual for Esther—their characteristic ways of responding to the admonition to be penitent—there can be no peace for the "two troubled minds" that now meet privately at last (ch. 36, p. 449).

In this scene, Lady Dedlock tells Esther how she has been wandering without exodus in "the desert," and that "useless remorse" and her own denial of maternal love are "the earthly punishment I have brought upon myself" (pp. 452, 450). Here Dickens naturalizes the sin and the divine punishment that Aunt Barbary had alluded to in chapter 3 ("pray daily that the sins of others be not visited upon your head"; p. 19), recalling the first commandment in Exodus 20:5 forbidding worship of idols (" . . . for I the Lord thy God *am* a jealous God, visiting the iniquity of the fathers upon the children . . . "). Lady Dedlock *has* betrayed her first loyalties of the heart— not to God but to child and lover—for the idolatry of social position; to the puritanical aunt, however, her sister's sin would be more appropriately glossed by Leviticus 18:25, in which God threatens to "visit the iniquity . . . upon [the land]" for sexual transgressions. Combining this idea from Leviticus with the generational curse from Exodus, Aunt Barbary had taken it upon herself to carry out jealous Jahweh's visitation upon little Esther, "degraded from the first of these evil anniversaries" (p. 19).

Now so much later in life, as Esther reads her mother's remorseful confession, she reports that she "could not disentangle all that was about me; and I felt as if the blame and the shame were all in me, and the visitation had come down" (p. 453). Momentarily in chapter 36 she has no New Testament verses with which to combat this virulent legacy of past Law. Crushed by her first full awareness of the web of sins and deceptions in which she has been enmeshed simply by being born, Esther herself pronounces the curse against her birth, not even alluding to the aunt's early words but adopting them as her own authentic expression of "the real feelings that I had":

> I hope it may not appear very unnatural or bad in me, that I then became heavily sorrowful to think I had ever been reared. That I felt as if I knew it would have been better and happier for many people, if indeed I had never breathed. (p. 453)

Esther's parallel sentences moving the curse backward in time recall the regressive form of Job's curse in the deepening of his despair ("Let the day perish wherein I was born, and the night *in which* it was said, There is a man child conceived"; 3:3). Esther reiterates her confession, not with Job's vehemence but with his compulsion:

> I was so confused and shaken, as to be possessed by a belief that it was right, and had been intended, that I should die in my birth; and that it was wrong, and not intended, that I should be then alive. (p. 453)

"Why died I not from the womb?" Job cries. . . .

> For . . . then had I been at rest,
> With kings and counsellors of earth, which built desolate places for them-
> selves; . . .
> Or as an hidden untimely birth I had not been; as infants *which* never
> saw light. (3:11, 13, 14, 16)

Lady Dedlock will flee that desolate place where she has built her deceptive noble position; Esther longs for release in the hiddenness of never having been born at all. If there is providential care in the world, Esther's sorrowful words imply, it has not been "intended" for these sisters of Job.

Esther's fantasy of her own evil influence outside any benevolent order next unleashes a gothic influx near the Ghost's Walk, temporarily obscuring her religious hope. But her "augmented terror of [her]self" (p. 454) as the instrument of doom to her mother is an indulgence of fantasy guilt;[52] her descent into the depths is yet to come. With the restoration of the domestic security that does much to sustain Esther's faith, loving letters from Ada and Jarndyce arrive to counter Lady Dedlock's written confession. Now the better memory of a New Testament text expels the darker remembrances of grim Old Testament passages. Esther sees

> very well how many things had worked together, for my welfare; and that if
> the sins of the fathers were sometimes visited upon the children, the
> phrase did not mean what I had in the morning feared it meant. I knew I
> was as innocent of my birth as a queen of hers; and that before my Heav-
> enly Father I should not be punished for birth, nor a queen rewarded for
> it. (pp. 454–55)

With the recall of Romans 8:28 ("And we know that all things work together for good to them that love God, to them who are the called according to *his* purpose"), Esther forces closure on her Joban doubts of God's providence. Her remembrance of a saving New Testament passage also leads to her implicit identification with the "queen" whose people were nearly punished for their birth but were saved from a genocidal law by a wonderful "concurrence of providences."

For all her eloquence at this climax, however, Esther's struggles are hardly over.[53] Her Romans 8:28 echo may also remind us that the human "conspiracy to make [her] happy" at Bleak House (p. 437) has not worked altogether for the good of Dame Durden. The closing tableau of chapter 36 bears out once again the irony of the New Testament allusion. When Esther hears "my darling calling as she came up-stairs, 'Esther, my dear. . . . Little woman, dear Dame Durden!' " (p. 456), she is "called" to her "purpose" like "them that love God"; but as Ada's pet names imply, this calling is to become only a little woman, when Esther becomes "like a child" in the Madonna / Ada's arms (p. 456). In the context of these infantilizing human providences, therefore, to recognize her birth as "innocent" from inherited sexual fault is also a way for Esther to deny her adult identity; and on a second, skeptical reading, her apparently inspiring association with Queen Esther becomes a disloyal declaration of independence from tainted Lady Dedlock—that very denial of kinship which the biblical queen had to overcome. Esther Summerson must still come to terms with her own fleshly nature and that of the mother she has agreed to conceal with the help of "the providence of God" (p. 449)—a god wanted, the reader notes ironically, to protect from public shame rather than to empower full and open forgiveness.

In these ways Esther's saving texts only point to her unresolved dilemmas. Indeed, if it is in the Christian spirit of St. Paul's Epistle to the Romans that she has meant to rewrite her mother's Law-ridden letter, the terms of Esther's self-deception are also deducible from a central opposition developed in Romans 8. Esther in fact reverses her aunt's misapplication of the Old Testament only to substitute her own like-minded interpretation of the New: in this Victorian reading, Lady Dedlock becomes one of those for whom "to be carnally minded is death," while the "spiritually minded" Esther chooses the path to "glory" by adopting the mortification of the flesh, seemingly confirmed by her "providential" disfigurement ("if ye through the Spirit do mortify the deeds of the body, ye shall live"; 8:13). In this way, as Lawrence Frank has observed of Esther's mechanisms, she "fix[es] herself . . . in a state beyond temptation" and avoids her mother's carnal misdeeds,[54] hoping thereby to secure salvation from spiritual anxiety. As one of "the children of God . . . heirs of God, and joint-heirs with Christ" (8:16, 17), Esther then gains a spiritual parentage to replace the fleshly one she has rejected; and in "the Spirit of adoption" she can "cry, Abba, Father" (8:15) not only to her "Heavenly Father" (p. 454) but also to the aging father-husband in her chaste marriage to John Jarndyce. Ironically, Romans 8 read in this way authorizes that very betrayal of the heart, represented by marriage to an older, sexually impotent man of position, that to Dickens was her mother's most serious misdeed.

The "child" Esther becomes at the end of her double crisis in chapters 35 and 36 may have exchanged the nobody's child she rightly disowns for the redeemed child of God, but the woman has not been wholly renewed despite the imprimatur which biblical allusions seem to place upon her resolution of crisis. In the chapters that follow her queenly declaration, what might have been progression is merely a "return" to Bleak House, not the "general new beginning altogether" she claims it is (see Rom. 8:22). Again we hear the burden of the same old Calvinist tune: " 'Once more, duty, duty, Esther,' said I; 'and if you are not overjoyed to do it, more than cheerfully and contentedly, through anything and everything, you ought to be' " (ch. 38, p. 472). Until her second baptismal trial in chapter 59, Esther remains captive to the unresolved battles of her texts.

Esther's greatest potentiality for healing comes at her point of deepest distress with the pursuit, discovery, and public recognition of Lady Dedlock as her mother. Reliving in this second crisis the *de profundis* experience of her illness only to find herself more fully implicated in human misery than ever before, Esther gains the power to revise one of the skeptical narrator's earlier chapters in the spirit of the New Testament—this time, without incurring irony at her own expense. Chapter 32, "The Appointed Time," is a blasphemous account of Krook's death and demonic resurrection, a dark Easter parody; there, Jobling and Guppy experience meaningless death in the godforsaken "troublous valley of the shadow of the law" (p. 391). The other narrator had already replayed some motifs from this chapter in the scene of Tulkinghorn's death, but had offered no answer to the question, "What does it mean?" except the unmeaning flourishes of the "paralysed dumb witness" (an unredeemed Roman) on the lawyer's allegorical ceiling (ch. 48, p. 585). In Esther's extended crisis narrative (chs. 62, 59), an allegorical journey into the "abyss" of evil, Dickens conveys the only kind of human answers he knows—a humanistic one—to the question of meaning in the face of death: a Victorian progress through the depths to love.

In chapter 57 Esther is roused from sleep only to lose her "right mind" (p. 674) so that she might enter into the horror of a "dream" (p. 676), a more extended allegory of her inner life than the terrifying visions of her fever. In the intensity of the search after Lady Dedlock, Esther "retrace[s] the way" (p. 678) of her earlier illness, which had left her irresolute. As before, time becomes "an indefinite period of great duration," stretching back to the beginnings of her selfhood and incorporating all the intervening years of struggle ("I seemed, in a strange way, never to have been free from the anxiety under which I then laboured," she confesses; p. 687). Now the fearful dream-images are directly of her mother confronting an Esther who gazes in horror at that which she has been seeking all along in her preoccupation with loss. Like Job foundering in cross-seas of internal debate and self-defense, in chapter 59 Esther "torment[s herself] with questioning . . . and discussing . . . [and] long dwelling on such reflections" that are impossible to answer because her thoughts of her mother darkly "reflect" herself (p. 703). Meanwhile the horses slip and founder in a labyrinthine, liquid landscape that resembles her mind losing direction, "miss[ing] the way" (p. 687) it normally follows in its dutiful progress by diurnal platitudes. Instead of the usual evasions, Bucket and Esther drive on "through streams of turbulent water" (p. 703) that rise, and rise again, in a dark baptismal flood.

In the midst of this ritual crisis, Bucket, a benign godfather reversing the gloomy "godmother," renames the plucky Esther "Queen" (p. 704), recalling for the reader her own declaration of innocent birth. But while these are necessary "encouraging words . . . under those lonely and anxious circumstances," the pair must plunge ever deeper into the unknown Joban regions where fairytale identities do not save, where Esther is not unambiguously innocent, and where the baptismal immersion becomes a penetrating contamination. "Descending into a deeper complication" of "the narrowest and worst streets in London" (p. 704), Esther meets new tests of her maturity. At Snagsby's, a crucial stage on the way, Esther becomes a Job figure in several impressive aspects—at once a comforter of the "poor soul" Guster, a fellow-sufferer with her, trembling and weeping, and an inquirer after the truth though it lead to the unthinkable (p. 712).

Further still Esther travels into "ways . . . deep" with falling sleet, where narrow courts close in and "stained house fronts put on human shapes and [look at her]." This weatherbeaten landscape of urban gothic reproduces, in its inchoate guilt and liquidity, the place of horrors to which Jobling and Guppy were brought in Krook's shop. Here Esther meets her "appointed time" when "great water-gates seemed to be opening and closing in [her] head, or in the air" (pp. 712–13); her "roarings are poured out like the waters. For the thing which I greatly feared is come upon me" (Job 3:24–25). Again, as with Jobling and Guppy, in the early morning hours Mr. Woodcourt, Mr. Bucket, and Esther have descended into a claustral space, where "a thick humidity . . . like a disease" makes everything as loathsome to touch and smell as Krook's fleshly "liquor" in his sepulchral shop. Just as Dickens's earlier witnesses had at first misread the unstable signs of Krook's demise ("he is *not* there!" p. 402), so Esther uncharacteristically mistakes the signs she sees of her mother's disappearance: "On the step at the gate, drenched in the fearful wet of such a place, which oozed and splashed down everywhere, I saw, with a cry of pity and horror, a woman lying—Jenny, the mother of the dead child" (p. 713).

Now Esther finds that words have "no meaning [attached] to them," like the speechless witnesses to Krook's death; nor can Esther, normally quick "to read a face" (ch. 64, p. 750), "comprehend the solemn and compassionate look in Mr. Woodcourt's face." "Shall she go?" asks a voice (p. 713; cf. Jobling's "Shall I go?" (p. 402). Esther at last "go[es] down" (p. 402) into the burial place to read accurately the sign of her mother's reappearance, not as charred bone like Krook but again as the merely material form of a human being: "I passed on to the gate, and stooped down. I lifted the heavy head, put the long dank hair aside, and turned the face. And it was my mother, cold and dead" (p. 714). Unlike Jobling and Guppy, with their cry of "O Horror" (p. 403), Esther does not immediately "run away" from the evil she recognizes; it is with "pity and horror" that she discovers her kinship with the woman she associates with "my mother"—and with all such "distressed, unsheltered, senseless creature[s]" (p. 713) in England whom the dead figure emblematizes.

"I pray to Heaven it may end well!" Esther had pleaded at the start of this journey into the depths (ch. 57, p. 675). In her discovery of death by the dead letter, death without the forgiveness that would have saved the woman alive, Esther offers the only help she can, a wordless gesture of love and acceptance. No longer the child cradled in Ada's arms, Esther has become the mourning adult survivor in a pathetic pieta. Chapter 59 ends; there are no further words for this eloquent, chilling tableau, no coda of moral indignation (as at the end of chapter 32), no easy reassurances of "our hope to be restored in Heaven!" (p. 389). In her final gesture before the closed gate,

Esther shows she has learned the lesson of a Scripture text important in *Bleak House* which urges the full gospel and not some cheerful evasive substitute for it: "the end of all things is at hand. . . . above all things have fervent charity among yourselves: for charity shall cover the multitude of sins" (I Pet. 4:7, 8). For Dickens, apocalypse may never come to right the world, but death unquestionably is here: therefore, have love.

The alternating, sometimes unstable biblical texts involved in Esther's provisional progress ground her suffering and gradual (if flawed) maturity in the common experiences of *Bleak House*, which even the comic Guppy and Jobling undergo; indeed, the very ways she uses the Bible point to the internal demons she must overcome. Her inductions into the depths have the effect of authenticating her charity and making her more humanly convincing than an unrelieved portrait of a "Saint Summerson" would have done (ch. 43, p. 524). Like Job she moves from knowing herself as "one *that* comforteth the mourners" (29:25) to recognizing herself as "one who mourns" (the meaning of Job's name; see 30:28), finally embracing instead of denying her human condition, the condition to which the other narrator has faithfully born witness.

The popular nineteenth-century preacher Charles Haddon Spurgeon mused on this favorite theme of Joban sermons:

> A man is never made thoroughly useful unless he has suffering. . . . We must first suffer in our heads and hearts the things we preach, or we shall never preach them with effect. . . . Then take heart. Perhaps the Lord designs thee for a great work. He is keeping thee low in bondage, and doubt, and fear, that he may bring thee out more clearly, and make thy light like the light of seven days, and bring forth thy righteousness "clear as the sun."[55]

Although Dickens did not admire Calvinists like Spurgeon, and though other parts of his novel most effectively protest just this kind of religious rationalization, the final disposition of Esther's case illustrates this common notion in Victorian theodicy. When romance triumphs in her final chapter—with what seems to many readers an engineered concurrence of providences that prove not God's care but the author's need for happy closure—Esther is rewarded for the gain in maturity her provisional realistic narrative has forwarded up to this point. The story shifts away from realism; we have arrived at Job's (and Queen Esther's) folktale ending. And indeed Summerson finds that her "age shall be clearer than the noonday; [she] shalt shine forth, [she] shalt be as the morning" (Job 11:17; cf. Apoc. Est. 11:11). This is her "usual time" (p. 717) and the setting for her last acts of writing "early in the morning at [her] summer window" (p. 768). In the seventh, creative year of her restoration, this creator can write of her pilgrimage, confident that whatever her battles with "bondage, and doubt, and fear," whatever her misuse of texts that kill and of others that would bring life, the end of her Victorian progress will be greater than her beginning.

Notes

1. *The Implied Reader: Patterns of Communication in Prose Fiction from Bunyan to Beckett* (Baltimore: Johns Hopkins Univ. Press, 1974), p. 288.

2. "Jesuitism," in *Latter-Day Pamphlets*. Vol. 20 of *The Works of Thomas Carlyle*, ed. H. D. Traill, Centenary ed., 30 vols. (London: Chapman and Hall, 1907), p. 323.

3. *The City of Dickens* (Oxford: Clarendon Press, 1971), pp. 141, 228. This assumption of biblically sponsored harmony underlies Michael Wheeler's reading of *Hard Times* in *The Art of Allusion in Victorian Fiction* (New York: Barnes and Noble, 1979), pp. 61–77, and all of the full-length books that treat Dickens's uses of the Bible except, perhaps, Dennis Walder's wider-ranging *Dickens and Religion* (London: G. Allen and Unwin, 1981). Although often sensitive to the elusiveness of Dickens's transactions with Scripture, Welsh is concerned with a unifying culture-myth based on the Christian apocalyptic tradition of the heavenly and earthly cities; Bert G. Hornback, in *"Noah's Arkitecture": A Study of Dickens's Mythology* (Athens: Ohio Univ. Press, 1972), traces underlying Genesis motifs; Andrew Sanders, writing more generally of death and resurrection themes in *Charles Dickens: Resurrectionist* (New York: St. Martin's, 1982), undertakes to show how consistently Dickens demonstrated his religious convictions in his novels; and less sophisticated students of Dickens, from such early apologists as C. H. MacKenzie, *The Religious Sentiments of Charles Dickens* (London: Walter Scott, 1884), to Jane Vogel, *Allegory in Dickens* (University: Univ. of Alabama Press, 1977), and Theresa R. Love, *Dickens and the Seven Deadly Sins* (Danville, Ill.: Interstate Printers and Publishers, 1979), have sought to identify a Christian philosophy in the fiction.

4. *Bleak House*, ed. George Ford and Sylvère Monod, Norton Critical Edition (New York: Norton, 1977), p. 389. Subsequent references to this edition are given parenthetically in the text.

5. *Sartor Resartus*. Vol. 1 of *The Works of Thomas Carlyle*, p. 157.

6. Dickens to Rev. R. H. Davies (Christmas Eve, 1856), quoted in John Forster, *The Life of Charles Dickens*, ed. A. J. Hoppe, Everyman's ed., 2 vols. (London: Dent; New York: Dutton, 1966), II, 380.

7. *The Life of Our Lord* (London: Associated Newspapers, 1934) is symptomatic of an age in which the Bible had been, as Dickens complained, "the subject of accommodation, adaptation, varying interpretation without end" (Dickens to W. F. de Cerjat, 25 Oct. 1864. *The Letters of Charles Dickens*, ed. Walter Dexter. 3 vols. [Bloomsbury: Nonesuch Press, 1938], III, 402). It represents not only his desire to simplify the New Testament's language for children's hearing but also his own need to harmonize the four divergent gospels in one "History," to suppress certain biblical doctrines, and to re-create Jesus Christ as the exemplary human being (not the divine Son of God, although he raises the dead) who teaches us to "DO GOOD always" so that we may be forgiven and "live and die in Peace" (see *The Life of Our Lord*, pp. 11, 127–28).

8. With Dickens we are in what George P. Landow describes as "the hazy, ill-defined borders between religious and secular discourse in an age when these territories continually shifted"; Dickens takes a Broad Church position that types were not divinely instituted signs of specific historical events but general symbols of religious ideas. See Landow's *Victorian Types, Victorian Shadows: Biblical Typology in Victorian Literature, Art, and Thought* (Boston and London: Routledge and Kegan Paul, 1980), pp. 225, 31. Dickens's infamous literalistic misreading of Millais' painting, *Christ in the House of His Parents*, suggests how alien to his thought orthodox typology was. Queen Esther's typology has been read variously: while she can be seen as a type of Christ, more common is St. Jerome's interpretation of her as "a type of the church [who], frees her people from danger and, after having slain Haman whose name means iniquity, hands down to posterity a memorable day and a great feast"; see "To Paulinus, on the Study of Scripture," Letter 53, in *St. Jerome: Letters and Select Works*, Vol. 6 of *A Select Library of Nicene and Post-Nicene Fathers of the Christian Church*, Second Series. trans. and ed. Philip Schaff and Henry Wace (New York: Christian Literature; Oxford: Parker, 1893), p. 101. Cf.

Jonathan Edwards, who reads this book as "an history that is a shadow of gospel things and times" and sees Esther as "the church [presented] as a chaste virgin to Christ," in *Notes on the Bible*, Vol. 9 of *The Works of President Edwards*, ed. Edward Williams and Edward Parsons, 10 vols. (1847; rpt. New York: B. Franklin, 1968), pp. 191–93. Catholic commentaries in the Reformation period treated Esther as a type of the Blessed Virgin: see Lewis Bayles Paton. *A Critical and Exegetical Commentary on the Book of Esther*, International Critical Commentary (New York: Scribner's, 1908), p. 108.

9. *The Realistic Imagination: English Fiction from Frankenstein to Lady Chatterley* (Chicago and London: Univ. of Chicago Press, 1981), p. 4.

10. Dickens to Rev. David Macrae, rpt. in Macrae, *Amongst the Darkies, and Other Papers* (Glasgow: John S. Marr, 1876), p. 127.

11. Dickens, "The Sensational Williams," *All the Year Round*, 13 Feb. 1864, pp. 14–15.

12. Walder, *Dickens and Religion*, p. 160.

13. In its new complexity, Esther's Narrative represents a kind of halfway station between *David Copperfield* and *Great Expectations*, the *Bildungsromane* Jerome Hamilton Buckley discusses in *Season of Youth: The Bildungsroman from Dickens to Golding* (Cambridge, Mass.: Harvard Univ. Press, 1974), pp. 28–62. Although Esther's is distinctively a woman's "Progress," through her Narrative Dickens came to explore some of the psychodynamics of "guilt and inner conflict" and (through Esther's doubles in *Bleak House*) "the thin line between respectability and illicit impulse" which we find in Pip (Buckley, pp. 42, 46).

14. Esther's central encounter with the incongruous—her discovery of the surprising kinship with Lady Dedlock—is in concentrated form akin to many other moments of confusion, disorientation, and "shock" in her narrative (see, e.g., Chancery discoveries in ch. 5, p. 52). The establishing and disrupting of configurations, a process essential to learning and to reading (as Iser argues in *The Implied Reader*), does go on in Esther's Narrative for her and for Dickens's reader, though not as a steady progression toward conclusive knowledge; in *Bleak House* knowing is much more uncertain, as we suspect even in Esther's last halting, broken-off sentence.

15. For other appreciations of Esther's psychological portraiture which have influenced this essay, see William Axton, "The Trouble with Esther," *Modern Language Quarterly*, 26 (1965), 545–57, and "Esther's Nicknames: A Study in Relevance," *The Dickensian*, 62 (1966), 158–63; Q. D. Leavis, "*Bleak House:* A Chancery World," in F. R. Leavis and Q. D. Leavis, *Dickens the Novelist*, 1st Amer. ed. (New York: Pantheon Books, 1970), pp. 118–79; Alex Zwerdling, "Esther Summerson Rehabilitated," *PMLA*, 88 (1973), 429–39; Crawford Kilian, "In Defence of Esther Summerson," *Dalhousie Review*, 54 (1974), 318–28; Lawrence Frank, " 'Through a Glass Darkly': Esther Summerson and *Bleak House*," *Dickens Studies Annual*, Vol. 4, ed. Robert B. Partlow, Jr. (Carbondale and Edwardsville: Southern Illinois Univ. Press, 1975). pp. 91–112; and Paul Eggert, "The Real Esther Summerson," *Dickens Studies Newsletter*, 11 (1980), 74–81.

16. A phrase from Dickens's will; rpt. in Forster, *Life*, II, 422.

17. Scriptural citations are from the King James Version of the Bible.

18. Barry V. Qualls. *The Secular Pilgrims of Victorian Fiction: The Novel as Book of Life* (Cambridge: Cambridge Univ. Press, 1982), p. 115.

19. Dickens opposed the doctrine of Original Sin, yet the vast extent to which his characters and settings are mired in evil and darkness suggests a more ambivalent attitude.

20. As Michael Ragussis has rendered Dickens's interpretation of this biblical role, Summerson "finds herself in the wilderness of ink, in 'the immense desert of lawhand,' like her Old Testament counterpart, the orphan 'Queen' . . . who reserves Haman's law of the dead letters in a striking prefiguration of the New Testament"; see "The Ghostly Signs of *Bleak House*," *NCF*, 34 (1979), 264–65. See also Edwin M. Eigner, *The Metaphysical Novel in England and America: Dickens, Bulwer, Melville, and Hawthorne* (Berkeley and Los Angeles: Univ. of California Press, 1978), p. 198: "Her name is Esther, and her fate, like that of the Biblical

heroine, is to rise from a despised birth to become the beautiful and redeeming queen of her oppressed, leaderless people."

21. For an exposition of Job's type, see *Job to Song of Solomon*, Vol. 3 of *Matthew Henry's Commentary on the Whole Bible* (McLean, Va.: MacDonald Publishing, n.d.), pp. 2 ff. Ford and Monod identify the allusion to Job 7:8–10 in chapter 1, when "the very little counsel drops, and the fog knows him no more" (p. 10, n. 3); Susan Shatto. "A Commentary on Dickens's *Bleak House*," Diss. Univ. of Birmingham 1974, connects the phrasing of "Jarndyce and Jarndyce has stretched forth its unwholesome hand to spoil and corrupt" (p. 8) with Job 1:11–12. These and other Job allusions are clues to larger affinities: chapter 1 strikes a Joban mood of accursed creation and piles up mud like Job's dung-heap on a day of "mourning without the sun" (Job 30:28); much wrangling in *Bleak House* is a reminder of Job's debates about divine justice; the title recalls his ruined habitations motif. I discuss the striking thematic, imagistic, structural, and stylistic affinities between *Bleak House* and Job in a forthcoming article, "The Book of Job According to *Bleak House*: Biblical Reading in the Later Dickens," to appear in *Dickens Studies Annual* in 1984.

22. Tennyson called Job "the greatest poem of ancient and modern times," and Carlyle heard in it "sublime sorrow, sublime reconciliation; oldest choral melody as of the heart of mankind" ("The Hero as Prophet"); see *The Dimensions of Job*, ed. Nahum N. Glatzer (New York: Schocken Books, 1969), p. ix.

23. Ford and Monod identify this reference: see *Bleak House*, Norton ed., p. 100, n. 9. See also Skimpole to Esther, p. 726: "then, if I never allude to an unpleasant matter, how much less should you!" Skimpole is often Esther's dark angel; his reduction of her fine traits to self-serving, empty gestures caricatures and draws attention to her limitations. Caddy Jellyby criticizes Esther's habits of evasion in chapter 4: "Don't tell stories, Miss Summerson" (p. 44).

24. Zwerdling, "Esther Summerson Rehabilitated," p. 433, points out that the first-person point of view is "useful to a writer whose response . . . is fundamentally divided," as Dickens's was toward self-sacrifice; he can "study the psychological roots of selflessness . . . without committing himself to either praise or blame."

25. Joseph I. Fradin, "Will and Society in *Bleak House*," *PMLA*, 81 (1966), 95–96. It seems necessary to dualistic treatments of *Bleak House* to insist on Esther's consistency, lucidity, and exemplary religious orientation in order to distinguish her sharply from the other narrator; for critics bound to the form of this distorting argument, see. e.g;, J. Hillis Miller, *Charles Dickens: The World of His Novels* (Cambridge, Mass.: Harvard Univ. Press, 1958), pp. 210–11, 213; Leonard W. Deen, "Style and Unity in *Bleak House*," *Criticism*, 3 (1961), 207, 214; Robert A. Donovan, "Structure and Idea in *Bleak House*," *ELH*, 29 (1962), 200–201; and W. J. Harvey, *Character and the Novel* (Ithaca: Cornell Univ. Press, 1965), pp. 89–99.

26. See Carey A. Moore, ed. and trans., *The Anchor Bible: Esther* (Garden City, N.Y.: Doubleday, 1971), p. xlvi; and Robert Alter, *The Art of Biblical Narrative* (New York: Basic Books, 1981), p. 34. Alter emphasizes the book's "schematic neatness unlike that of earlier historicized fiction in the Bible."

27. See *The Great Code: The Bible and Literature* (New York: Harcourt, 1982), pp. 169–72. Frye notes the embodiment of Esther's political story of Jewish "expectation of a *culbute générale* in the future . . . when those with the right beliefs . . . would emerge on top with their now powerful enemies rendered impotent" (p. 115).

28. *Joshua to Esther*, Vol. 2 of *Matthew Henry's Commentary*, p. 1121. Henry Melvill (chaplain to Queen Victoria) also emphasizes this theme in "The Sleepless Night" (on Esther 6:1) in *Sermons*, ed. Right Rev. C. P. M'Ilvaine (New York: Stanford and Swords, 1850), II, 51–60.

29. Matthew Henry sees the Book of Esther as a parable of right government (and, ironically, concludes with a paean to the British system). Especially as expanded in the apocryphal additions (which Dickens could have read in the family Bible, now in the collection of Dickens House, London), this book provides a relevant subtext for the *Bleak House* satire on "the pestilent behavior of them that are placed in authority unworthily" (Apoc. Est. 16:7); cf. "most

pestilent of hoary sinners" (p. 6) and "all authorities in all places . . . where false pretenses are made, and where injustice is done" (p. 403). Mordecai's apocalyptic dream (see Apoc. Est. 11:5–11) suggests motifs for Dickens's opening paragraphs. But *Bleak House* cannot renew faith in God's "most excellent" order (Apoc. Est. 16:16) for the nation as Esther does.

30. Demetrius R. Dumm, O.S.B., "Tobit, Judith, Esther," in *The Jerome Biblical Commentary*, ed. Raymond E. Brown, S.S., Joseph A. Fitzmyer, S.J., and Roland E. Murphy, O. Carm., 2 vols. in 1 (Englewood Cliffs, N.J.: Prentice-Hall, 1968), I, 632, 629.

31. Henry, *Joshua to Esther*, p. 1127.

32. The name "Esther" may also be derived from the Persian *stara*, star; see A. S. Yahuda, "The Meaning of the Name Esther," *Journal of the Royal Asiatic Society* (1946), pp. 174–78. The Hebrew equivalent for "Esther" is "myrtle," the plant sacred to Venus.

33. Henry, *Joshua to Esther*, p. 1127. Both Mordecai and Jarndyce refuse to bow down to the secular powers.

34. Not until she leaves the paternal relation with Jarndyce behind for the "court" of a more suitable mate (as Queen Esther leaves the fatherly Mordecai for the lover-king Xerxes' court) can Esther Summerson claim her exaltation as Woodcourt's "household goddess" (p. 605); she seems even coyly to claim the love-goddess name when she hints that at last she may become charming after all (see p. 770).

35. There seems to be for both Esthers conspiracies to make them happy and some degree of coercion in their marriages. Lawrence Frank, " 'Through a Glass Darkly,' " p. 104, notes that Esther Summerson "chooses to acquiesce once more to that 'conspiracy' to make her happy which has in it the element of coercion which even [she] can detect." Esther's sense of it is expressed in her use of "Bleak House" as a euphemism for her coming marriage to Jarndyce (see pp. 437; 602, 604). Queen Esther twice describes herself as a "desolate woman" (Apoc. Est. 14:3, 14).

36. Dumm, "Tobit, Judith, Esther," I, 630–31.

37. John Kitto, "Woman," in *The Kings of Israel*, Vol. 2 of *Daily Bible Illustrations* (New York: Robert Carter, 1872), p. 10.

38. Frank, " 'Through a Glass Darkly,' " p. 94. Even Summerson admits that her preoccupation with hiding her trouble blinds her to Ada's need to confide in her: see ch. 50, pp. 606–7.

39. Moore, *The Anchor Bible: Esther*, p. xxxiv.

40. Mordecai dreams that from the people's cry "as it were from a little fountain, was made a great flood, even much water. The light and the sun rose up, and the lowly were exalted" (Apoc. Est. 11:10–11); the river "is Esther" (10:6). *Bleak House* begins in a muddy world after a Deluge that has failed to renew the earth, then progresses through the lowly Esther's two baptisms (by fire, water) enabling her to become a renewing presence wherever "it rain[s] Esther" (p. 61—wherever Esther reigns), even if she cannot redeem the world.

41. Henry, *Job to Song of Solomon*, p. iii.

42. R.A.F. MacKenzie, S.J., "Job," in *The Jerome Biblical Commentary*, I, 515.

43. See Qualls, *The Secular Pilgrims*, pp. 114–19, for a pertinent discussion of this pilgrimage, a Romantic revision of the puritan progress to salvation.

44. Henry, *Job to Song of Solomon*, p. iv.

45. "Dickens' Working Plans," *Bleak House*, Norton Critical Edition, p. 786.

46. Froude, "The Book of Job," in *Short Studies on Great Subjects* (New York: Scribner's, 1884), p. 253. For a typical Victorian sermon on self-development through affliction, see Charles Haddon Spurgeon's meditation on Job 10:2 ("Shew me wherefore thou contendest with me"), in *Morning by Morning; or, Daily Readings for the Family or the Closet* (New York: Sheldon, 1886), p. 46; cf. Esther on Ada "more beautiful than ever" after her trials (p. 769) and Woodcourt on Esther "prettier than you ever were" (p. 770).

47. George H. Ford reminds us that Dickens's "most effective part as an actor was that of

Wardour, in *The Frozen Deep* . . . another example of renunciation"; see *Dickens and His Readers: Aspects of Novel-Criticism since 1836* (New York: Norton, 1965), pp. 67 ff.

48. Eigner, *The Metaphysical Novel*, p. 197.

49. This repeated Joban motif is parodied in chapter 1 of *Bleak House*, p. 10 (see n. 8); it recurs in the scenes of Krook's death (ch. 32, p. 402; cf. Job 7:10) and Tulkinghorn's murder (see ch. 48, p. 585). The link with Job's suicidal passages is appropriate, for both Krook and Tulkinghorn in different ways bring on their own deaths.

50. Ford and Monod identify this allusion: see p. 307, n. 3.

51. For an important discussion of this passage, see Qualls, *The Secular Pilgrims*, pp. 115–116.

52. Ann Ronald discusses "the superficial terror of the malleable Esther" as opposed to "true Gothic horror" elsewhere in *Bleak House* in "Dickens' Gloomiest Gothic Castle," *Dickens Studies Newsletter*, 6 (1975), 71–75.

53. Eigner, *The Metaphysical Novel*, p. 199, reads this passage as "the beginning of Esther's queenly power, which had long lain dormant"; Qualls, *The Secular Pilgrims*, p. 117, believes "the pattern of felt grace is on this meditation. Esther discovers in the random happenings of her life a divinely ordained pattern," like Bunyan, although the quest for innocence is Romantic. Zwerdling, "Esther Summerson Rehabilitated," p. 435, puts the emphasis (as I do) on what comes after her queenly declaration: "Although this has the ring of confidence, it should be noticed that Esther is planning to be vindicated in death, not in life." It is perhaps unintentionally ironic that Esther declares her innocence of birth from Romans 8:28, for this is also a key proof-text for the Calvinist doctrine of election so perversely motivating her aunt to persecute the illegitimate child; Spurgeon uses this text in Sermon V, "Election," in *Sermons of Rev. C. H. Spurgeon of London*, Second Series (New York: Robert Carter, n.d.), p. 73.

54. Frank, " 'Through a Glass Darkly,' " p. 101.

55. Sermon VI, "The Anxious Inquirer" (on Job 23:3) in *Sermons of Rev. C. H. Spurgeon of London*, Third Series (New York: Robert Carter, n.d.), p. 98.

Bleak House, I:
Suspended Animation   Robert Newsom*

> Everything was so strange—the stranger from its being night in the daytime, the candles burning with a white flame, and looking raw and cold—that I read the words in the newspaper without knowing what they meant, and found myself reading the same words repeatedly.
>
> —*Bleak House*, chapter 3

I

It is rapidly becoming a commonplace of literary criticism that while the proper study of mankind may be man, the proper study of literature is literature—that both the appropriate subject for and the subject characteristi-

*Reprinted from *Dickens on the Romantic Side of Familiar Things: "Bleak House" and the Novel Tradition* (New York: Columbia University Press 1977), 11–45. © 1975, 1977 by Robert Newsom. Reprinted by permission of the author.

cally belonging to literature are its own technique and method. This is the message brought to us by students of rhetoric, linguistics, and structuralism, and this is the message which has been brought to bear upon Dickens studies most notably in recent articles by J. Hillis Miller and Steven Marcus.[1] "*Bleak House*," Hillis Miller asserts at the beginning of his Introduction to the Penguin English Library edition of that novel, "is a document about the interpretation of documents."[2] And while it is true that *any* literary production may be said in a general sense to have its own methods as its subject, it is in a more particular sense true of Dickens's literary productions, and especially true of *Bleak House*.

Miller shows that not only does the novel place the reader in precisely the situation of all those characters who are trying to solve mysteries, but that the writer and the novel as a whole are placed in the perplexed situation of posing what are perhaps *Bleak House*'s most famous questions:

> What connexion can there be, between the place in Lincolnshire, the house in town, the Mercury in powder, and the whereabout of Jo the outlaw with the broom, who had that distant ray of light upon him when he swept the churchyard-step? What connexion can there have been between many people in the innumerable histories of this world, who, from opposite sides of great gulfs, have, nevertheless, been very curiously brought together! (16)

For Miller, the ultimate answer is that there is no answer—at least none that can be articulated, because "The villain is the act of interpretation itself, the naming which assimilates the particular into a system, giving it a definition and a value, incorporating it into a whole."[3] Miller justifies this judgment by pointing on the one hand to the tremendously long list of detectives in the novel whose interpretations are either flatly wrong (like Mrs. Snagsby's) or whose interpretations, while right in themselves, come too late to do any good (like Mr. Bucket's), and on the other hand to the names of characters in the novel, virtually all of which are either "openly metaphorical . . . or seem tantalizingly to contain some covert metaphor lying almost on the surface of the word."[4] "This overt fictionality," Miller continues, "is Dickens's way of demystifying the belief . . . that the right name gives the essence of a thing." On the contrary, "The metaphors in [the characters'] names reveal the fact that they are not real people or even copies of real people. They exist only in language."[5]

Here Miller is going considerably beyond his assertion—which no one I think will disagree with—that "*Bleak House* is a document about the interpretation of documents." To say that characters exist *only* in language demystifies of course a good deal more than the authority of "documents." Curiously, Miller seems to have put himself in the camp of those critics who come upon Dickens from precisely the opposite direction, those who, insofar as they come to Dickens with the tenets of realism ineradicably in mind (Robert Garis is perhaps the best example here), inevitably find Dickens wanting.

Certainly Miller does not want to find Dickens wanting, and it is precisely the tenets of realism that he sets out to demystify. But he overshoots his mark and, brilliantly, demystifies fiction itself.

Bleak House is indeed a document about the interpretation of documents, and of course a large part of the novel is about the falsity of certain kinds of documents; but *Bleak House* itself is presented as an authentic document: nothing in it suggests that we are to question its own authority. There is nothing in Esther's narrative to suggest that she is not telling the truth, and there is nothing in the third-person narrative to suggest that it is not telling the truth. We know *Bleak House* is a novel and that therefore its characters "exist only in language." But what we know is not necessarily the same as what we believe, and I suggest that most readers of the novel believe in its characters. This is even true, I suggest further, of those readers who say things like "there never was such a person as Esther." The very form and ambiguity of such statements attest to the reality of Esther as "a person." And yet Miller is quite right, I believe, to center on the problematic relationship between fiction and reality.

Every reader of the novel quickly recognizes that something peculiar is going on in the way the story is told: the double narrative not only comes upon us without warning in chapter 3, but the very conditions of that narrative are never explained. Esther begins her narrative by telling us that "I have a great deal of difficulty in beginning to write my portion of these pages, for I know I am not clever." But how can Esther know of the existence of the other narrator? The other narrator is an omniscient third-person narrator familiar in the English novel since Fielding. He is one of those characters of whom we may say that he exists "only in language." But by the very rules of his profession, so to speak, his existence cannot be known to Esther, who, as a character in the novel, is a character of an entirely different order. We are not presented, in other words, with a case of multiple narration in which different characters narrate a single story in turn. Nor are we even presented with a first-person narrative supplemented by an omniscient third person narrative, as would be the case if Esther were being helped by an unseen hand. She does see the other hand, and it is that fact that confounds the reader. Rather than being given a shifting point of view, we are given two points of view which are somehow incompatible. Here a fictional reality is not being demystified, but, on the contrary, made doubly problematic.

Of course, it is not only through the double narrative that Dickens makes reality strange. The famous beginning of the novel places us in a world which is both dazzlingly real and dazzlingly unreal:

> LONDON. Michaelmas Term lately over, and the Lord Chancellor sitting in Lincoln's Inn Hall. Implacable November weather. As much mud in the streets, as if the waters had but newly retired from the face of the earth, and it would not be wonderful to meet a Megalosaurus, forty feet long or so, waddling like an elephantine lizard up Holborn Hill. Smoke lowering down from the chimney-pots, making a soft black drizzle,

with flakes of soot in it as big as full-grown snow-flakes—gone into mourning, one might imagine, for the death of the sun. Dogs, undistinguishable in mire. Horses, scarcely better; splashed to their very blinkers. Foot passengers, jostling one another's umbrellas, in a general infection of ill-temper, and losing their foothold at street-corners, where tens of thousands of other foot passengers have been slipping and sliding since the day broke (if this day ever broke), adding new deposits to the crust upon crust of mud, sticking at those points tenaciously to the pavement, and accumulating at compound interest.

Bleak House begins like a newspaper story, with a dateline. It begins in Lincoln's Inn Hall on the last day or so of November. But it also begins in the early days of the Creation (for "the waters had but newly retired from the face of the earth") or just after the Flood. Or it begins at the end of time (for the flakes of soot have "gone into mourning, one might imagine, for the death of the sun"). Here we have a literal mixing of fact and fancy, and here we can say Dickens is in the most obvious sense dwelling upon "the romantic side of familiar things." But the "romantic" and "familiar" perspectives are not paradoxical or puzzling inasmuch as the perspectives here are quite plainly those of the real eye and the mind's eye.

This opening paragraph is one of the passages Robert Garis has used in defining Dickens's "theatrical mode," and he recalls Gissing's objection that "This darkness visible makes one rather cheerful than otherwise, for we are spectators in the company of a man who allows nothing to balk his enjoyment of life."[6] Gissing's objection becomes Garis's point. "I would amplify Gissing's remark," he tells us, "to say that the source of Dickens's enjoyment here is not only the scene before him, but his own skill in rendering that scene, and that he consciously and proudly offers us that skill for our enjoyment and applause."[7] And presumably this would be Miller's point as well, for the fictionalizing of reality here is entirely overt, as the phrase "one might imagine" makes clear.

If the narrative itself is not puzzling, the scene it narrates surely is. Something *is* wrong in reality, and that something wrong is the fog and mud which render things and people "undistinguishable." Of course we shall almost immediately learn that the fog and mud "stand for" the central evil and confusion, "most pestilent of hoary sinners," the High Court of Chancery. It is because Dickens has chosen as his subject something as bewildered and bewildering as Chancery that the fanciful imaginings of the opening paragraphs are not gratuitous, and not even in that sense fanciful. The "familiar" things here, the fog, the mud, and Chancery—and Chancery was almost as familiar to readers of the newspapers in 1850 as the fog and mud which were a part of their almost daily experience[8]—not only encourage such imaginings, but virtually impose them. That point becomes explicit much later in the novel when Miss Flite says to Esther about Chancery that "there's a dreadful attraction in the place. . . . There's a cruel attraction in the place. You *can't* leave it. And you *must* expect" (35). Miss Flite is of course mad, and her referring to the "spell" of Chancery is her way of signifying that she knows she is mad: she is never so lucid as in this scene with Esther. Chancery has driven her mad as it drives others in the novel mad (most prominently, Tom Jarndyce, Gridley—"mad" in another sense— and, less dramatically, but even more fatally, Richard). But that her madness is an appropriate and even logical response to Chancery is testified to by Esther's comment on first witnessing Chancery proceedings, that "there seemed to be no reality in the whole scene, except poor little Miss Flite, the madwoman, standing on a bench, and nodding at it" (24). Therefore it is *not* especially wonderful that the narrator of the opening pages should fancy himself in a scene at the beginning of time or at the end of time. His own fanciful imagination, we may say, is an important, perhaps essential, part of the reality he is describing.

The "familiar" things in the novel, Dickens is saying, belong to a reality so astonishing that we have to call it unreal, and so astonishing, indeed, that we can no longer experience its components as "familiar." We should be reminded here of the beginning of the novel's preface, which says, among other things, precisely that the reality Dickens is describing is itself too absurd to be represented in a work of fiction. Reality is its own satire.

Thus, even in speaking of *Bleak House*'s opening paragraphs, there is something unsatisfactory about speaking of a mixture of fact and fancy: that formulation misses the problematic quality of Dickens's reality. It misses too Dickens's fascination with the problem; for it is on the problem that his interest clearly centers. More than being concerned to *teach* us how documents which purport to represent reality are misleading and even false, he is, I think, concerned with *dwelling*, to use his own word, on precisely that point in experience when what we have come to think of as the "familiar" suddenly ceases to be so, and strikes us instead as something the very opposite of the "familiar," the "romantic." And the converse, as I hope to show, is true as well: *Bleak House* dwells also on the "familiar" side of "romantic" things.

II

Almost all books that have general arguments may be described as seeking to move the reader from a "familiar" to a "romantic" perception of a thing or from a "romantic" to a "familiar" one. The latter is usually the overt strategy. An author begins with an idea that is new and even bizzare to us— the ideas of natural selection or unconscious motivation, for example. If he has argued well, then at the end of his book his idea will have passed from being something strange and even offensive to being accepted as something we can and must live with. If he has argued with genius, that idea will pass into a commonplace, something we have grown so accustomed to that it becomes an essential part of ourselves. But an author can just as well move us in the opposite direction, from a perception of a thing as "familiar" to a perception of it as "romantic." Malthus, for example, does this in the *First Essay* with the idea of "necessity," an idea straight out of the common language and overlooked for just that reason. By the end of the *First Essay*, the idea of necessity, transparently understood at the outset, has become opaquely understood: it has passed from invisible familiarity to visible strangeness—and frightening reality. Of course, authors of books with such arguments usually move us in both directions at once: Darwin and Freud make old, familiar ideas strange to us while they are familiarizing us with new ones. The notion of free will becomes positively an astonishing conception to us by the time we have read through the first part of the *Introductory Lectures on Psycho-Analysis*.

The point in all of this is that an author with an argument of this kind wants to persuade us of something, which necessarily involves moving us from one position of certainty to quite another position of certainty, and to do this he must take us through some critical peripety. The greater the genius, the more dazzling the peripety is likely to be, and the more likely it is that we as readers will return to that peripety to be dazzled by it again and again. But the peripety is not the point. It really is something we are supposed (by the author) to be carried *through*. In *Bleak House*, we shall see, it really is the point, and it is the point suggested by "the romantic side of familiar things."

We have already seen a few of the ways in which reality is both made strange and is strange in *Bleak House*. But perhaps the best demonstration of how Dickens dwells upon "the romantic side of familiar things" comes from a rather detailed examination of how the whole opening number works, of what questions and expectations, in other words, the first monthly installment raises in its readers. Most importantly, what rules has the opening number set up for the novel's narrative?

One pattern becomes apparent on the novel's first page as the narrator describes the literally chaotic scene before him—literally chaotic because of the war of earthly elements described and perhaps too because this world of *Chancery* suggests a punning connection with not only the "chance people" of the second paragraph but with Chance as one of the traditional rulers of Chaos.[9] The pattern of the opening, and indeed the pattern of things described, is circular. The first four paragraphs of the novel complete a full circle.[10] We begin with "the Lord Chancellor sitting in Lincoln's Inn Hall," move out into the neighboring streets, take in a view of the "Essex marshes" and the "Kentish heights," return again to the London streets and finally to Temple Bar and Lincoln's Inn Hall again. We can only move in circles, moreover, because the world of Chancery is itself circular. It is a world of "interminable briefs" and on this particular afternoon is "mistily engaged in one of the ten thousand stages of an endless cause." Both statements, of course, are wholly self-contradictory—briefs are the opposite of interminable, and a cause that is endless cannot have a finite number of stages—unless those briefs and stages are ranged round a circle. John Jarndyce, in fact, will later speak of "the wheel of Chancery" (35), referring to both the instrument of torture and the wheel of Chance or Fortune. Even the suit in which he is a party, Jarndyce and Jarndyce, is, as its name implies, circular.

> Jarndyce and Jarndyce drones on. This scarecrow of a suit has, in course of time, become so complicated, that no man alive knows what it means. The parties to it understand it least; but it has been observed that no two Chancery lawyers can talk about it for five minutes, without coming to a total disagreement as to all the premises. Innumerable children have been born into the cause; innumerable young people have married into it; innumerable old people have died out of it. Scores of persons have deliriously found themselves made parties in Jarndyce and Jarndyce, without knowing how or why; whole families have inherited legendary hatreds with the suit. The little plaintiff or defendant, who was promised a new rocking-horse when Jarndyce and Jarndyce should be settled, has grown up, possessed himself of a real horse, and trotted away into the other world. . . . but Jarndyce and Jarndyce still drags its dreary length before the Court, perennially hopeless.

The circular nature of Chancery asserts itself in both the smallest and the largest ways. The "foggy glory" round the Chancellor's head is but the first of an endless series of expanding concentric circles, "and even those who have contemplated its history from the outermost circle of such evil, have been insensibly tempted into a loose way of letting bad things alone to take their own bad course, and a loose belief that if the world go wrong, it was, in some off-hand manner, never meant to go right." No two Chancery lawyers can talk about Jarndyce and Jarndyce "for five minutes without coming to a total disagreement as to all the premises"—they cannot, that is to say, talk about it without immediately becoming deadlocked within one of the smaller circles. And the circles have a life of their own. Jarndyce and Jarndyce was once but a small circle, a mere "scarecrow of a suit," which has grown so large that it now "drags its dreary length before the court, perennially hopeless," rather like that "Megalosaurus, forty feet long or so," whom "it would not be wonderful to meet . . . waddling like an elephantine lizard up Holborn Hill," for like the Megalosaurus it belongs to the distant world out of which we came, and which "no man alive" now understands.

The circle Dickens traces for us in the first four paragraphs is repeated throughout the chapter:

> On such an afternoon, if ever, the Lord Chancellor ought to be sitting here—as here he is—with a foggy glory round his head. . . . This is the Court of Chancery. . . .
> Thus, in the midst of the mud and at the heart of the fog, sits the Lord High Chancellor in his High Court of Chancery.

At first we can understand the world of Chancery no better than those who live in it. We are like those "chance people on the bridges peeping over the parapets," or like "the uninitiated from the streets, who peep in through the glass panes in the door [of Lincoln's Inn Hall]," or like the "little mad old woman" who stands "on a seat at the side of the hall, the better to peer into the curtained sanctuary," or even like the Chancellor himself, "outwardly directing his contemplation to the lantern in the roof, where he can see nothing but fog." We are like them, and they are all like one another, for the fog that at once revels and conceals the world makes everyone and everything look like everything else. The gas masquerades as the sun, for it looms "through the fog in divers places in the streets, much as the sun may, from the spongy fields, be seen to loom by husbandman and ploughboy." The crowds in the street are anonymous "foot passengers" obscured by mud and fog and their little army of umbrellas, and are "losing their foot-hold at street-corners, where tens of thousands of other foot passengers have been slipping and sliding since the day broke." They are, like everyone else, mired "in one of the ten thousand stages of an endless cause." The Chancery practitioners are hardly less anonymous:

> Eighteen of Mr. Tangle's learned friends, each armed with a little summary of eighteen hundred sheets, bob up like eighteen hammers in a pianoforte, make eighteen bows, and drop into their eighteen places of obscurity.

This circular mirroring of people, places, and images with one another does not let up throughout the whole course of the novel. Nothing that is introduced in the first pages fails to return either in its own shape or only slightly modified. The Megalosaurus of the first paragraph returns in the same chapter as the legendary suit itself, which "drags its dreary length before the court," but also recurs again and again in later chapters. The "wagons and hackney coaches" of the London streets roar along "like one great dragon" (10). Judy Smallweed "appears to attain a perfectly geological age, and to date from the remotest periods" (21); and her grandfather's god, we are told in the same chapter, is "Compound Interest," which also refers us back to the novel's first paragraph. "The hot water pipes . . . trail themselves all over the house" in the "antedeluvian forest" at Chesney Wold (28), "where old stone lions and grotesque monsters bristled outside dens of shadow, and snarled at the evening gloom over the escutcheons they held in their grip" (36). Miss Flite calls Chancery simply "the Monster" (35). The blue bags containing Chancery documents are "stuffed, out of all regularity of form, as the larger sort of serpents are in their first gorged state" (39). Mr. Krook's cat, Lady Jane, goes "leaping and bounding and tearing about . . . like a Dragon" (39). "The Duke of Poodle sends [to Tulkinghorn's funeral] a splendid pile of dust and ashes, with silver wheel-boxes, patent axles . . . and three bereaved worms, six feet high, holding on behind" (53), while Lady Dedlock is as "indifferent as if all passion, feeling, and interest, had been worn out in the earlier ages of the world, and had perished from its surface with its other departed monsters" (48). And so on.

The Megalosaurus is but the first image in the novel, and we could draw up equally long (or longer) lists for the other images of the first few paragraphs. The "smoke lowering down from Chimney-pots . . . with flakes of soot in it as big as full-grown snow-flakes" recurs at several points, but most dramatically as presaging Krook's death:

> "Why, Tony, what on earth is going on in this house tonight? Is there a chimney on fire?" [asks Mr. Guppy.]
> "Chimney on fire!"
> "Ah!" returns Mr. Guppy. "See how the soot's falling. See here, on my arm! See again, on the table here! Confound the stuff, it won't blow off—smears, like black fat!" (32)

And so too does the confusion between up and down in which the smoke is involved return—in fact in the paragraph following the one I have just quoted:

> They look at one another, and Tony goes listening to the door, and a little way up-stairs, and a little way down-stairs. Comes back, and says it's all right, and all quiet.

In the same chapter, "Mr. Weevle has been down and up, and down and up [from Krook's shop] . . . oftener than before" and, as he converses with Snagsby, glances "up and down the court." Bleak House itself is "one of those delightfully irregular houses where you go up and down steps out of one room into another" (6). Reading an article aloud to the circle at Chesney Wold, Sir Leicester interrupts himself at several points, each time "invariably losing his place after each observation, and going up and down the column to find it again" (29). These repeated up-and-down patterns signify confusion, of course, but also suggest a particularly restless and uneasy variant of the larger pattern of circular repetitions. Allan Woodcourt, "who appears in some inaptitude for sleep to be wandering abroad rather than counting the hours on a restless pillow, strolls, . . . often pauses and looks about him, up and down the miserable by-ways [of Tom-all-Alone's]" (46). The novel's central restless pacer, perhaps, is Lady Morbury Dedlock, the ghost of The Ghost's Walk, who in life had been lamed by a horse and thereafter "tried to walk upon the terrace; and with the help of the stone balustrade, went up and down, up and down, up and down, in sun and shadow, with greater difficulty every day" (7).

In his classic exposition of *Bleak House*, Hillis Miller notes that the novel's first chapter creates a world in which everything is in motion, but "it is a motion which does not move anywhere."[11] Reading the opening chapter is like watching the workings of a complex machine when all the gears have been disengaged, but continue to turn under their own momentum; indeed, like being caught up in such a machine ourselves. The state we find described and the state in which we find ourselves is therefore literally one of suspended animation, and this becomes especially clear at the very end of the first chapter. While it describes no real events, the chapter does describe a good deal of activity, and at its end brings us to the brink of a real event. The Chancellor is being waited upon by a boy and girl, wards of Chancery, whom he is about to see in his private room. No sooner is this announced than the chapter closes, and we too are made to wait his decision as to whether they shall live with their uncle or not. The second chapter, "In Fashion," abruptly intervenes, and appears to remove us to an entirely different world. But the difference between being "In Fashion" and "In Chancery" is only apparent. The two worlds explicitly mirror one another: they are "not so unlike," for "both are things of precedent and usage" (2). Both, that is, are devoted to repeating patterns of the past. And the two worlds mirror one another also in what might at first seem small details. The evil of the world of fashion is "that it is a world wrapped up in too much jeweler's cotton and fine wool," which certainly recalls the Chancellor's sitting in Lincoln's Inn Hall, "softly fenced in with crimson cloth and curtains" (1) and the woolsack upon which he sits in the House of Lords and which symbolizes his office.

Again, we are both moving in circles and having them described to us. But the energy with which the circles of the first chapter are turning is here running down, and there is far more suspension than animation in the fashionable world. Lady Dedlock has her "dim little star[s] revolving about her" and is herself turned about the fingers of her tradesmen and servants, as Mr. Sladdery the librarian tells us. But those spits in the kitchen described in the chapter's first paragraph have indeed stopped, and it will be long before they "shall begin to turn prodigiously!"

When we first met Lady Dedlock she is in the midst of flight:

> My Lady Dedlock has returned to her house in town for a few days previous to her departure for Paris, where her ladyship intends to stay some weeks; after which her movements are uncertain.

Having been led by our guide out of Chancery and out of London into Lincolnshire, we find ourselves back in London again, at the Dedlock house in town. And at that house

> upon this muddy, murky afternoon, presents himself an old-fashioned old gentleman, attorney-at-law, and eke solicitor of the High Court of Chancery, who has the honour of acting as legal advisor of the Dedlocks, and has as many cast-iron boxes in his office with that name outside, as if the present baronet were the coin of the conjuror's trick, and were constantly being juggled through the whole set. Across the hall, and up the stairs, and along the passages, and through the rooms, which are very brilliant in the season and very dismal out of it—Fairy-land to visit, but a desert to live in—the old gentleman is conducted, by a Mercury in powder, to my Lady's presence.

This is Mr. Tulkinghorn, "surrounded by a mysterious halo of family confidences," like the Chancellor's "foggy glory." His arrival simply completes another circle, for Lady Dedlock is involved in a case in Chancery, and he has come to her this afternoon to advise her what has been doing—though nothing, of course, "has been done."

     Mr. Tulkinghorn takes out his papers, asks permission to place them on a golden talisman of a table at my Lady's elbow, puts on his spectacles, and begins to read by the light of a shaded lamp.
     " 'In Chancery. Between John Jarndyce—' "
     My Lady interrupts, requesting him to miss as many of the formal horrors as he can.
     Mr. Tulkinghorn glances over his spectacles, and begins again lower down. My Lady carelessly and scornfully abstracts her attention. Sir Leicester in a great chair looks at the fire, and appears to have a stately liking for the legal repetitions and prolixities, as ranging among the national bulwarks. It happens that the fire is hot, where my lady sits; and that the hand-screen is more beautiful than useful, being priceless but small. My Lady, changing her position, sees the papers on the table—looks at them nearer—looks at them nearer still—asks impulsively:
     "Who copied that?"
     Mr. Tulkinghorn stops short, surprised by my Lady's animation and her unusual tone.
     "Is it what you people call law-hand?" she asks, looking full at him in her careless way again, and toying with her screen.
     "Not quite. Probably"—Mr. Tulkinghorn examines it as he speaks—"the legal character which it has, was acquired after the original hand was formed. Why do you ask?"
     "Anything to vary this detestable monotony. O, go on, do!"
     Mr. Tulkinghorn reads again. The heat is greater, my Lady screens her face. Sir Leicester dozes, starts up suddenly, and cries, "Eh? what do you say?"
     "I say I am afraid," says Mr. Tulkinghorn, who had risen hastily, "that Lady Dedlock is ill."
     "Faint," my Lady murmurs, with white lips, "only that; but it is like the faintness of death. Don't speak to me. Ring, and take me to my room."

The completion of this circle takes us back to the very beginning, to the title of the first chapter. And no sooner is this circle completed than the novel finally appears to get under way, after some dozen or so pages, and presents us with its first real event. It is the event, moreover, which springs the action of the whole novel, for it is Lady Dedlock's "imprudence" here, her being "taken by surprise" (40), that sets Tulkinghorn off on the investigation that will finally expose her and lead to his own death. Only the merest *chance* sets things in motion. It "happens" that the fire is too warm and that Lady Dedlock's hand-screen—the symbolism is obvious—"is more beautiful than useful." "Changing her position," her attention, which she had "carelessly and scornfully" abstracted, is now drawn to the paper Mr. Tulkinghorn is reading, and recognizing the hand as Captain Hawdon's she lets down her guard for an instant and "asks impulsively" her fateful question. But no sooner has the question been asked and the action begun than it comes to a stop again. "Mr. Tulkinghorn stops short, surprised by my Lady's animation and her unusual tone." Immediately we are back again in the "detestable monotony" of the suspended animation of the fashionable world. Mr. Tulkinghorn takes up his reading again, and Sir Leicester, though he "appears to have a stately liking for the legal repetitions and prolixities," has fallen into a doze and back into the world of Rip Van Winkles and sleeping beauties invoked at the beginning of the chapter. Lady Dedlock grows ill and faint, and Sir Leicester is awakened and "starts up suddenly," but he wakes in a world that is itself still largely asleep. The "stopped spits in the kitchen" have not yet begun "to turn prodigiously," and Sir Leicester can explain away his Lady's faintness by remarking that "the weather is extremely trying—and she really has been bored to death down at our place in Lincolnshire."

As we have seen, *Bleak House* is not a novel that gets under way easily. The opening chapter leaves us on the brink of an event, is interrupted by another chapter which finally does present us with an event, only to lapse again into sleepy obscurity. It is not surprising that the third chapter, introducing Esther's narrative, should repeat the pattern:

> I have a great deal of difficulty in beginning to write my portion of these pages, for I know I am not clever. I always knew that. I can remember, when I was a very little girl indeed, I used to say to my doll, when we were alone together, "Now Dolly, I am not clever, you know very well, and you must be patient with me, like a dear!" And so she used to sit propped up in a great arm-chair, with her beautiful complexion and rosy lips, staring at me—or not so much at me, I think, as at nothing—while I busily stitched away, and told her every one of my secrets.

Like the Chancellor, who has his "satellites" (8) and Lady Dedlock, who has her "dim little star[s] revolving about her" (2), Esther is at the center of a circle and is the center of her world. Her name means "a star"[12] and there is of course a pun intended in her surname: she is the summer sun. But her world does not at first seem very much to resemble that of the Chancellor or of Lady Dedlock. It is removed from theirs in place and time. Windsor lies outside the apparent orbit we have described around Chancery, Chesney Wold, and the Dedlock house in town, and we have evidently left the "muddy, murky afternoon" on which the novel began. Esther's doll does recall—and comment upon—the Chancellor and Lady Dedlock, for she sits "propped up in a great arm-chair, with her beautiful complexion and rosy lips, staring at . . . nothing." And like Mr. Tulkinghorn she is the (literally) "silent depository" (2) of family secrets. Esther too is a silent observer. "I had always a rather noticing way," she says, "a silent way of noticing what passed before me." Nevertheless, what seems to be missing from her world are the mud and the fog of the first chapter, and the kind of animation-in-suspension which they create. The story of her early life, which begins her narrative, appears to be a succession of orderly and intelligible events. But Esther gets no more than a couple of pages into her story before our way again becomes obscure.

> It was my birthday. There were holidays at school on other birthdays—
> none on mine. There were rejoicings at home on other birthdays, as I knew
> from what I had heard the other girls relate to one another—there were
> none on mine. My birthday was the most melancholy day at home, in the
> whole year.
>
> I have mentioned, that, unless my vanity should deceive me (as I
> know it may, for I may be very vain, without suspecting it—though indeed
> I don't), my comprehension is quickened when my affection is. My disposi-
> tion is very affectionate; and perhaps I might still feel such a wound, if such
> a wound could be received more than once, with the quickness of that
> birthday.

The meaning of this important passage is generally clear: Esther is about to
relate the story of an especially awful birthday, one which, because of her
unusual sensitivity, has been so deeply wounding that the pain of it can be
recalled only partially. It is the kind of passage, further, that is not especially
liable to stop us on a first reading (like our first view of Lady Dedlock) for we
are eager to know just what that wound might be. If we do pause, however,
we see that the second paragraph here in fact does not really make sense.
The trouble begins in the parenthetical clause, "I may be very vain, without
suspecting it—though indeed I don't." "Don't" what? "Don't" *not* suspect it,
which is what the syntax seems to demand, but the sense would make
nonsensical? The problem is not simply grammatical, but logical. Esther is
caught up in a vicious circle: she may be vain, without suspecting it, but she
clearly *does* suspect it, so her first statement cannot be true. The rest of the
paragraph poses even greater logical problems:

> . . .my comprehension is quickened when my affection is. My disposition
> is very affectionate, and perhaps I might still feel such a wound, if such a
> wound could be received more than once, with the quickness of that
> birthday.

The implicit conclusion to the first few clauses is clear. If her understanding
is greater when her sympathies are engaged, and if they are usually engaged
(as her having a "very affectionate" disposition would imply), then she is
usually quick to comprehend—a complete contradiction of her earlier statement that she "had always a rather noticing way—not a quick way, O no!"
Esther is caught again in the same confusion I have just discussed. On the
one hand she suspects and understands, and on the other something prevents her either from suspecting or understanding, or from admitting that
she both suspects and understands. This confusion—so typical of Esther, and
so annoying to many of her critics—manifests itself in various ways in the
paragraph. There is no logical connection between the first two clauses of the
last sentence. What do comprehension or an affectionate disposition have to
do with still feeling "such a wound"? The "wound" appears out of nowhere,
for it refers not to anything she has already mentioned but to the recollec-
tions she is about to relate. And the last two clauses are entirely ambiguous.
Does she mean that she might still feel such a wound if it could be felt again

with the quickness with which she first felt it, or that it is the nature of such wounds to be felt with such quickness only once? Does "quickness," in other words, refer to feeling or to receiving the wound? What, finally, is the connection between comprehension, feeling, and receiving, which seem to be equated here but which are not at all the same things?

Esther seems to be talking more to herself than to her audience here. The tone is musing and abstracted, and that would both account for the incoherence of her thoughts and provide us with another way of understanding them. For it is characteristic of such states that they present us with what are apparently quasi-logical connections in syntax which only serve to obscure the real train of our thought.[13] We have seen that the connections here simply don't work, and that the logic of Esther's thoughts is only apparent. Indeed, we can perhaps dispense with them as artifacts. What this leaves us with is the following series of words: "comprehension . . . quickened . . . affection . . . disposition . . . affectionate . . . wound . . . quickness." This series might not at first seem meaningful, but it does in fact have its own inner coherence. "Comprehension" and "quickness" are obviously related: a "quick" person being one who is unusually perceptive. But "quickness" is also related to "affection." Being "quickened" can mean the same thing as being "affected"; that is, being deeply stirred. "Affection" in turn can mean any emotional "disposition" and also, in its medical sense, something like a "wound." Similarly, a "wound" can mean the raw flesh of the "quick," and "quickness" takes us back to "comprehension."

Esther's thought proceeds not by logical steps but by a series of words with overlapping meanings, and a series, moreover, which is circular. It is in the very texture of her thoughts, in other words, that we are presented with the same kind of stop-and-go, circular motion that seems to be the external condition of things in the worlds of Chancery and of fashion. The mud and fog of the first two chapters, signifying confusions in the external relations between things and people, have in the third been internalized and become the inhibited condition of a particular kind of thinking. Chancery thus represents both society and a state of mind—specifically Esther's state of mind, and the state of mind, therefore, of a large part of the novel itself.

One of the other most important circular reverberations of Esther's first chapter with the worlds of Chancery and fashion comes when Esther relates the stories of her melancholy birthday and of her godmother's death:

> . . . my godmother and I were sitting at the table before the fire. . . . I happened to look timidly up from my stitching, across the table, at my godmother, and I saw in her face, looking gloomily at me, "It would have been far better, little Esther, that you had had no birthday; that you had never been born!"
>
> I broke out crying and sobbing, and I said, "O, dear godmother, tell me, pray do tell me, did mama die on my birthday?" . . .
>
> Her darkened face had such power over me, that it stopped me in the midst of my vehemence. . . .

"Your mother, Esther, is your disgrace, and you were hers. . . . Forget your mother and leave all other people to forget her who will do her
unhappy child that greatest kindness. Now go!"

She checked me, however, as I was about to depart from her—so
frozen as I was!—and added this:

"Submission, self-denial, diligent work, are the preparations for a life
begun with such a shadow on it. You are different from other children,
Esther, because you were not born, like them, in common sinfulness and
wrath. You are set apart." . . .

It must have been two years afterwards, and I was almost fourteen,
when one dreadful night my godmother and I sat at the fireside. I was
reading aloud, and she was listening. . . . [I] was reading, from St. John,
how our Saviour stooped down, writing with his finger in the dust, when
they brought the sinful woman to him.

" 'So when they continued asking him, he lifted up himself and said
unto them, He that is without sin among you, let him first cast a stone at
her!' "

I was stopped short by my godmother's rising, putting her hand to
her head, and crying out, in an awful voice, from quite another part of the
book:

" 'Watch ye therefore! lest coming suddenly he find you sleeping.
And what I say unto you, I say unto all, Watch!' "

In an instant, while she stood before me repeating these words, she
fell down upon the floor. I had no need to cry out; her voice had sounded
through the house, and been heard in the street.

Various things in these two episodes recall Lady Dedlock's happening to
recognize Captain Hawdon's handwriting. In both Esther is sitting with her
godmother before the fire. In both reading is involved, though in the first it
is only the reading of Miss Barbary's face. Writing is mentioned in the
second, for Christ is "writing with his finger in the dust." In the first episode,
Esther simply "happens" to look up at that moment at her godmother, and
what she sees moves her to ask an impulsive question. She is given no real
reply and her godmother's darkened face stops her "in the midst of [her]
vehemence." After she is given the only answer Miss Barbary is willing to tell
her, she is again "checked" and "frozen," recalling Lady Dedlock's "freezing
mood." In the second scene, it is Miss Barbary who is so disturbed by what is
read to her (the story of the woman taken in adultery in John 8:7) that she
swoons, and indeed soon dies:

She was laid upon her bed. For more than a week she lay there, little
altered outwardly; with her old handsome resolute frown that I so well
know, carved upon her face. Many and many a time, in the day and in the
night, with my head upon the pillow by her that my whispers might be
plainer to her, I kissed her, thanked her, prayed for her, asked her for her
blessing and forgiveness, entreated her to give me the least sign that she
knew or heard me. No, no, no. Her face was immoveable. To the very last,
and even afterwards, her frown remained unsoftened.

Miss Barbary's "old handsome resolute frown," her "carved" and "immove-able" features and her absolute unresponsiveness combine features of Lady Dedlock's "freezing mood," Esther's doll, and the Chancellor, who is "legally ignorant of [the man from Shropshire's] existence after making it desolate for a quarter of a century" (1). Indeed, Esther here is precisely in the position of Miss Flite, "the little mad old woman" who expects "some incomprehensible judgment,"[14] and the quotation with which Esther's godmother counters her reading from St. John in fact foretells the Day of Judgment (Mark 13:35–37).

More important than the resonance with Miss Flite, however, is the structural similarity between these scenes with Esther's godmother and the scene between the woman who is her real mother and Mr. Tulkinghorn. And as we shall see, the connections the texts ask us to make, indeed, even imposes on us, are important precisely because there is no real connection in plot established between them at this point in the novel: the connections are merely, or purely, structural.

One further detail should link these scenes, and that is the reappearance just after Miss Barbary's death of "the gentleman in black" who had called on Esther two years before, just as Mr. Tulkinghorn, another gentleman in black, has called on Lady Dedlock. Mr. Kenge does not begin, as Mr. Tulkinghorn had, with a repetition of the words with which the novel had opened, "In Chancery." But he does almost as well: "our young friend," he says of Esther, "has no doubt heard of—the—a—Jarndyce and Jarndyce." Here the first real connection in plot between Esther's narrative and the first two chapters is apparent, although precisely what the connection is long remains secret.

With Esther's removal to Greenleaf under the secret guardianship of a party in Jarndyce and Jarndyce, she enjoys "six quiet years," she tells us, of respite from a world that the reader has by now come to know as "Chancery." But the respite ends with a summons from Kenge and Carboy to London. In fact, Esther returns to Chancery on the "same mirey afternoon" described in the first two chapters. The temporal circle begun with Esther's story of her early years has closed, and at precisely the same moment that the third-person narrator is guiding us through the public side of Chancery, Esther is hidden away with Richard Carstone and Ada Clare in the Chancellor's private room.

With Esther's arrival in court, the interrupted thread of events in the first chapter is at last taken up again and the novel may finally be said to have gotten under way. But Esther's experience of Chancery of course duplicates the picture of it in the opening chapter, so that even while we feel that at last we are moving forward we are also aware of having returned to the beginning and of still being in a state of animation-in-suspension. Esther writes of waiting in Mr. Kenge's office:

> Everything was so strange—the stranger from its being night in the
> day-time, the candles burning with a white flame, and looking raw and

cold—that I read the words in the newspaper without knowing what they meant, and found myself reading the same words repeatedly. As it was no use going on in that way, I put the paper down, took a a peep at my bonnet in the glass to see if it was neat, and looked at the room which was not half lighted . . . and at a bookcase full of the most inexpressive-looking books that ever had anything to say for themselves. Then I went on, thinking, thinking, thinking; and the fire went on, burning, burning, burning; and the candles went on flickering and guttering, and there were no snuffers—until the young gentleman by-and-by brought a very dirty pair; for two hours.

At this point the two narratives have perfectly linked up, for they are describing precisely the same things from two different points of view. They are describing not only a particular world, but our experience of that world. Like Esther, we read the words of the novel without quite knowing what they mean (that is, without yet knowing how they relate to one another), and find ourselves reading what amount to the same words repeatedly. But from this point on, the two narratives split up again, and though they overlap almost entirely in regard to the characters they encompass, they will not come to describe the same events again (except, occasionally, at second-hand) until chapters 56 and 57 (at the juncture of numbers 17 and 18) where Esther takes up the search for Lady Dedlock at exactly the moment when the third person narrator leaves off.

In a sense it is here that the novel's prelude ends and the action of the novel proper begins, but in saying this I am also choosing a somewhat arbitrary point, for in the following chapter, the last of the opening number, we are presented with the Jellyby family and material that is at once new to us and familiar. Mrs. Jellyby's home obviously mirrors the chaos of Chancery. Her room is "strewn with papers and nearly filled by a great writing-table covered with similar litter," reminiscent of "the registrar's red table . . . with bills, cross-bills, answers, rejoinders, injunctions, affidavits, issues, references to masters, masters' reports, mountains of costly nonsense, piled before [the Chancery solicitors]" as well as Miss Flite's "small litter . . . which she calls her documents" (1). But beyond this there does not seem at first to be any connection between Mrs. Jellyby's philanthropic activities and Chancery. Mrs. Jellyby's world clearly has little use for "precedent and usage" and her plan to place "two hundred healthy families cultivating coffee and educating the natives of Borrioboola-Gha, on the left bank of the Niger" would seem as far removed from Chancery as it is possible to be. Nevertheless, Dickens links Chancery and Mrs. Jellyby's philanthropic schemes by pointing out that they share a central notion, the idea of a "cause." Being in a cause or having a cause is the one thing that unites the worlds of the Jellybys, Chancery, the Dedlocks, and indeed everyone in the opening number. Exploring the meaning of that idea and tracing its implications is a task that will take Dickens the whole rest of the novel to accomplish, but we are already in a position to make some generalizations about the novel based upon our reading of the opening number.

III

Concerning the opening chapters of *Bleak House* Hillis Miller writes:

> The narrative line of *Bleak House* shifts continually from one space-time to another apparently simultaneous with it but otherwise unconnected. It is not until we are far into the novel that relations between widely separated actions and milieus begin to appear. At first it seems that Dickens, inexplicably, has chosen to write two or three novels at once, and to alternate with no apparent rhyme or reason from portraits of the aristocratic world of Lady Dedlock at Chesney Wold to the very different stories of Esther Summerson and the wards in Jarndyce. Moreover, a great number of minor characters are presented who have no obvious relation to the major stories.[15]

This would be true if by "relations" we meant only fully understood causal relations. But of course this is not all that "relations" means. The one thing we do know about all the events and characters in *Bleak House*'s opening number is that they are related because they are all involved in the same kind of suspended animation and the same kind of inhibited or circular activity. Indeed, it is just because the causal relations between these people and events are not from the outset understood that the relations between them are perceived virtually as identity. This is the force of the mirroring of the different worlds we are shown at the novel's beginning. To hold causal relationships in suspension and to portray a series of worlds which share a number of overlapping attributes and details prevents us from making any clear discriminations between them, and tends rather to make us see reflections even where no obvious overlapping exists. The invocation of the world of fairy-tales in relation to the fashionable world at the beginning of the second chapter, for example, does not serve to distinguish the world of fashion from that of Chancery, which has its reference in the cosmologies of the Bible, Milton, and Victorian geology, but instead adds another kind of legendary framework relevant to Chancery. And the converse is true, though at this point in the novel (in chapter 2) we can know this only semiconsciously or implicitly by allowing our imagination to give free rein to the mirroring of the two worlds. Only later in the novel will the religious and geological aspects of the fashionable world be explicitly revealed (for example, in the discussion of religious "Dandyism" [12] or the geological references to Chesney Wold and the Dedlocks discussed above).

The insistent mirroring of the novel's worlds (conveyed in the specific train of mirror imagery in the novel as well as in its general structure) not only tends to make for the identification or confusion of all these worlds but also paradoxically provides Dickens with a device whereby he can prepare us for the important "revelations" in the rest of the novel. If we look for causal relationships in the novel's opening number, we shall not find them, and the novel will indeed appear, as Miller suggests, to be made up of unrelated people and events. If, however, we relax our conscious search for such relations, and allow the tendency for separate people and events to fuse—if, in other words, we give ourselves up to the confusion of *Bleak House,* then we will find that no event in the novel can come as a true surprise to us; rather every "new" development will strike us with a sense at once of familiarity and inevitability.

Let us take, as an example one of the central mysteries in the novel, the question of Esther's identity. What really do we learn about it in the opening number? In terms of hard evidence, almost nothing. We are led to believe that she is an orphan, and illegitimate. We know that her guardian is Mr. Jarndyce and that he is in a Chancery suit, but we have no way of knowing how he came to be her guardian. Nevertheless, if we allow the parallels between Esther and Lady Dedlock as evidence of another kind, we shall find that we know a great deal. The obvious parallels are primarily between the scene in which Lady Dedlock recognizes the handwriting of the manuscript Tulkinghorn reads to her, and the scene on Esther's birthday and her reading to her godmother, as well as the intervening visit of Mr. Kenge. We are told that Lady Dedlock is childless, and we sense that her childlessness is at the root of her being put "quite out of temper" and the mask of boredom that conceals her uneasiness. But we also know that Lady Dedlock has a secret— perhaps having a connection with Jarndyce and Jarndyce, but in any case one whose hold over her is so strong that the mere sight of a particular handwriting is enough to make this grand woman fairly swoon. We know that Miss Barbary holds a similar secret, also one that is possibly connected with Jarndyce and Jarndyce, and also one whose hold over *her* is so great that simply hearing the story of Jesus writing in the dust and being presented with the woman taken in adultery is enough not only to make her swoon but in fact to kill her, though her characteristic resolute and handsome composure is as firm as Lady Dedlock's. We might also suspect that Miss Barbary's secret has to do with Esther's identity, for several reasons, but most clearly because of the parallel between the biblical story and Esther's illegitimate birth. Dickens places just one serious obstacle in the way of our causally connecting Lady Dedlock and Miss Barbary and Esther, and realizing that Lady Dedlock and Miss Barbary are sisters in fact as well as in spirit, and that is our supposition that Lady Dedlock is childless and that Esther is an orphan—although the latter is ambiguous.

That we are prepared for every event in the novel of course does not mean that we are conscious of that preparation, for the parallels between images, characters, or events are generally drawn by references to apparently indifferent common denominators which are veiled because they appear in successively different contexts. Thus, when we learn that Mrs. Jellyby is devoted to a philanthropic "cause" (4) we probably shall not consciously connect her cause with Chancery causes, because the everyday sense of the language selects for us quite different meanings for the word in these two contexts. Nevertheless, it is through such delicate punning that we can pinpoint the relatedness of the Jellybys and Chancery and that we can understand that both worlds have their reference in the idea of a "cause" not only in its various particular senses, but in its most general and abstract sense. We have already seen this kind of punning in the circle of words with overlapping meanings that Esther constructs to describe the anxious confusions of her childhood. It is a confusion that not coincidentally is expressed by the relative absence of causal (that is, logical) relationships in her thoughts and indeed is explicitly about her failure to understand her own causal relations with the world—"What did I do to [my mother]?" she asks Miss Barbary, "How did I lose her? Why am I so different from other children, and why is it my fault, dear godmother?" (3). Though Esther does not use the word "cause" here, nevertheless she is implicitly carrying on the elaborate play on the word that has begun in the first chapter with "the cause" of Jarndyce and Jarndyce and that in many ways forms the novel's real subject or asks the central question—"Where do I come from?" It is, of course, the most basic question that we can ask about ourselves, and the question our most basic myths seek to answer.

Bleak House is about "causes" and "relations" in every conceivable meaning and combination of meanings of those two words. It begins, we should recall, with a picture of causal relationships that have been entirely dislocated and turned upside down. This is the especial horror of Chaos, and this too is what makes the pun the most important device by which we can understand or make connections within the world of the novel, for it is in the very nature of puns that they can be intuitively understood without one's consciously making the logical connections between their various meanings. And it is this fact that makes the suspense of the opening number not only bearable, but pleasurable. The mirroring of the novel's various worlds and the tendency to see reflections even where there is no explicit overlapping of details (itself a kind of punning on a grand scale) is just what allows us, in spite of all the apparent discontinuity in the first four chapters, to know, if only at the back of our minds, that indeed the connections exist, and that Lady Dedlock and Esther are related by the profoundest of ties.

The circular patterns I have been tracing in *Bleak House*'s opening number are of course not perfectly circular: things do not repeat themselves with exactness, but rather with variation. When Esther's narrative catches up with that of the third-person narrator, we find ourselves almost exactly where we had been left at the end of the first chapter, but not quite: only a door separates us from our former selves. As skillful as Dickens is in maintaining his circles, he is equally skillful in playing out his variations—variations sometimes so complex as to all but hide from us the fact that we have moved in circles. The experience for the reader is thus one of *déjà vu*. We are continually being made to feel that we have been here before while at the same time we know that we have not, and this is especially the case in those scenes which structurally and dynamically echo previous ones without there being a manifest connection (generally in plot) between them. It is this circular experience of *déjà vu* (doubly circular, really, for it is circular in itself and circular in that it is itself repeated) that represents for me a kind of continual peripety and that represents for me further one structural embodiment of Dickens's dwelling "on the romantic side of familiar things." Peripety means of course literally "a falling round"; what we have seen in the beginning of *Bleak House* is a falling round and round and round, and one that continually makes the familiar strange and the strange familiar.

This is precisely the experience we have already seen described by Esther as she waits for the Chancellor in the passage I have taken as my epigraph, and it is an experience that is not restricted to the labyrinthine world of Chancery, but one that pervades even the relatively secure worlds of *Bleak House*. Indeed, it pervades Bleak House (the house) itself, as Esther tells us in describing it in the next number, for "you might, if you came out at another door [of Mr. Jarndyce's room] (every room had at least two doors), go straight down to the hall again by half-a-dozen steps and a low archway, wondering how you got back there, or had ever got out of it" (6).[16]

Notes

1. J. Hillis Miller, "The Fiction of Realism: *Sketches by Boz, Oliver Twist*, and Cruikshank's Illustrations," in *Dickens Centennial Essays*, ed. Ada Nisbet and Blake Nevius (Berkeley: University of California Press, 1971), pp. 85–154, and Steven Marcus, "Language into Structure: Pickwick Revisited," *Daedalus*, 101 (1972), 183–202.

2. *Bleak House* (Harmondsworth: Penguin, 1971), p. 11.

3. *Ibid.*, p. 22.

4. *Ibid.*

5. *Ibid.*, p. 23.

6. Quoted by Robert Garis, *The Dickens Theatre: A Reassessment of the Novels* (Oxford: Clarendon, 1967), pp. 15–16. The quotation is from George Gissing, *Charles Dickens* (New York, 1924), p. 228.

7. Garis, p. 16.

8. The classic demonstration of the topicality not only of Chancery abuses, but also of all the major social satire in *BH* is in John Butt and Kathleen Tillotson, "The Topicality of *Bleak House*," in *Dickens at Work* (London: Methuen, 1957), pp. 177–200. Their work follows the lead of Humphry House in *The Dickens World* (Oxford: Oxford University Press, 1942). Notable among the more recent scholars of *BH*'s topicality are Philip Collins, K. J. Fielding, and Trevor Blount. Their numerous essays can easily be located in the bibliographies listed in the bibliographical note at the end of this volume.

9. It is particularly instructive to compare the first few paragraphs of the novel with Milton's description of Chaos in Book II of *Paradise Lost*. See esp. ll. 890–900, 907–19, 927–42, 947–50. I use the edition by Merrit Y. Hughes (New York: Odyssey, 1962), which follows the second edition of 1674.

10. J. Hillis Miller in *Charles Dickens: The World of his Novels* (1958; rpt. Bloomington: Indiana University Press, 1969), pp. 187–90, is the first critic to discuss a pattern of circular repetitions in *BH*. H. M. Dalseki in *Dickens and the Art of Analogy* (New York: Schocken Books, 1970), pp. 156–90, has discussed the circles of *BH* at length in what I think is the best of recent essays on the novel.

11. Miller, *Charles Dickens*, p. 165.

12. There is also perhaps an allusion to the biblical Esther, also a queen, who "obtained favor in the sight of all them who looked upon her" (Esther 2:15.), for Esther Summerson seems to be explicitly recalling these words when she says that she "found some favour in [Allan Woodcourt's] eyes" (25).

13. This is what Freud refers to in *The Interpretation of Dreams* as secondary revision or elaboration, a function of both the dream-work and of waking life.

14. One of Esther's nicknames at Bleak House, of course, is "Little Old Woman" (8).

15. Miller, *Charles Dickens*, p. 164.

16. An analysis of the quite long description of Bleak House will show an incredible number of resonances not only with Chancery, but with all the worlds of the novel we have encountered thus far, as well as most of the other actual houses in the novel. In "The Titles for *Bleak House*," *The Dickensian*, 65 (1969), 84–89, George Ford has demonstrated many connections between Bleak House and the rest of the novel.

The Ghostly Signs of *Bleak House*   Michael Ragussis*

Even the title is duplicitous, signaling from the outset that this is a novel whose mysteries are linguistic. When the Lord Chancellor remarks that Bleak House is "A dreary name," Mr. Kenge counters with, "But not a dreary place."[1] This divergence between name and place, between signifier and signified, infects every aspect of the novel's language, and the division between name and place is echoed more gravely in the division between name and person. *Bleak House* is a novel of misnomers, a mystery story in search of the "proper name" (x, 117), where names—even the novel's own name— seem like "the impromptu name" (xx, 255) Jobling takes. Kenge makes us see that the words "Bleak House" can be taken as mere words, independent of any particular object or meaning, and the reader begins to see that the novel's title names, from different angles, different objects. It names, for example, not one dwelling, but two, perhaps even three: Tom Jarndyce's house (bleak in fact); John Jarndyce's Bleak House (bleak in name only); and Esther's Bleak House, "namesake" (lxiv, 753) of the former and Jarndyce's gift to Esther at the novel's close. These latitudes in the name's meaning seem less significant, however, than the particular discrepancy between name and place that Kenge raises. There is a kind of nostalgia in the novel for that time when words did simply name the objects they represented—"when [for example] Turnstile really was a turnstile" (x, 119). In the process of bestowing names all the time, the narrator puzzles over such discrepancies, and seems to take his cue for Bleak House (and *Bleak House*) from examples like "Turnstile." If Bleak House, at least at present, is a pleasant place with a bleak name, it is no wonder (in this topsy-turvy world of names) that there is

*From *Nineteenth-Century Fiction* 34, no. 3 (December 1979): 253–80. © 1979 by the Regents of the University of California. Reprinted by permission.

"a rather ill-favoured and ill-savoured neighbourhood, though one of its rising grounds bears the name of Mount Pleasant" (xxi, 257). Place names seem to function not so much as signposts, but more as ironic commentaries on the present text of the place, or even as deliberate masks, like those false names so many of the characters assume. Places seem to mime the characters in the novel in this way, and my analogy is not farfetched given that the houses and places (like "Tom," Dickens's abbreviation for the place-name "Tom-all-Alone's") in *Bleak House* are so consistently personified: places and characters present themselves to each other, to the reader, even to the writer, as a series of imposters. Words cloak and veil rather than discover, and the question the novel asks, pertinaciously, is: "Do . . . words disclose the length, breadth, depth of . . . [the] object . . . or, if not, what do they hide?" (xxix, 364). As signposts, place names seem false directions to the traveler who, apparently defrauded, fails to recognize in the destination what the name has suggested to him: go to Bleak House, go to Turnstile, go to Mount Pleasant, even go to Lincoln's Inn Fields, and you will discover a world whose mysteries, immediately, are linguistic. Dickens's embroidery of this last name subtly finds in it a tragic or cynical truth, explaining how these are in fact fields where "the sheep are all made into parchment" (xlii, 514), a brilliant suggestion that takes us to the heart of the novel's dark understanding of how places and people alike are reduced in words. Man and beast are lost, in the celebrated opening paragraphs of the novel, in a fog that obscures all signposts in London, obliterating even the distinctions between man and beast. It is the fog of language, taking us back to a primitive time when language did not distinguish man from beast—the time, this novel tells us, of nineteenth-century England, when Jo, unable to read and write and unfavorably compared to a dog, grows into a symbol of linguistic disorder that touches everyone.

This problem of naming has its most serious side in the question of personal identity. If London is a city where signs confuse rather than enlighten—where streets and houses are masked in the fog of a language that is downright misleading—it is as well populated by "anonymous character[s]" (xxix, 363), where people are simply unnamed (Jo and Guster, for example, have no "Christian sign," xxii, 278), or where they have taken impromptu names or aliases and suppressed their true names (Jobling / Weevle, Mr. George, Nemo), or where they do not know their true names (Esther). Dickens extrapolates place names and personal names with the Bagnet daughters, showing a simple, if comical, solution to the problem of naming: the Bagnet family anchors its children to the places where they were born, Malta and Quebec being constant reminders to their parents, and to themselves, of their birthplace, a log or seaman's diary that records the military family's travels. Comical as such names are, they ironically echo "Tom-all-Alone's," where person and place become identical, with human subjectivity sinking into the thingness of impersonality. "Tom," with its personified houses and human vermin and dead-alive characters like Nemo, symbolizes such tragic confusions, and Dickens's comedy plays counterpoint to a tragic motif. The problem of naming is solved most easily, but with a self-conscious irony (given that some characters are misnamed, or are in search of a name), when the author himself names his characters by a leading characteristic, such as Woodcourt, Flite, or Krook. The examples are numerous, and they are what we expect in Dickens.[2] But what flows athwart this typical flood of appropriate names—and what makes us reconsider this characteristic of Dickens's style—is the central problem of the novel: Esther is "friendless, nameless, and unknown" (xvii, 213), and like her father (alias "Nemo," and called "Nimrod" by Mrs. Snagsby) or her mother (ironically named "Honoria"), she shows us the dissociation between name and person. Boythorn makes the dissociation a question of morality—"It is morally impossible that his name can be Sir Leicester. It must be Sir Lucifer" (ix, 108)—and Dickens's characters adjust, and improve upon, the names their author bestows: Sir Leicester becomes Sir Lucifer; Nemo, Nimrod; and Mrs. Snagsby, Guster; as we shall see.

The novel, then, has two broad linguistic categories, each presenting a problem about naming. In the first there are the characters who are nothing but words—the sheep are in fact turned into parchment, into paper and words, in an ironic self-reflection on the writer's own job. Here the appropriateness of the name is not merely a genuine indication of meaning; rather it swallows up the person, allowing him no identity apart from that sounded in the word. Meaning ironically twists back upon itself—the name does not bestow meaning, but robs the individual of the rich world he is, or might be: the letter killeth, and the name lives off the person (in one of the deepest implications of the novel's imagery of parasitism). Through a pun on the word "character"[3] Dickens suggests just this about his own fictive world: his characters are nothing but characters, that is, letters, parts of words, so much ink on paper.[4] Mr. Guppy looks as if he "had inked himself" (iii, 28) in his first appearance, but his ink is a suggestion of how he still bears the signs of his creation at Dickens's hand; and Caddy's "inky condition" (v, 57) seems her natural state. Dickens expects us to see that these characters are so much ink and nothing more. Caddy may complain that "I am only pen and ink" (xiv, 169) to her mother, but she is the same, in a more literal way, to her more original parent. Similarly, Chesney Wold looks like "a view in Indian ink" (ii, 11) because, at one level, it is just that. Indeed, the "black drizzle" that covers London in the novel's first paragraph is the black drizzle of ink ("a rain of ink," x, 124) turning up in the rooms, and on the persons, of Gridley, Richard, Nemo, Caddy, and Charley, to name a few.

But Esther suggests the opposite problem: here the appropriateness of the name Summerson ("They said there could be no East wind where Somebody was; they said that wherever Dame Durden went, there was *sunshine* and *summer* air," xxx, 378; italics mine) is suddenly insufficient.[5] It is not that Esther is misnamed—her name certainly does not stand in opposition to what she is (the way the names "Bleak House" or "Mount Pleasant" or

"Honoria" do). But she requires her original name, if she is to have a history, if she is to know who she is. She still only seems Somebody unnamed, and Matthew Bagnet's birthday celebration, with the easily answerable questions "What is your name? and Who gave you that name?" (xlix, 587), reminds us of Esther's poignant birthdays, or even of Ada's (meant to echo Esther's, and therefore appropriately termed at one point in the novel "somebody's birth-day," 1, 600). The orphan's birthday is always a reminder that he or she is only somebody. Esther couples the idea of her name with her very existence: "I had never, to my own mother's knowledge, breathed—had been buried—had never been endowed with life—had never borne a name" (xxxvi, 452). To assume her true identity, Esther needs her name. This is what Miss Barbary means when she threatens that Esther will be at one stroke "friend-less, nameless, and unknown." Like the first category of characters, Esther is robbed of a history because of her name. But unlike them it is not the name itself that robs her: it is the absence of a name. And all the symbolic names in the world (like "Summerson"), no matter how appropriately they point to characteristics in Esther, seem finally only to make more apparent that her true name is unknown: "This was the beginning of my being called Old Woman, and Little Old Woman, and Cobweb, and Mrs. Shipton, and Mother Hubbard, and Dame Durden, and so many names of that sort, that my own name soon became quite lost among them" (viii, 90). Where do signifier and signified meet, without one overwhelming the other? Can per-sonal identity exist through the true name, or through what Dickens is to call, with fine ambiguity, the "proper name"?

The question of the proper name is directly broached in the chapter "The Law-Writer," in which the description of the ghostly remains of the writer at once presents the reader with one of the novel's central mysteries and retrospectively throws into tragic relief the chapter's earlier, and more comic, exploration of naming. Dickens's use of the idea of metamorphosis—this is a world in which people and things, even words, have "writhed into many shapes" (i, 8)—takes many forms in the novel. The kind of metamorpho-sis that "The Law-Writer" presses (beyond making Tulkinghorn a crow, or Snagsby "greasy, warm, herbaceous, and chewing," x, 121) is the way in which names develop such latitude that they name two people at once. While Guster and Mrs. Snagsby must be, from the viewpoint of personality, sheer opposites, Dickens questions the notion of the proper name by suggest-ing Mrs. Snagsby is a "Guster": "This proper name [Guster], so used by Mr. Snagsby, has before now sharpened the wit of the Cook's Courtiers to re-mark that it ought to be the name of Mrs. Snagsby; seeing that she might with great force and expression be termed a Guster, in compliment to her stormy character." If the name seems proper for Guster, it is only a make-shift name for her; in fact, like those places I have already surveyed (Mount Pleasant or Bleak House), it suggests an origin that cannot be quite read—she is "by some supposed to have been christened Augusta" (x, 117). She is the comic or pathetic mirror of Esther, or Jo, or any of Dickens's orphans.

Like Jo, she has no last name, and her first, or proper name, is only a nickname (like Esther's many nicknames, or even like "Jo"), an abbreviation for some unknown whole: these characters are fragments. The orphan's name is never proper enough: it always, of necessity, must have this kind of latitude because it never names adequately, or sufficiently, its person; therefore, it overflows traitorously, perhaps even promiscuously (after all, it sometimes names a bastard), into the world beyond the self, seeming as much the possession of another person.

The same chapter, "The Law-Writer," suggests a case in which the name coincides with what it means in a curiously direct way, so that allegory, a particular kind of naming, becomes itself allegorized into "Allegory," and particular words become, before our very eyes, names, and allegorical names at that: in one paragraph in the chapter, "rumour" undergoes a subtle metamorphosis into the capitalized, and named, "Rumour" (x, 119, 118). Here there is no distance at all between signifier and signified—name and object or idea coincide. In all these cases—Guster / Mrs. Snagsby, allegory / Allegory, rumour / Rumour—individual identity disappears through the name. Identity, no longer individual, becomes common and confused. In fact allegory is a method of naming that confuses subject and object, consciousness and matter, and suggests man's loss of his proper right (even his birthright—after all, the idea of property is naturally joined in *Bleak House* to the ideas of patrimony and the father's name) to language. As techniques in writing, allegory and personification are double-edged: the writer's own verbal ability endows objects or ideas with life, and his characters often shrink, comparatively, into mere fictive nothingness. The ideas allegory and rumour grow into characters, Allegory and Rumour: they are embodied sometimes with movement, always with gesture, while two characters become mere gusters—literally the air and wind that words are (as the text will make clear in a traditional but crucial comparison between words and breath).

"The Law-Writer" opens with two apparently comic paragraphs which, by directly bearing on this idea of names, anticipate in the most subtle way the tragic implications of the law-writer's death. Ominous echoes of *Hamlet*, sometimes turned comic—in the image of Peffer's ghost hiding at the cock's crowing at dawn; in the theme of Tulkinghorn's indecision; in "bodkins" as a reminder of a particularly relevant and well-known passage[6]—are clues that this chapter is about the lost, or dead, father. In fact, well before the novel discloses the true identity of Esther's father, or for that matter, simply who Nemo is, these echoes suggest the answer: the dead father, the ghostly parent, is Esther's. The linguistic dimension of this problem appears immediately, beyond the fact that the father is the law-*writer*, even beyond the clue "bodkins," where the instrument of suicide contemplated by Hamlet is a writing implement in Snagsby's shop. It is a matter of one name's displacing another: the name Nemo displaces Hawdon, the way Summerson displaces Hawdon, or even the way Guster displaces Mrs. Snagsby. "PEFFER AND

SNAGSBY, displacing the time-honored . . . PEFFER, only," is simply the first step in the total effacement of Peffer's name, or of what amounts to the same thing, Peffer himself. Smoke wreathes itself around Peffer's name (the way fog, at the outset of the novel, obscures all signs, smoke and fog creating death wreaths for the name) until it has "quite overpowered the parent tree" (x, 116). The loss of name in paragraph one here leads naturally to the ghost story of paragraph two (not to mention the ghost story of Nemo and the end of the chapter): the loss of the name is the loss of the parent, or more particularly, of the father. The parent is most clearly the source of the child's ultimate identification and therefore is symbolically a name, a symbolic name—a name which, once elided, makes parent and child alike ghosts. This is why the charge against Turveydrop is that "he wouldn't let his son have any name, if he could take it from him" (xiv, 173), and why the name he does bestow on his son, as Caddy points out, "sounds like [that of] a dog, but of course he didn't christen himself" (xiv, 169). No one christens oneself, and therefore the orphan begins his life in a special linguistic vacuum: his name is the most arbitrary of all, with no father's name, and with a proper name like "Jo" or "Guster" or "Prince" (Turveydrop's symbolic attempt to orphan his son). In the last case, it seems no accident that the character has a dog's name: misnamed by the father, in fact almost unnamed by him, Prince shares that common identity with dogs that the fog creates in the novel's opening paragraph, and reminds us of Dickens's elaborate comparison between the illiterate Jo and a dog. The final consequence of his poor linguistic start in this world is that Prince, as Caddy (quintessentially pen and ink) tells Esther, is not much of a writer: "he puts so many unnecessary letters into short words, that they sometimes quite lost their English appearance" (xiv, 176–77).

The parent of importance, as I have suggested, is not Peffer but Hawdon, or "The Law-Writer" (as the chapter calls him), or the Captain (as Mr. George calls him, knowing him only by his earlier profession), or Nemo (as he calls himself), or Nimrod (as Mrs. Snagsby calls him), or the mighty hunter (as Dickens calls him, using Nimrod's epithet), or Our Dear Brother (as Dickens calls him in mock-pathetic fashion). The novel's "anonymous character" seems to encourage names and nicknames, and as they proliferate (the way words seem to proliferate, almost intemperately, at the hand of the law-writer) they remind us of the numerous names and nicknames the daughter has and of the real name she needs. In a chapter where Dickens has shown that some names are allegorical signposts ("Allegory," "Rumour," even "Guster" is an allegorization of sorts), and where the parent's name is eminently effaceable ("Peffer"), it is not surprising to wonder over the Captain's proper name—in fact to see that Nemo, his pseudonym (writers, even law-writers it seems, use pseudonyms), is proper, and even more, that the misnomer (if "misnomer" in this case isn't itself a misnomer, as is the "proper name") "Nimrod" is perhaps the most proper of all. The text makes clear, of course, how Nemo has in death "established his pretensions to his name by becoming indeed No one" (xi, 126). With No one as her father, with no father, or what amounts to the same thing, with a nameless father. Esther herself is no one: she thinks to herself, "I was no one" (iv, 45). And of course the text suggests, in many passages, how no one is the anonymous someone at the heart of the law in two paradoxical senses—as its father or originator and as its helpless victim. All Londoners experience "diving through law and equity, and through that kindred mystery, the street mud, which is made of nobody knows what, and collects about us nobody knows whence or how" (x, 123). Here nobody (I mean both the word "nobody" and the nameless narrator who is, after all, like the law-writer, a no one to the reader) explains how no one and someone (Nemo, someone named No one) are responsible for the law, and how *Bleak House*'s mystery is a mystery of "kindred," where the law has made out of our proper kin nobodies and somebodies (we remember Esther is called "Somebody").

But the name "Nimrod"—the name farthest from his proper name, at two removes from Hawdon, being Mrs. Snagsby's comically incorrect rendering of Nemo—establishes perhaps the largest mythical framework for understanding Hawdon as "the law-writer." About Nimrod, the mighty hunter, the Old Testament tells us, "the beginning of his Kingdom was Babel" (Gen. 10.10). Nimrod thereby gathers together the novel's apparently casual or irrelevant references to "the tower of Babel" (xx, 247), "a Babel of iron sounds" (lxiii, 742), a "confusion of tongues" (xlix, 590), and even "Chadband's piling verbose flights of stairs, one upon another" (xix, 237). This confusion of tongues is expressed in Dickens's world, not simply through the boundaries that separate one nation from another, but within England itself through geographical location and class structure, so that in Cook's Court we find "the many tongues of Rumour" (x, 116), while at Chesney Wold "the fashionable intelligence, a mighty hunter before the Lord, hunts with a keen scent" (xii, 144)—that same intelligence, we recall, that "is weak in English, but a giant refreshed in French," scattering Dickens's prose with such phrases as "*élite*" and "*beau monde*" (xii, 138). Beside the law-writer's bed, when Tulkinghorn finds him dead, is "a tower of winding sheet" (x, 124), where "sheet" doubles as shroud and sheet of paper (in fact the latter becomes the former in this world where all the sheep are turned into parchment), a tower of babel that the law-writer seems at once to create and die from, after the fashion of spontaneous combustion. The reference to him "as dead as Phairy" (xi, 126) does not now seem so anachronistic as at first, and the description of the room as "a wilderness marked with a rain of ink" (x, 124) suggests Dickens's brilliant use of "the great wilderness of London" (xlviii, 583), that "immense desert of law-hand" (xlvii, 567), as the Old Testament desert, but with this difference: the Law of God, the divine Word, has itself degenerated into babel, and the Father has become the tyrannous, and dead, Pharaoh.

When we hear that "the bar of England is scattered over the face of the earth" (xix, 232), we remember the Lord's punishment for making Babel:

"Come, let us confound their language, that they may not understand one another's speech. So the Lord scattereth them abroad from there upon the face of all the earth" (Gen. 11.8). "The bar of England" is subtly associated with the "bars" that strike down "crookedly" (connecting the legal bar with the mock Lord Chancellor, Krook) across Lady Dedlock's portrait (xii, 138). It also multiplies into "the bars of the gate" (xvi, 202) that close Hawdon in the graveyard between lover and daughter: the reader's last view of Lady Dedlock shows her "with one arm creeping round a bar of the iron gate, and seeming to embrace it" (lix, 713). The "great eternal bar" (xv, 193) of death shows how the deadly law divides this family from itself: the bar that keeps Lady Dedlock from final union with Hawdon, the bar makes Esther's mother "cold and dead" (lix, 714) before the daughter can reach her, is finally the legal bar, establishing the precedent of false names and thereby making the tragic mystery of Bleak House, substituting the "kindred" of law and mud for the kindred of Nemo, Honoria, and Esther Summerson, all of whom are imprisoned behind the bars of false names. The "great eternal bar," built of "walls of words" (i, 6), the everlasting house of death, is the bleakest house in all of *Bleak House*.

A contaminating disease that "taints everybody" (xxxvii, 463), failing to respect even the boundaries of class and geography, fills the house of death in *Bleak House*. Jarndyce christens the business of the law, not with any Christian sign, but appropriately with a nonsense word that captures its foolishness as well as its deadly work: "ceremoniously, wordy, unsatisfactory, and expensive . . . I call it, in general, Wiglomeration. How mankind ever came to be afflicted with Wiglomeration, or for whose sins these young people ever fell into a pit of it, I don't know" (viii, 91). Neither a Christian sign nor a conventional medical term, "Winglomeration" is Jarndyce's name for a wordy affliction that directs us to the conjunction between words and disease and to the novel's most notable example of this conjunction, namely the stained and polluted graveyard of the law-writer. Language as disease is suggested through a word-play in the description of this graveyard, "pestiferous and obscene, whence malignant diseases are communicated to the bodies of our dear brothers and sisters" (xi, 137). The suggestive use of "communicate" here suggests its primary meaning, reinforced by the novel's emphatic self-reflections on language and naming, as well as its medical meaning: language is London's communicative / communicable disease. The vocabulary of stain, spot, mark, and trace, as I will show, consistently refers in *Bleak House* to this conjunction between language and disease: such words represent the marks of writing, grammatological signs, as well as the symptoms and effects of disease. Lady Dedlock tries to hold back from the "stains contaminating her" (xvi, 202) at the law-writer's grave, but the contaminating stain—an inky disorder that is the ubiquitous "black drizzle" that covers London—is inescapable: it marks the law-writer's desk, his grave, and all his relations. The word "Inkwhich" (xvi, 200) describes an inquiry that discovers ink as the cause of death (or words as the cause of the affliction "Wiglomeration"), but the law, in its inquest into

Hawdon's death, misses the clue which Jo's malapropism inadvertently detects. It is ironic, then, that the English fear "contaminating a language spoken in the presence of the Sun" (xiii, 152)—not that English is spoken there, as the novel's opening paragraph makes clear, where "the death of the sun" gives way to that "black drizzle" that seems to cause a "general *infection* of *ill*-temper" (italics mine). And at the heart of the drizzle and the obscuring fog is Chancery, "which has . . . its dead in every churchyard" (i, 6): Chancery (chancre) is an "ill name" (v, 51), like Jarndyce and Jarndyce (jaundice),[7] and ill names spread their infection, communicate it to the nameless and the titled alike.

The legalism of the dead letter—Jarndyce in fact calls the will "a dead letter" (viii, 88)—covers a multitude of sins, not the least of all the diseases and deaths in the novel. In fact, "the death of the sun" may be the novel's boldest pun, for the dead son (or Son) is precisely what the legalism of the dead letter produces: it erases through words, if you will, the bond between father and son, and throws London back into a primitive world, that Old Testament world of the Law, awaiting anew the appointed time when the Law will be superseded. The novel's "Appointed Time" is an ironic shadow of this, when the Lord Chancellor (or at least his shadow, Krook) goes up in flames. Even Krook's "crooked mark" (v, 55) (a phrase that suggests the crime of the law is language itself) on the wall is Biblical, foretelling (and inscribing in his own hand) his own doom the way the writing on the wall that Daniel reads foretells the tyrant's downfall. The Roman, Allegory, is a similar writing on the wall (or ceiling) that foretells the doom of another of the law's tyrants. All this writing on the wall culminates in Lady Dedlock's fear that her story will be "chalked upon the walls" (xli, 508). Esther is the son (Summer-son), or in the case the daughter, who finds herself in the wilderness of ink, in "the immense desert of law-hand," like her Old Testament counterpart, the orphan "Queen" (lix, 704), who reverses Haman's law of the dead letters in a striking prefiguration of the New Testament. In this way Dickens combines the two apparently diverse plots of Esther and Chancery: by making Esther's father the law-writer, Dickens makes Esther the victim of Wiglomeration; hence her disease is implicitly compared to Rick's fever of the blood in chapter xxxv, and Esther can appropriately speak of her own "little trial" (xxxv, 437), her illness.

The novel's ever-present stain, a sign of the disease of language, explains the convergence of discourse with intercourse, of inkstain with bloodstain. The stain is at once a point of origin (the stain of the love letters, the father-writer's stain of procreation) and an end point (the stain of Hawdon's grave, the stain of Lady Dedlock's shame that forces her to this same grave, the stain of blood on Tulkinghorn's floor). Hawdon's stained desk is the center of the novel: the inkstain on this desk is as inescapable as his past (in fact his writing does lead back to his past, and to his ultimate identification). This stained desk is the workplace of the sin of language, where the father's name is blotted out, erased, only to give rise to a series of false names that make a ghost of the father—a sin that is visited upon the daughter. And although Lady Dedlock holds back from the "deadly stains contaminating her" (xvi, 202) when Jo shows her Hawdon's grave, she is led finally to its "spot" (lix, 713), and everywhere she travels becomes a "deserted blighted spot" (lvi, 674). Lady Dedlock of course realizes that she is "the stain and blot upon this place [Chesney Wold]" (xli, 510). By reaching Chesney Wold, the stain naturally reaches Lady Dedlock's husband: Sir Leicester ironically insists that until Tulkinghorn's murderer is discovered, "I almost feel as if there were a stain upon my name" (liii, 630)—as he shortly will discover is all too true. Nor does the stain neglect the great lawyer. In "The Law-Writer" Tulkinghorn is magisterially placed before "the red bit, the black bit, the inkstand top, the other inkstand top, the little sand-box" (x, 120). Tulkinghorn becomes the carrier of the disease that plagues London (he literally carries the Hawdon-Honoria letters), and seems, whether placed before his inks or carrying the letters, to turn Guster's comic appreciation of the law into a tragic truth: red bits, black bits, letters (of all kinds, including the "dead letter"), the bodkins of the opening paragraph of "The Law-Writer" are indeed the "awful implements of the great torture of the law" (x, 121). Tulkinghorn dies of the disease he carries and spreads, and the lawyer provides himself, unfortunately, with only a single witness—with Allegory, a "dumb witness" that cannot speak (where words seem so self-reflexive that all they do is name themselves, and point dumbly beyond), "pointing at an empty chair, and at a stain upon the ground before it that might be almost covered with a hand" (xlviii, 585). The stain is its own witness: it speaks the deadly tale, as usual.

The stain of ink follows most closely the mystery of Esther's father. The novel develops a wide network of images—traces, tracks, marks, spots, and signs—which leads back, inevitably, to the law-writer's stain. The novel impresses insistently upon the reader that Esther has behind her a writer—not merely Dickens himself (whose black drizzle creates the fictional Esther), not even just the law-writer, but finally Miss Barbary (who, as writer, is meant to remind us of these first two): "the writer had bred her in secrecy from her birth, had blotted out all trace of her existence, and . . . if the writer were to die before the child became a woman, she would be left entirely friendless, nameless, and unknown" (xvii, 213). The writer seems to have, through his ink, absolute power over his creation, able to blot out all traces of its existence; upon the death of the writer, the creature becomes, once again, nameless and unknown, a mere black drizzle, a fragmentary word, an anonymous character (what an author himself becomes when he hides behind a pseudonym, and what an omniscient narrator necessarily is, as in *Bleak House*). The writer then has complete authority over identity—he is in fact the author of identity, holding its secret within the power of his pen and ink. The stain, by suggesting both blood and ink, shows how blood relations are defined linguistically, through the name, and how the writer's ink has the power of life and blood over its creations. Esther is stained, then, by the writer: Hawdon bears her in that special stain of love that does not bear her a name. The stain of the love letters, then, does not point to illicit love except insofar as it points to a linguistic failure, and this makes of love a stain—a stain meant to remind us of ink, the blot upon the name that erases the name and all identity.

Boythorn makes the point that wrong names are moral impossibilities; the failure to bestow the proper name, in *Bleak House*, becomes an act of immorality. The sinful or criminal stain uses language to hide the identity of the father, and the father betrays the daughter into the hands of anonymity—into the kindred mystery of mud and fog, of aliases and pseudonyms. The sin of the writer is to fail to take responsibility for his acts and words, to hide behind his ink. The law-writer stands for this kind of anonymity—he is an "anonymous character" because he is an unknown character in Dickens's fiction, and because he is an anonymous letter, unattached to a readable language, a mere fragment or abbreviation, like the hieroglyphic abbreviations Esther sees in the letters she receives from the law. With brilliant irony Dickens has Esther, and not another character or the omniscient narrator, report to us Nemo's advertisement and compare it to the letters she receives from the law. This is the most she ever sees of her father—just his law-hand, and his name, or more precisely, his false name "Nemo": no kindred sign, not even a mark of individuality. The law-writer's anonymous writing is copying, and copying produces anonymity; but Hawdon does not realize he copies a law that makes of himself, and of those near and far to him, "outlaw[s]" (xvi, 197), whether it be Jo or his own long-lost daughter, or all the anonymous victims of the law's disease, all the nobodies who flounder, and die, in the mud. The law (Law), then, is the absent father (Father) who refuses to be properly named—who fathers, but leaves us nameless. In Gridley's case, for example, the law attempts to rob him of his rightful father: "the Master . . . inquired whether I was my father's son—about which there was no dispute at all." Losing his paternal name, he is no longer Gridley but only "the man from Shropshire" (xv, 193). The law even denies Esther her aunt—"Aunt in fact, though not in law" (iii, 21)—and in this way the law stands for that language which confounds all familial ties and sends what it produces and copies (or reproduces)—namely, words and children—into the world unknown and nameless. "The writer had bred her in secrecy" now means that the writer breeds without naming. He sows and breeds (to use the dominant imagery of Hawdon's burial), but neglects his further responsibilities: it is, in short, a deathly reproduction, and ends with the lovers' final reunion in the "obscene" (xi, 137) burial ground. The legal letter is symbolized finally by Krook's markings: the ultimate law-writer and interpreter of the law (the mock Lord Chancellor) cannot even read and write, and knows not what he reproduces in the only linguistic act he can perform, namely to copy senselessly. The black drizzle of ink and the dust of Krook's chalkings are signs—signs of a deadly incontinence, at once verbal and sexual.

Language masks identity, but it also categorically identifies: aliases and pseudonyms can hide family names, but the love letters, where the hand and heart commit themselves to the act of love in a final signature, identify Esther's parents. Names may deceive, but the hand gives us away, generously. This is the hand that Lady Dedlock is in search of, even after it is too late—"Of any hand that is no more, of any hand that never was, of any touch that might have magically changed her life" (xxviii, 356). Tulkinghorn searches for Hawdon's hand as well, though clearly to a different end; in fact, Lady Dedlock's fate is joined to Tulkinghorn's through the hand (eventually leading to a contract of sorts between them) in their first encounter in the novel. Lady Dedlock's impulsive question, upon seeing Hawdon's handwriting—"Who copied that?"—tries to mask itself with the apparently careless and bored question, "Is it what you people call law-hand?" Tulkinghorn's answer is an identification of sorts: "Not quite. Probably . . . the legal character it has, was acquired after the original hand was formed" (ii, 16). The life-giving hand Lady Dedlock seeks becomes the deadly, and dead, hand of the law-writer: her life is beyond all magical changes. And as for Tulkinghorn, the dead letter erupts to take its revenge. Tulkinghorn's search for the same hand ends ironically with "the murderous hand" (xlviii, 587) that shoots him through the heart. Again the point of origin is at the same time a deadly end point: the hand of the love letters is finally confused with the murderous hand.

The institution so given over to pen and ink cleverly withdraws, at crucial moments, from the written word. In this way the law epitomizes what I have called the sin or crime of writing—namely, the act of writing which refuses responsibility, when an author refuses to be named as the author of his own work, embodied simply by the criminal Hortense in those anonymous letters accusing Lady Dedlock of Tulkinghorn's murder. Hence Guppy is quick to explain, "Being in the law, I have learnt the habit of not committing myself in writing" (xxix, 359). And Bucket's position on letter writing is equally telling: "He is no great scribe . . . and discourages correspondence with himself in others, as being too artless and direct a way of doing delicate business. Further, he often sees damaging letters produced in evidence, and has occasion to reflect that it was a green thing to write them. For these reasons he has very little to do with letters, either as sender or receiver" (liii, 629). Lady Dedlock, no longer green, gives up the hand of self-identification at the end. The letters she writes at the close of the novel, while clearly hers, suggest a desire for anonymity: while in her letters to Sir Leicester and Esther she takes full responsibility for her actions, still she flees, still she wants to be unrecognized in death, unidentified, seeking the kind of anonymity her lover did. Having learned full well how letters, and the hand, identify one, in her last communication to Esther she writes, "I have nothing about me by which I can be recognised. This paper I part with now" (lix, 710). She wishes to die the nameless death of No one, and goes to the same burial ground. Seeking in death the anonymity which she was responsible for, at least in part, in her daughter's life and in her lover's, "she hurries from herself" (lv, 667). Esther tries to protect her mother by burning the letter in which Lady Dedlock recounts the facts of Esther's birth, an ironic twist for the daughter who, searching to discover this familial language all along, must destroy it immediately and "never . . . interchange another word, on earth" (xxxvi, 450) with her mother; but this fire is insufficient, for while this letter is burned, the original love letters survive Krook's fire, and identify the lovers.

However much Lady Dedlock tries to protect the living from her stain, she is unsuccessful: language, as an infectious disease, does come to her husband, and "the stain upon the name" at Chesney Wold takes the form of a verbal disorder in Sir Leicester. If Lady Dedlock wants no self, no identity, Sir Leicester, against his will, loses all self, all identity. Sir Leicester, who used to be so "persuaded of the weight and import to mankind of any word he said that his words really had come to sound as if there were something in them," is reduced to "mere jumble and jargon." He loses the power of speech, and able only to write, writes "in a hand that is not his" (lvi, 668). Sir Leicester becomes another example of how the dissociation of the self is defined verbally. Finally, Sir Leicester's chalking upon the slate reduces him almost to the illiteracy of Krook. Miss Flite tells Esther she thinks the woman who took the handkerchief (Lady Dedlock) is the Lord Chancellor's wife and that his wife "throws his lordship's papers into the fire" (xxxv, 439)— another subtle doubling of Sir Leicester and Krook, because of course Lady Dedlock does want Krook's papers, containing the incriminating love letters, burned. These two slate writers, husband (Sir Leicester) and mock-husband (Krook), are also subtly connected to Lady Dedlock's fear that her shame will be "chalked upon the walls." That Sir Leicester becomes a double for Krook (who already is a double for the Lord Chancellor) suggests the novel's extravagant metamorphoses, all things writhing into the same shape, copies (like what the law-writer himself makes) of the law-writer, as the contaminating language of the law seems to spread, reducing the English, who so guard the language spoken in the sun, to illiteracy, to the dumbness of Jo. Jo's open admission of linguistic incompetence—his "can't exactly say" (xi, 138)—could be a genuine model for all speakers and writers in this world. We remember how Jo's disease is sown abroad on the winds, and seems to reach all people: "death levels all distinctions" (liii, 631), and the dead letter spreads its stain everywhere, and on everyone. In this way Dickens's conjunction of "No one" and "Every one" (xi, 131) shows that Hawdon's double role—as the father, or source of the dead letter, and as the helpless victim—is everyone's role.

Esther, I have shown, is a "no one" like her father, a copy of Nemo. Her illness makes this connection clearer, for it seems to write on Esther's face her origin. Esther, praised for being able "to read a face" (lxiv, 750), clearly bears the traces of her parentage, even if she cannot quite decipher them: they are her "scars," or the "deep traces of . . . illness" (xliv, 539) that are, we remember, linguistic (she catches the communicable disease from Jo, whose constant habitat, when not being told to move on, is Tom's and the law-writer's stained burial ground). The "deep traces" of her illness track it down to Hawdon, reminding the reader of the origins that Esther seeks: Hawdon "lies there, with no more track behind him, that any one can trace, than a deserted infant" (xi, 131). Hawdon's origin is traceless because he is anonymous: Tulkinghorn and Krook, at least at first, find "not a morsel of an old letter, or of any other writing" (xi, 129). Eventually the trace of ink becomes the track that does identify him, just as it will Esther. After all, Esther is originally traceless too; she is in fact the "deserted infant" in this "desert of law-hand" that Hawdon appears to be. But her illness eventually traces her origin, links her now indelibly to her father, even though she innocently thinks her scars will hide, not discover, her parentage by obscuring her resemblance to Lady Dedlock. These traces, clearly the symbols of the inky father's disease, write a plain enough tale in Esther's "namesake" (l, 602), Caddy's baby: "It had . . . curious little dark marks under its eyes, like faint remembrances of poor Caddy's inky days" (l, 599). These inky marks, which originate on the desk "marked with a rain of ink," seem to make of everyone in the novel—even Mr. George, innocent of Tulkinghorn's murder but guilty of the name-changing and obscuring of kindred that is the novel's major crime—"a marked . . . man" (lii, 620), as Mr. George calls himself.

Esther's ultimate reaction to her "deep traces" is to transform them into signs on paper, to use them to trace her history. Esther's childish confessions to Dolly (another dumb witness, like Allegory, or even like Esther's deaf-and-dumb namesake) turn into her confessions to us, curiously making "the unknown friend" (lxvii, 767) to whom she writes—namely, the reader—another dumb witness; the word "unknown" ironically reminds us of its earlier conjunction with "nameless," making us aware of our own silent and nameless participation in this tale of many words and names. In any case, Dolly stands both for all dumb witnesses, and for the dumb self Esther has been all along—some "no one" or nobody whose name can be simplified into an allegorized thingness. "Dolly," with no proper name (allegory's names are necessarily common), and no father's last name. Dolly is buried in the garden of childhood as Esther steps beyond her childish home into the world of experience—the inky world of London, where the fog and the inky Guppy are her first impressions, and where she must find her name. She enters the world of the dead letter to make it in the world of the spirit, and in this sense she is the summer Son: "Forasmuch as ye are manifestly declared to be the epistle of Christ ministered by us, written not with ink but with the Spirit of the living God; not in tables of stone but in fleshly tables of the heart . . . for the letter killeth, but the Spirit giveth life" (2 Cor. 3.3–6). She enters the world, to have her history in it: she writes to reclaim the name that is her own. Esther's origin, then, requires of her a deeper immersion in ink and words, to trace through page after page her history, as if to regain the meaning that has been absent from it for so long.[8] The novel's gap between name and object (or subject), between signifier and signified, is what Esther's narrative attempts to bridge—to give meaning to the dead letter, to make it spirit, to breathe into it the breath of life. If my analogies here seem God-oriented, it is no accident that Esther finishes her narrative at the point of having been mistress of Bleak House—the new Bleak House, the name-

sake of the old—for "full seven happy years" (lxvii, 767): Bleak House, like
the work she has just written (Bleak House and *Bleak House* come together
here), is modeled on God's creation in seven days, and Esther can look at
both now and see that they are good. Rick's failure "to begin the world" (lxv,
762) is realized in Esther. Rick is petrified into a silent "stone figure" (like the
tables of stony law), his final chance to use language against the law "stopped
by his mouth being full of blood" (lxv, 761). Esther is the transfer from old to
new: she begins the world in the new way, through the spirit.

I have explained the force of Esther's role in the novel through a Biblical
analogy: she is the Son who is to save us from the letter. To transform the
letter into the spirit is, to use another example from the Bible, to remove the
veil that obscures the spirit: "for until this day remaineth the same veil
untaken away in the reading of the old testament; which veil is done away in
Christ" (2 Cor. 3.14). It is precisely such a veil that *Bleak House* pictures:
"Over all the legal neighbourhood, there hangs . . . some great veil of rust,
or gigantic cobweb" (xix, 233). When Jarndyce says, "It rained Esther" (vi,
61), the rain (or reign) of Esther stands as the new covenant, superseding the
"wilderness marked with a rain of ink" (x, 124) that her dead father's house
represents. Even her symbolic role as housekeeper shows her, like the
woman in the child's rhyme, ever about "to sweep the cobwebs out of the
sky" (viii, 90); she is like Jo, who "sweeps his crossing all day long" (xvi, 197),
symbolic and real orphans at work to rend the veil from the legal neighborhood. Lady Dedlock wears the same veil, the veil of the letter: Esther's final
act toward her mother is to lift the veil of hair that, even in death, tries to
obscure the mother. After her illness, Esther performs this act for herself as
she lifts "a veil of my own hair" (xxxvi, 444) to look into the mirror. Whether
symbolically sweeping the veil of cobweb from the legal neighborhood or
lifting the veil from her mother's face, she attempts a finer reading of the
world around her. And to be face to face with her mother, and face to face
with herself, is to read the text of who she is, for the face and the heart, are
written with the spirit. Vholes the lawyer throws up his hands at the thought
("Who can read the heart, Mr. C?" xxxix, 487), but if Vholes only looked he
would see what Esther sees, "the commentary upon it now indelibly written
in [Rick's] handsome face." Again, all the characters in *Bleak House* are
marked: Rick shares with Esther those written "traces" (li, 612) of the letter
that show the disease from which he dies. And Esther becomes not only a
writer but also a reader: she lifts the veil, she is quick "to read a face."

The relationship between the Law and the Gospel, particularly on the
idea of a symbolic patrimony, further suggests Esther's role in *Bleak House:*
"the relation of God's promise to Abraham and the Mosaic legislation . . .
Paul works out by using the analogies of a will and a codicil and of a minor's
coming of age."[9] Esther comes of age by discovering her parentage: Esther's narrative, as a solution to this mystery, is the enlightenment of
langauge, the solution of the novel's central linguistic mystery. But she
inherits nothing here, except the deep traces of her illness. Even the

father's ink-stained desk is "inherited" (xx, 256), curiously enough, by the next lodger, Jobling, who fulfills the position of law-writer, or copier, by taking an alias. What her surrogate father gives her, as her inheritance for coming of age, is not the patrimony from the legal case of Jarndyce and Jarndyce—that, we remember, is eaten up in costs. He gives her words, with a symbolic meaning: she always remembers "the day when he took me to the porch to read the name" (lxvii, 769). Esther is given Bleak House made new, the namesake of the house she transformed through love— Bleak House, where the letters spell just a bleak house, but where the spirit's meaning is clear. The surrogate father, unable to name her authentically (Dame Durden and Little Woman are only nicknames), names her house for her, and this is what she inherits: Esther finally inherits a name, even if it is only the name "Bleak House."

But Jarndyce is not Esther's father, just as the Bleak House he gives her is not Bleak House but its namesake, only a symbolic patrimony from a symbolic father.[10] Names are only shadows, and to try to make them more usually backfires. The letter may remind us of the spirit, but the spirit turns out to be a mere ghost, insubstantial, the way signs are, and the way allegory, bled dry, is. We may try, like Rick, to substitute for the shadow a substance: "the fighting with shadows and being defeated by them, necessitates the setting up of substances to combat; from the impalpable suit which no man alive can understand, the time for that being long gone by, it has become a gloomy relief to turn to the palpable figure of the friend who would have saved him from this ruin, and make *him* his enemy" (xxxix, 489). The time for understanding is long gone, somewhere outside history, and the dead letter has left us only a spiritlike ghost or shadow: in *Bleak House* a phrase like "shades of names" (lii, 620) comes to suggest how names, really all words, are mere ghosts, and moreover, how human beings, ghostlike, can be possessed by names (where people are only shades of names). Once again we have the dissociation of name and object: there is a wish for the word to embody, to be substantial, to take us to the thing itself, instead of being a mere symbol, but Rick's substitution of the palpable for the shadow ends with a literalism that makes enemies of friends and makes Rick himself a dead shadow, a mere abstraction. Words are insubstantiality itself: "Words . . . are but air" (xxix, 364), we learn, in an ironic reversal of the traditional identification of the word with the spirit. In fact, the air of *Bleak House*, including its gusters and east winds, is anything but creative, being a "poisoned air" (xi, 137), one further reminder of language's infection: "Even the winds are [Tom's] messengers" (xlvi, 553), messengers or communications as potent as the deadly letter itself.

Bleak House then is a world of signs and marks, where fragments make a linguistic puzzle that is never quite successfully solved and where mystery becomes a semiology: the novel shows that it is in the nature of language to present a mystery, actually to make a mystery, even a ghost story. Again, Jo teaches us a lesson: words are in fact "mysterious symbols" (xvi, 198), not only to the illiterate, but also to the writer and the reader of *Bleak House*. The novel's mystery story seeks to find the real name behind the alias and the pseudonym; to find the author of anonymous letters, and even signed letters; to compare handwritings to see if they are "in the same hand" (liv, 642); to see if different letters have used "corresponding ink and paper" (liv, 651). The novel's mysteries, if solved, are solved too late: they turn up the dead father and the dead mother, and the mystery becomes a ghost story. The lifting of the veil (an image that suggests, because of its New Testament association with hermeneutics, how all reading and writing are of mysteries) occurs in death: Esther pushes away the veil to discover her mother cold and dead. The tracking down of the hand, warm and alive, that wrote the letter finds only the dead hand, whether in Lady Dedlock's search for the hand that might magically have changed her life, or Esther's search in "The Track" for the mother's hand, so recently warm and alive in the apologetic letter written to Esther and given Guster to deliver. This final letter that Lady Dedlock is so eager to separate herself from is like the dead mother herself, a ghostly reminder, divided from the life and meaning who are its source. Esther discovers only the corpse of meaning, the ghostly sign. Meaning is "deadly meaning" in this novel: "So, it shall happen surely, through many years to come, that ghostly stories shall be told of the stain upon the floor . . . and that the Roman, pointing from the ceiling, shall point . . . with far greater significance than he ever had in Mr. Tulkinghorn's time, and with a deadly meaning" (xlviii, 585–87). The sign points to death—all its meaning comes to it at the moment of death, and all its stories are therefore ghost stories, stories about the deadly stain. Such stories are in the past tense, reconstructions back to an origin that is necessarily always lost, always at one already with death. The origin in *Bleak House* is always "the beginning of the end!" (viii, 89).

Bleak House is a fractured verbal world, where the comic abbreviations of legal jargon ("clt," "abt," "rece," "forded," "clks," "offe," iii, 27) or of the fashionable intelligence (" 'Vayli'—being the used-up for 'very likely,' " liii, 633) suggest the tragic side of language. It is a world where the signifier becomes an unreadable abbreviation, never quite taking us back to the original whole: in short, it is a trace, to use Derrida's term,[11] and Dickens's. Words survive their authors, and seem mere ghostly traces of a life that used to be. The great fire at Krook's still leaves intact the love letters; his room is "ghostly with traces of its dead inhabitant, and even with his chalked writing on the wall" (xxxix, 492). In fact these traces of a former life, like the will itself—"a stained discoloured paper" (lxii, 738)—survive the suitors of Jarndyce and Jarndyce. The "dead letter" has (like Krook's cat, who survives the fire along with the love letters and chalkings) nine lives, or more: it is the final dumb witness that watches over life and death, unable to tell its mean- ing. In this light words seem to epitomize the novel's idea of parasitism and vampirism: the lawyers of Chancery are "in the habit of fleshing their legal wit upon [Jarndyce and Jarndyce]" (i, 8). We do not use language; language uses us as its tools. Caddy's complaint, "I can't do anything hardly, except write" (iv, 44), is a modern cry, like something a character in Beckett's fiction might utter: it could serve as the writer's epitaph, the law-writer's painful confession of his senseless linguistic incontinence, and every writer's confession of language's tyrannical reign (a black and deadly drizzle), the word's use of him. In this sense not only Krook but all the characters in *Bleak House* are lost in a "monomania," "possessed of documents" (xxxii, 401): this phrase, like "shades of names," contains a syntactical ambiguity that makes people (and quite logically, ghostlike people) the property of language. There is then a reversal of the role of the author: the letter is the parent, assuming a curiously superior role in one's life (this is a further explanation of how Hawdon is at once father and deserted infant, criminal and victim). The letter originates and directs my life; it witnesses and survives my death. Language is the ghostly parent who betrays me into an unknown world where I am, necessarily, friendless and unknown; where I, like the other incomplete signs or characters that surround me, speak only in fragments, in nicknames, in misnomers; where identity is withheld from me; where names are not what they seem; where the name, not only surviving the death of the character, predicts it, like "Richard's name in great white letters on a hearse-like panel" (li, 611); where each letter is like "another missive from another world," part of an otherworldly alphabet that reminds me that my father and mother are imprisoned behind the bars of death; where "all the living languages, and all the dead, are . . . one" (lvi, 668); where the proper name is a common name, shared by others, and where names seem misnomers, so that misnomers themselves are sometimes proper. The proper name is so common that it is one of many copies or namesakes, and "No one" is simply a nameless copy of "Every one": the law-writer, who copies, stands for the copy that everyone is, mere "blank forms" (x, 115)—the blank form Father, the blank form Son or Daughter. To call yourself Somebody now looks like an impertinence.[12] Like Rick and Ada you are encouraged to see "a new page turned for you to write your lives in" (xxiv, 303), but you cannot escape a text, a life-role, that has already been written for you by an anonymous author: the book of life becomes all too soon the harrowing "book of fate" (liii, 629). And the father himself is hunted, and haunted, in these curious role reversals: the mighty hunter (Nimrod) is hunted down as the sign goes in search of its own meaning, of what is proper to it. Again it finds only "deadly meaning" because all tracks and traces lead to the same "spot." Likewise Lady Dedlock is hunted down ("Hunted, she flies," lv, 666), as if the mighty hunter does finally track her down, and is united with her only in death. Esther tracks them down in the graveyard, and finds the blot that obscures the precise features of meaning.

I have said that *Bleak House* is a mystery, a ghost story, a story told in the past tense—and it is as well a history that leads Esther back to two fathers, the real and the symbolic. History seeks to fill in the nameless gap, to fill in the empty pages of the book of life, or at least to interpret those lacunae in a text that has been censored. Here the sign contains its own requirements for history, for it brings us "to the brink of the void beyond" (ii, 11): it is a fragment that requires completion, sometimes a gulf that requires filling, like the "vast blank" which Chesney Wold becomes (here a full history of the Dedlock family, and all its generations and ghost stories, boils down to nothing, to Sir Leicester's silences and the impotent "echoings and thunderings" of a defeated pantheon, lxvi, 766), like "every void in the place" (xlvi, 551) that darkness (itself a void) fills in Tom-all-Alone's, like the "blank forms of legal process" (x, 115) that stand for the law's intransigent emptiness and the sign's fragmentary nature. But the novel shows that the void is only filled by a trace, or in other words, that it is never filled. The real father (who is always symbolic at the same time) is dead before the reader (or Esther, for that matter) ever gets to see him: he enters the novel as a ghost, already dead. By entering the novel only as a dead man, Hawdon shows us once more the conjunction of beginnings and endings. In this way he is like Tom Jarndyce, and both Esther's own personal story and the more general story of Jarndyce and Jarndyce (in other words, the novel's two plots) are joined by these muddy beginnings, where the point of origin, the father, lies outside of the narrative itself. History leads to prehistory, to that time which words cannot cover, or which they cover so as to obscure—to fill in the blank, the way Mr. Snagsby coughs (a substitute for words that still manages to suggest the idea of language as disease) "to fill up all the blanks" (xlii, 515). The origin is a mystery: "How mankind ever came to be afflicted with Wiglomeration, or for whose sins these young people ever fell into a pit of it, I don't know."

This idea of language pointing to a meaning that lies beyond it brings us back to the Roman, Allegory, and shows the ironic connection between history and allegory. The alternative to history (where language is already a trace, losing its race against time) is allegory, where language is equal to itself, with no anteriority: in allegory meaning is so common (as in the names allegory bestows), so general, as to have no meaning at all, except in the end—at the deadly moment when allegory becomes history, when the hand finally points out a meaning beyond itself, and enters the historical world of traces and stains and ghosts. Finally, if the real father is absent, a mysterious symbol or sign from the start, beyond the knowable (or historical) past, his replacements are equally symbolic, almost allegorical. The father in *Bleak House* is, for example, only a surrogate, like John Jarndyce, whom Esther calls "Father" (iii, 27): he cannot bestow upon Esther her true name, and Miss Flite's name for Esther, "Fitz-Jarndyce" (xxxv, 438), poignantly suggests a surrogate name. The father is only the object of a distant address, for he is absent and nameless. He is only "my Heavenly Father" (xxxvi, 454), an unsatisfactory abstraction that reminds us of Skimpole's naïve formulations on parentage: "we are all children of one great mother, Nature" (xliii, 528), or "[Ada] is the child of the universe" (vi, 68). Jo's illiteracy—his "can't exactly say"—unwittingly becomes a telling reticence, so that while repeating the prayer "Our Father" after Woodcourt, the orphan without any Christian sign stops short at a particularly relevant point: "Hallowed be—thy————" (xlvii, 572). Again, we are like Jo, "stone blind and dumb" (xvi, 198) when it comes to knowing our father's, or Our Father's, name. Our Father stands for that symbolic silence where the name should be, but is not.[13] He is the final unknown and nameless friend that we, like Esther in her narrative, address; the final dumb witness, like Allegory; a copy of the flesh-and-blood father we desire—the most ghostly sign of all.

Notes

1. *Bleak House*, ed. George Ford and Sylvére Monod, Norton Critical Edition (New York: W. W. Norton, 1977), ch. iii, p. 31. Subsequent references to this edition are given parenthetically in the text and indicate chapter and page number.

2. The question of names in Dickens's novels, a popular critical subject, usually leads to the critic's explanation of the appropriateness of characters' names. The most suggestive treatment of the subject I have seen is contained in J. Hillis Miller's brilliant introduction to the Penguin edition of *Bleak House* (Harmondsworth: Penguin Books, 1976), pp. 11–34. Miller emphasizes that Dickens "seems to remain in that realm of fiction where names truly correspond to the essence of what they name" (p. 23), and briefly explains how Dickens's characters become linguistic fictions. He does not address what is for me the center of the problem of naming in the novel—the death of the father and Esther's names (or namelessness). Also see, on *Our Mutual Friend*, the following useful studies: G. W. Kennedy's "Naming and Language in *Our Mutual Friend*," *NCF*, 28 (1973), 165–78, and U. C. Knoepflmacher's *Laughter and Despair: Readings in Ten Novels of the Victorian Era* (Berkeley and Los Angeles: Univ. of California Press, 1971), pp. 143–50.

3. See, for example, Dickens's explanation of Tulkinghorn's stargazing: "If he be tracing out his destiny, that may be written in other characters nearer to his hand" (xli, 507). The word "characters" refers first to the starry writings above Tulkinghorn, and also to the more present danger he often neglects or underestimates, namely Mademoiselle Hortense and Lady Dedlock, the chief "characters" Tulkinghorn has to fear in the ominous pair of chapters, "In Mr. Tulkinghorn's Room" and "In Mr. Tulkinghorn's Chambers."

4. See J. Hillis Miller's *The Form of Victorian Fiction* (Notre Dame, Ind.: Univ. of Notre Dame Press, 1968), pp. 36–44 and 105–13, for a fine dicussion of the narrator's awareness in *Our Mutual Friend* that his fictional characters and their world are only words.

5. Critics have been quick to acknowledge the symbolic appropriateness of the name "Summerson." See, for example, Joseph I. Fradin's "Will and Society in *Bleak House*," *PMLA*, 81 (1966), 107, and Norman Friedman's "The Shadow and the Sun: Notes Toward a Reading of *Bleak House*," *Boston University Studies in English*, 3 (1957), 154. Even while my argument accepts such a reading, I am suggesting that the novel impels the reader, as it does Esther, to look behind this name and all the nicknames she is given. In *Bleak House* the reader has a text which is itself wary of its own words, its own bestowal of names (perhaps this is why the novel itself, in a certain sense, is misnamed). In fact, perhaps in the very appropriateness of symbolic names we begin to suspect that the self or place so named is only a fiction, a mere linguistic trick.

6. "For who would bear . . . / . . . the law's delay . . . / When he himself might his quietus make / With a bare bodkin?" *Hamlet*, III.i.70–76.

7. See F. R. Leavis and Q. D. Leavis, *Dickens the Novelist* (London: Chatto and Windus, 1970), p. 124: " 'jarndyce' was the old-fashioned pronunciation of 'jaundice.' "

8. Considerations of Esther's role in the novel have largely been given over to justification or condemnation of her character. See, for example, William Axton, "The Trouble with Esther," *Modern Language Quarterly*, 26 (1965), 545–57, or Alex Zwerdling, "Esther Summerson Rehabilitated," *PMLA*, 88 (1973), 429–39. Such essays, and even that large group of critical essays on the dual point of view in the novel, have neglected Esther's actual role as a writer. Judith Wilt's recent article, "Confusion and Consciousness in Dickens's Esther," *NCF*, 32 (1977), 285–309, is an admirable exception, opening with a few pages on the actual style—the use of dashes and parentheses in what Wilt calls "the grammar of suspension" (p. 288)—of Esther's writing.

9. R. M. Grant, *The Letter and the Spirit* (London: S.P.C.K., 1957), p. 49.

10. Critics have usually suggested that Esther's inheritance of the new Bleak House "points the way toward the lifting of the fog." See Alice van Buren Kelley, "The Bleak Houses of *Bleak House*," *NCF*, 25 (1971), 268. Most recently, however, critics have begun to suspect, and to argue tentatively, that even in Jarndyce's gift of the new Bleak House and in Esther's marriage to Woodcourt, there are some troubling ironies. See, for example, John Kucich's "Action in the Dickens Ending: *Bleak House* and *Great Expectations*," *NCF*, 33 (1978), 98. My approach to the novel, through the idea of language, suggests serious ironies in the roles of Jarndyce as surrogate father and the second Bleak House as namesake.

11. See Jacques Derrida, *Of Grammatology*, trans. Gayatri Chakravorty Spivak (Baltimore: Johns Hopkins Univ. Press, 1976), p. 30: "The trace is not only the disappearance of origin—within the discourse that we sustain and according to the path that we follow it means that the origin did not ever disappear, that it was never constituted except reciprocally by a nonorigin, the trace, which thus becomes the origin of the origin." The trace, Derrida's crucial notion of grammatological "difference" (the difference and deferment in all language), is similar to Dickens's understanding of language in *Bleak House*. I have sought throughout my essay to avoid projecting onto Dickens's text a philosophical terminology that might seem foreign. Instead I am suggesting certain contiguities between Dickens's and Derrida's work. After all, one of the great values of Derrida's work is simply to make manifest a tradition about language, and often true to Derrida's thesis, *Bleak House* shows with great emphasis—especially in its insistent vocabulary of trace, track, and mark—how Dickens is situated in a broad historical tradition. In other words, Derrida has given us a terminology, particularly in such a word as "trace" (with its French suggestion "track"), that is far more traditionally grounded than we at first might realize, or than Derrida himself sometimes makes evident.

12. Compare my discussion of the idea of the proper name in "The Law-Writer," and *Bleak House* generally, with *Of Grammatology*: "The proper name has never been, as the unique appellation reserved for the presence of a unique being" (p. 109). Dickens's text is filled with meditative and playful explorations of the idea of proper names, often in line with Derrida's notions (indebted, of course, to Rousseau and Lévi-Strauss). See, for example, Smallweed's taunt, "Dear me, that's not a common name, Honoria, is it?" (liv, 642). Well, the proper name "Honoria" is in fact also a common name insofar as it allegorically represents a common idea (Honoria, Honor) and, moreover, insofar as Smallweed means that the great Lady Dedlock has debased, or made common, the name.

13. Derrida sees God as the center of the Western metaphysical tradition, and *Of Grammatology* as a deconstruction of this logocentrism: "God's name holds death in check" (p. 71; see also p. 98) and allows the whole idea of naming. I argue, on the contrary, that God is not named, that he is in fact the ineffable, and therefore represents a shadowy surrogate-father, or the ghostly sign itself, or the trace (to use Derrida's term). See Sigmund Freud, *The Standard Edition of the Complete Psychological Works*, trans. and ed. James Strachey, 24 vols., XIX (London: Hogarth Press and the Institute of Psycho-Analysis, 1961), 85: "to begin with, we know that God is a father-substitute; or, more correctly, that he is an exalted father; or, yet again, that he is a copy of a father."

Bleak House: Iconography
of Darkness
Michael Steig*

The illustrations for *Bleak House* are far more uneven in quality than those for the three preceding novels. Most of the comic plates—with a few important exceptions—are technically weak, even sloppy, and many of those which feature the novel's protagonist, Esther Summerson, are relatively uninteresting, though usually done with care. Mrs. Leavis finds Browne's work here "disappointing" because the illustrator "does nothing to actualize the Chancery fog," and there "is little in the way of background and almost no interesting detail," and she decides that in any case illustrations for this novel and those that follow "would have been unnecessary but for the habit of having illustrations," because of the extent to which Dickens' own art had matured.[1] Further, she finds those illustrations which do make use of emblematic detail to be inappropriate to Dickens' art, since the "Hogarthian satiric mode" is no longer Dickens.'[2] Yet *Bleak House* contains some of Browne's finest and most complex work in that Hogarthian mode, fully appropriate to Dickens' own effects. Both in combination with and transcending this mode, the illustrator employs the dark plate technique to convey graphically what is for the Dickens novels a new intensity of darkness. Some of this intensity is retained in the illustrations for *Little Dorrit,* but in other ways Browne's work for that novel definitely shows a falling-off which is then almost embarrassingly apparent in his last collaborative effort with Dickens, *A Tale of Two Cities.*

The complexity of Dickens' conception, the many interweaving plot strands and symbolic and thematic parallels of the text, is reflected in some respects from the outset in the complexity of Browne's emblematic conception in the *Bleak House* monthly cover. Because this design includes a number of identifiable characters, Browne must have had quite explicit directions, or at least some explanation of Dickens' purposes. The novelist had completed the first number by mid-December 1851, and so could have shown Browne the manuscript (chapters 1–4) well before it was published in March 1852; it is conceivable that Browne saw in addition at least a portion of the second number—which was already in proof, with the illustrations completed, by 7 March—before he finished his work on the wrapper design.[3] But three of the vignettes involving specific characters could not have been derived from a reading of the first six chapters, and this together with the fact that the vignettes are connected both visually and in relation to the plot indicates that Dickens explained his intentions in some detail. On the right side of the design we see Lady Dedlock taking a walk beside her carriage (an incident not occurring until Part IV, ch. 12); linked to this panel by a generalized depiction of a young couple with a distressed cupid between them is a

*From *Dickens and Phiz* (Bloomington: Indiana University Press, 1978), 131–60. Reprinted by permission.

third panel, of Nemo the "law-writer" (actually Captain Hawdon, Lady Dedlock's former lover and Esther's father). Although he is mentioned by Miss Flite in chapter 5, Nemo's opium addiction, indicated in the design by an apothecary's bottle on the table beside him, is not referred to until Part III, chapter 10.

These three vignettes together adumbrate the story of Lady Dedlock and Captain Hawdon, estranged in their youth, and now presented in the novel in early middle age. As I pointed out before, there may have been something of a private joke between Dickens and Browne in the fact that the scrivener is called "Nemo," since this was the *nom de crayon* Browne first adopted as illustrator for *Pickwick*. Like Browne, the Nemo of *Bleak House* works at a lowly paid task, hiring out as a free-lance to others, and willing (as Snagsby puts it in chapter 10) to "go at it right on end, if you want him to, as long as ever you like" (p. 95).

The other details in the crowded, though not confused, design relate in one way or another to Chancery, which provides the unifying theme for the wrapper as well as for the novel. The notion of Chancery as a gigantic game is expressed by Richard Carstone's remark that it is "wanton chess-playing," the suitors like "pieces on a board" (ch. 5, pp. 41–42). The two other game metaphors employed in the cover are battledore-and-shuttlecock, with lawyers as players and suitors as shuttlecocks, and across the top of the design, a panoramic game of blindman's bluff, with the Chancery attorneys and officials, appropriately, the "blindmen," and a host of terrified men, women, and children their fleeing victims. The image of the stumbling blindmen suggests that Browne read the first chapter, in which we find "some score of members of the High Court of Chancery bar . . . tripping one another up on slippery precedents, groping knee-deep in technicalities, running their goat-hair and horse-hair heads against walls of words" (p. 2). It has recently been shown that the battledore-and-shuttlecock vignette resembles a cut by George Cruikshank for Gilbert à Beckett's *The Comic Blackstone* (1846);[4] despite the resemblance, however, the portrayal of human beings as shuttle-cocks goes back at least as far as Gillray, and was used twice by John Doyle ("HB"), in 1831 and 1840. Although Cruikshank's cut takes priority as a probable direct source because of its more recent date, many motifs from HB cartoons do turn up in Phiz's illustrations, including the chess game played with human pieces of the *Bleak House* cover.[5]

The blindman's bluff image includes at the right a man thumbing his nose at the proceedings, perhaps representing the author's standpoint, or, since he wears shabby clothing, expressing the contempt of a pauper ruined by Chancery toward a court which can do him no more harm. The placement of this vignette at the top puts the most extensive metaphor of Chancery's blindness, incompetence, and random destructiveness in the most prominent position, and also suggests a structural relationship to the rest of the wrapper. Two men, some money, and papers spill over the inside border of the design which is formed of thin sticks acting as an espalier for a grapevine.

This vine, winding in and out of the various panels in the wrapper (just as Chancery insinuates itself into life in *Bleak House*), is evidently barren, a suggestion of the moral sterility of the Court; and the fragility of the supports implies—given the clear hint of collapse in the topmost vignette—that the whole structure is liable to come crashing down, a foreshadowing of the author's warning in chapter 32 of the possible spontaneous combustion of the system of government and law. (We may recall a similar hint in the structures of ledgers, cash boxes, and playing cards in the *Dombey and Son* wrapper.)

The only element structurally opposed to the blindmen is the depiction in the bottom center vignette of Bleak House itself and its owner, John Jarndyce; but the prospect is not really a very hopeful one, for Jarndyce, wearing the hat with ear-straps mentioned in chapter 3 (p. 16), has his back turned to both the sinister game above him and the representative figures who surround him. These include a "telescopic philanthropist" embracing two black children; a man blowing a toy trumpet while seated in a cart whose label, "Bubble / Squeak," hints at the commercial bubbles of philanthropic projectors and the squeak of their noise (it also implicitly compares them to the cockney hash); two arguing women; and two fools, one holding a roll of plans marked "Humbug" and another bearing a sign, "Exeter Hall," the site of evangelical meetings. Jarndyce's habitual denial of the unpleasant is embodied in the weathervane pointing east, representing his defensive fiction that the "wind is in the east" whenever he hears anything distasteful about the philanthropists he supports.

Chancery is represented not only in the game metaphors but in two other vignettes, which together with the chess and battledore images make up the four corners of the inner design. At upper right Mr. Krook the mock Lord Chancellor writes "C R" on the wall for "Chancery Rex," suggesting that Chancery, understood in its broadest symbolic sense, rules modern British society. The corresponding left-hand vignette presents a bewigged man digging up papers with a shovel, which evokes Krook, the collector of papers; we are reminded that Dickens from the beginning conceived of him as the man *"who has the papers"* resolving the mystery of Lady Dedlock and the case of Jarndyce and Jarndyce.[6] Finally, just as the suitors pursued by Chancery spill over and threaten to land on Bleak House, so the dirt unearthed by the digging figure spills over its boundaries and seems to descend on Esther's head. To understand this symbol, we must turn to the vignette centering on Esther, perhaps the most puzzling element in the *Bleak House* cover.

Esther stands with her face in profile to us, looking down at a fox which assumes a supplicatory or anticipatory position, one paw raised; facing Esther is an impish man dancing through a foggy swamp, carrying a lighted lantern in one hand and holding a globe on his head with the other. The globe is a widely used symbol of the material world, and a man bearing it on his head often represents Man burdened down with materialism, although here that is not quite the case. For the lantern and the swamp suggest the will-o'-the-wisp, a prominent emblem used in nineteenth-century graphic art to represent temptation or the pursuit of foolishness and self-destructive undertakings.[7] The two emblems combined in this way imply the temptations of the material world. Phiz had already used the two together in another etching, the allegorical frontispiece to Albert Smith's *The Pottleton Legacy* (1849), in which the materialistic temptations of the *ignis fatuus* are made explicit (they had already been implied in the *Nickleby* wrapper), and a figure nearby bears a globe on his head.

But what of the fox? Recalling the weathervane fox above John Jarndyce may help to clarify matters, for this latter fox points directly to the one standing alongside Esther. It has been suggested to me[8] that the weathervane fox crystallizes Jarndyce's irritation with his society, and thus in a sense, like the East Wind, represents him. If this is so, then the fox next to Esther may be a kind of protective figure, guarding her against the world (symbolized not only in the globe but in the dirt being shoveled down upon her by the Chancery figure). Moreover, one possible reason to make this protective animal a fox is its conventional association with prudence; in emblem books foxes are often shown listening at the side of a frozen river to see if it is safe to walk upon the ice.[9]

The range and complexity of emblematic representation of the novel's themes are considerable in the *Bleak House* cover, and it should be remembered that the novel's original readers were confronted with this design— and thus were confronted with a visual summary of the novel's thematic concerns—once a month for nineteen successive months. Whether or not a reader took in all the details, he could hardly escape the wrapper's points made about Chancery in the three game metaphors, nor the position of John Jarndyce in the novel. The wrapper's design also hints at the past relationship between Lady Dedlock and the law-writer, an obvious reference when viewed with hindsight. While *Bleak House's* wrapper may not be the most unified in strictly visual terms, iconographically and structurally it complements Dickens' own achievements in the most emblematically unified of all his novels, in which Chancery, fog, mud, disease, and Tom-All-Alone's act as powerful organizing images.

After this promising start, the series of etchings begins weakly; the one attempt at fog, in "The little old Lady" (ch. 2), is puerile, and only with "The Lord Chancellor copies from memory" (ch. 5 [illus. 1]) does Phiz hint at the power of his best plates in this novel. In terms of plot sequence, the action depicted here is completed only at the end of the tenth part, with Krook's death in "The appointed time" (ch. 32), in which the junk dealer's black doll (of the earlier plate) appears to be shocked at the event. But in its ominous quality, "The Lord Chancellor copies from memory" also foreshadows the dark plates of the novel's second half. Phiz has taken his cue for most of the details from the text, but he adds a demonic mask which reminds us of Miss Flite's remark that Nemo was said to have sold his soul to the devil (ch. 5, p.

1. The Lord Chancellor Copies from Memory

40). The Lord Chancellor's pointing finger introduces a motif which will occur more importantly twice again, as we shall see; and Esther's almost completely hidden face, in this and the two preceding plates, is also a motif—one might almost say an emblem—which continues through the novel and links Esther visually with her mother.

Before discussing the long series of illustrations which connect Esther, Lady Dedlock, and some of the novel's themes, I want to take up the four plates in which Browne employs Hogarthian techniques with the greatest variety and force. Among the novel's sinister, grotesque, or comic figures, there are a number whom Browne seems to handle unenthusiastically. Mrs. Pardiggle, the Smallweeds, Tulkinghorn and Bucket, for example, are given nothing like the vividness and individuality of Phiz's Pecksniff, Gamp, Dombey, or Bagstock. But these deficiencies seem to me more than made up for by the inventive handling of Turveydrop, Chadband, and Vholes, three characters who embody the corrupt qualities of *Bleak House* society: dandyism, false religion, false politics, and law. Phiz shows his full powers only beginning in Part V, dated July 1852, when he is between assignments for Lever, having completed *The Daltons* in March or April; he will not begin *The Dodd Family Abroad* until September. (He had also been engaged on Ainsworth's *Mervyn Clitheroe* until March 1852, and worked on Smedley's *Lewis Arundel* during both 1851 and 1852, so it is understandable that he may have felt a bit tired and overworked at the start of *Bleak House*.)

"The Dancing School" (ch. 14) is the second of fourteen horizontal plates in *Bleak House*; with its long, sweeping dance floor and its twenty-five distinct figures the plate requires all of the unusually large space allotted to it. Stylistically it is in the mode of some of the best plates for *The Daltons* and *The Dodd Family Abroad*, though surpassing in satirical impact anything in Lever's novels. There is relatively little modeling (though some careful shading) in the faces of the characters, but the figures are carefully balanced and arranged (e.g., Prince Turveydrop's pupils form a diagonal from the smallest at left to the tallest at right, with the dancing master in the center), and the lines are controlled. The most significant aspect of the characters' placement involves two mirrors, one at either end, on parallel walls. Into one a very small pupil on tiptoe is barely able to gaze and admire her pert little face; in the other the back of Mr. Turveydrop's ornately styled coiffure (wig) and his spotless collar are reflected. Just as the chapter is entitled "Deportment," so this plate really focuses on the Master of Deportment, who stands taller than any other figure and oversees the labors of his son as though he somehow deserves credit for them. Mrs. Leavis' argument that Dickens becomes his own illustrator is given some credence by the marvelous description of Mr. Turveydrop, "a fat old gentleman with a false complexion, false teeth, false whiskers, and a wig" (ch. 14, p. 135); Browne can convey little of this in the mode in which he works.

But the illustration's function is a different one. Apart from the way its composition emphasizes the relative pretended and real positions of father and son, the plate comments upon Turveydrop's narcissism by paralleling him with the vain little girl; and it also unobtrusively makes visible the connection between Mr. Turveydrop and the Prince Regent, his suppposed model, referred to early in Esther's meeting with him. Esther feels that he sits "in imitation of his illustrious model on the sofa,"[10] and Mr. Turveydrop recalls when "His Royal Highness the Prince Regent did me the honour to inquire, on my removing my hat as he drove out of the Pavilion at Brighton (that fine building), 'Who is he? Who the Devil is he? Why don't I know him? Why hasn't he thirty thousand a year?' " (ch. 14, p. 137). A comparison of the Model of Deportment in this plate with an engraving by George Cruikshank of King George IV at the beginning of his reign will make it clear that Phiz is consciously using an old device from the days of "6d plain, 1/- coloured" political and social prints, the parodying of a well-known portrait to suggest a parallel between a contemporary and a figure from the past.[11]

It is especially interesting that the Cruikshank portrait—to my eye almost a caricature, though apparently intended to be taken straight—shows George IV standing with the Royal Pavilion in the background. The reference to a print of the Regent on a sofa is less easy to pin down, but it may enter into a later illustration by Phiz, in which Mr. Turveydrop's connection with the Regent is explored in far-reaching ways. That Dickens was reminded of the early nineteenth century's most famous British object of caricature is suggested by his note to himself in the number plan for the dancing school chapter:

> *Deportment.*

> Mr. Turveydrop—*Prince Turveydrop* George the Fourth, old Turveydrop's model of . . .
> *Deportment.*[12]

The graphic allusion to George IV in "The Dancing-School" is picked up again, this time solely in illustration, in Part VIII. Although this number, comprising chapters 22 through 25, contains many important serious episodes—such as Richard's decision to give up the law for the army, Jarndyce's request that Richard and Ada call off their engagement, Gridley's death, Mlle. Hortense's offer of herself to Esther as a maid, and Jarndyce's gift of Charley Neckett to Esther for that same purpose—Browne was directed to illustrate two scenes notable for their acid, grotesque comedy: "A model of parental deportment" (ch. 23 [illus. 2]), and "Mr. Chadband 'improving' a tough subject" (ch. 24 [illus. 3]). A glance at the two plates will reveal a connection between them which could hardly have been missed by those who read the novel in parts, when the two would have been placed together at the opening. Although no parallel between Turveydrop and Chadband is made explicit in the text, such a parallel is obvious in Phiz's depiction of the two men: each, with right hand raised, is in the process of bestowing what Esther calls "benignity" (ch. 23, p. 232) upon an assortment of followers and skeptics; in each plate a pair of true

2. A Model of Parental Deportment

3. Mr. Chadband "Improving" a Tough Subject

believers and a single doubter are similarly placed, Esther facing Turveydrop and Snagsby facing Chadband from the extreme left, while Caddy and Prince kneel close to the Model and Mrs. Snagsby and Mrs. Chadband sit near the "oily vessel."[13] Other details link these two etchings with "The Dancing-School": the mirrors of the earlier illustration have their counterparts in both plates, and the lyre decorating a wall of the dancing school is repeated in miniature on a chest in the Chadband illustration.

The broad significance of the parallels seems clear. Turveydrop and Chadband are just two characters who embody the theme of hypocrisy and false belief, but these two are linked by the special blatancy of their use of others' faith in them as a means to the gratification of selfish desires; yet without the graphic parallel one's impression might be that these fat men are merely two among a miscellany of grotesques who come off and on stage like music-hall performers. And there are at least two other graphic links between the illustrations, for each character is mirrored or parodied by a picture on the wall near the top center, and at the right hand of each there are upon a table objects which emblematize the character's major preoccupations. But further, the presence of such details is related to Browne's knowledge of his forerunners in graphic satire, and their special significance can best be inferred by examining those sources.

Few of the qualities usually associated with George IV as king or as prince regent are brought out in Dickens' treatment of Turveydrop; of the "First Gentleman's" licentiousness, gambling, drunkenness, gourmandizing and foppery, only the last two are present in his fictional emulator, and only the foppery is given much emphasis. Yet when we trace the derivation of old Mr. Turveydrop's image we find that the artist has subtly retained in attenuated form some stereotypical Regency qualities in the Model of Deportment. The immediate source appears to be George Cruikshank's wood engraving of George IV as Prince of Wales. "Qualification," the first illustration to William Hone's pamphlet, *The Queen's Matrimonial Ladder* (1820), which traces the course of the Prince's marriage to Caroline of Brunswick up to the year of his accession to the throne.[14] Despite the obvious differences, these two pictures contain three notable visual similarities: the position of the torso and legs of each figure; the almost identical placement of the head of the Prince and that of Turveydrop in front of a decorated tripartite screen; and the presence of similarly shaped objects upon a table near each figure's right arm.

But before going into these parallels, we must complete the derivation by going back to the source of Cruikshank's malicious caricature, Gillray's already sufficiently cruel portrait of the same man, "A VOLUPTUARY *under the horrors of Digestion*" (July 2, 1792; BM CAT 8112).[15] Not only are the poses of the two caricatures nearly identical, but Cruikshank picks up the details from Gillray and either repeats or alters them tellingly. In both designs empty bottles are piled beneath the Prince's chair and a dice box and dice are in evidence. But one of the upright decanters in Gillray is replaced in Cruikshank by an overturned and presumably empty bottle, while the dishes of mutton bones are replaced by two candles, burnt down to their holders and guttering—signifying the burning out of the Prince's life as the empty bottle suggests both repletion and exhaustion. Although Gillray in other prints frequently dealt with the Prince's notorious amours, this aspect is adverted to in his "VOLUPTUARY" caricature only by the bottles of nostrums for venereal disease; the artist was probably planning the ironically contrasting print which appeared a few weeks later, "TEMPERANCE *Enjoying a Frugal Meal*" (July 28, 1792; *BM Cat* 8117), in which the King and Queen dine on eggs and sauerkraut amidst emblems of miserliness, and he thus would have wished to emphasize gluttony in the first etching of the pair. But Cruikshank in his adaptation gives full play to lechery, showing on the screen Silenus upon an ass, a winged goat, and three voluptuous women (parodies of the Three Graces) dancing around a satyr's effigy, while a woman's bonnet hanging on a corner of the screen further intimates the Prince's main interest.

Where Cruikshank replaces the evidences of gluttony with emblems of a lecherous and spent life, Phiz in turn adorns Mr. Turveydrop's dressing table with implements of this character's main obsession, adornment of self: a mirror, and bottles of cosmetics which resemble in shape the candlesticks of Cruikshank's cut. In the Chadband plate, the corresponding table holds a dish of food, a decanter, two glasses, and an open Bible—together emblems of a gorging and preaching vessel (to use Dickens' terms). But there is another technique of iconographic expression in both plates which hints that Dickens' illustrator had in mind not only Cruikshank's caricature of the aging Prince, but its source in Gillray. Above the Prince's head in the Gillray is a portrait of Luigi Cornaro, "the author of . . . a discussion of disciplines and restraints which might be exercised in pursuit of longevity."[16] The irony of this allusion is paralleled in the companion satire of George III and Charlotte by an empty frame labeled, "The Triumph of Benevolence," and a picture entitled, "The fall of MANNA."

An ironic contrast of this kind is evident in the picture of John the Baptist directly above Chadband's head; the pose of the figure is similar to Chadband's, but nothing could be more pronounced than the contrast between Chadband's overfed and well-clothed body and the gauntness and rags of St. John (and of little Jo). The corresponding portrait in the "deportment" plate reflects Browne's sources even more directly. It appears to show Mr. Turveydrop as a younger man, scarcely less obese, but more luxurious and indolent in pose; in view of Esther's reference to the print of the Regent on a sofa, this may be intended for the Gillray original rather than the Cruikshank copy which shows an aged Regent in spite of its purporting to depict the Prince of Wales. In either case this picture, like that of John the Baptist, parallels the technique of contrasting portraits in Gillray's print; but there is enough resemblance in dress and pose between Turveydrop and the Cruikshank, and between the portrait and the Gillray, to suggest that Phiz may have been thinking of *both* caricatures. To parallel further his own Turveydrop plate with the Chadband one is to further imitate his own imitation of Cruikshank's imitation of Gillray—clearly, Browne was aware of his artistic heritage.

We may approach the interpretative significance of Browne's allusion by considering first what he makes of the folding screen. Cruikshank's bacchic and priapic emblems are transformed to decorous courtiers, ladies, and cupids, an attenuation of sexuality which is in line with Trevor Blount's view of Turveydrop as a "dehumanized neuter,"[17] but I think there is even more to it. Desexed as he may be, Turveydrop is not wholly asexual, as witnessed by the way Esther shrinks from his tribute: " 'But Wooman, lovely Wooman,' said Mr. Turveydrop with very disagreeable gallantry, 'what a sex you are!' " (ch. 14, p. 138). Beneath Mr. Turveydrop's impotent exterior lurks the remnant of a nasty sexuality which is emphasized by knowledge of Browne's graphic sources. There is also a possible parallel between the Model of Deportment's mistreatment of his late wife and the mistreatment popularly imputed to the Regent in regard to Caroline of Brunswick—the subject to which *The Queen's Matrimonial Ladder* is devoted. Ironically, while the middle and lower classes abhorred the Regent, by contrast in *Bleak House* two of the best, gentlest souls, Prince Turveydrop and Caddy Jellyby, blindly believe in Deportment. Thus in a sense the dandyism Dickens excoriates in the novel as typical of the upper classes has also infected the humbler orders of his age.

The parallel to Mr. Chadband suggests that this oily individual represents another case of the same thing—the deluding of the lower middle classes through a form of Christianity which is essentially no different from the religion of Deportment. Three details provide further comment on the specious preacher. Immediately beneath his outstretched arm and imitating its angle is a toy trumpet, which suggests that Chadband is blowing his own tinny little horn, like the self-puffer on the cover design. Above the chimneypiece are two symbols which suggest the spuriousness of Chadband's religious pretensions: a fish, one of the conventional symbols for Christ, is preserved under glass, but its mouth is open and its eyes regard Chadband with astonishment. And on the mantel a human figure resembling Jo huddles under a bell jar; on either side are shepherd figures with sheep. These elements represent the isolation of Jo from pastoral aid, the traditional church being indifferent to him and the pseudoclergyman Mr. Chadband preaching at him for self-aggrandizement rather than out of compassion.

This series of three plates, from the dancing school to Chadband is, as an example of Browne's use of the Hogarthian techniques of allusion, emblematic detail, and visual parallel between illustrations, on a level of artistic and interpretative accomplishment with the title page of *Martin Chuzzlewit*, the etching which shows Edith Dombey's final confrontation with Carker, and the first plate of *David Copperfield*.

In the depiction of Mr. Vholes, the eminently respectable solicitor for whose parasitic survival the archaic procedures of Chancery must be maintained. Phiz indulges in his last big splurge of emblematic invention for

Dickens. The techniques of "Attorney and Client, fortitude and impatience" (ch. 39 [Illus. 4]) are perhaps less brilliant than those of the Turveydrop-Chadband series, but a close examination of this etching's details and process of creation reveals much about one aspect of Phiz's art.

Q. D. Leavis has criticized this Vholes-Carstone plate on the grounds that it depicts Mr. Vholes in terms of a "Hogarthian satiric mode" which is no longer Dickens', and that Phiz "conveys nothing of the sinister ethos that emanates from Mr. Vholes in the text of the novel."[18] Mrs. Leavis' assumption is that the only proper function of illustrations like Browne's is to mirror the import of the text, but, as I have shown, an illustration may present a point of view and bring out aspects which are not overtly expressed in the text. Mrs. Leavis also fails to differentiate multiple purposes in Dickens. In describing Vholes's office, Dickens himself employs Hogarthian techniques, first conveying the decay and dirt, the "congenial shabbiness" of Symond's Inn, and then the "legal bearings of Mr. Vholes." The office is described in detail worthy of Hogarth, and then the narrative takes another turn and speaks of the "great principle of English law," i.e., "to make business for itself" (ch. 39, p. 386). Throughout the page-long discussion of the "Vholeses," Dickens uses metaphors which border on the emblematic: the law is a "monstrous maze," Vholes and his tribe, cannibals, and the lawyer is "a piece of timber, to shore up some decayed foundation that has become a pit-fall and a nuisance" (p. 386). In the interview with Richard, Dickens desribes some blue bags stuffed in the way "the larger sort of serpents are in their first gorged state," while the office is "the official den" of predators (p. 387). And most Hogarthian of all, and a detail which turns up in the illustration, "Mr. Vholes, after glancing at the official cat who is patiently watching a mouse's hole, fixes his charmed gaze again on his young client" (p. 388).

One can hardly blame Phiz for picking up this last detail as well as that of the maze, and elaborating these conceits into a multiplicity of images representing the predatoriness and confusion of the law; and there is nothing discordant between this elaboration and Dickens' own treatment. The three extant drawings indicate that Browne took a good deal of trouble with this plate. One, which I think is the earliest, shows Vholes at his desk much as in the ultimate etched version, but the desk is open beneath, and thus not the kind which would echo hollowly like an empty coffin (specified by Dickens). Richard stands with his back to Vholes, tearing his hair (as on page 387); even at this stage, most of the emblematic details are clearly visible, indicating that they were a part of the original conception. In a second drawing, the figures are placed as in the final version, but the details are somewhat sketchier and Phiz apparently was dissatisfied with Vholes's face, which is much less predatory in this version; another head, more like the one in the previous drawing, is sketched in the margin.[19] The drawing which was used for transferring the subject is much like the etching, only rather sketchy, and the head of Vholes is still not like the final one, which seems to come from the first drawing.

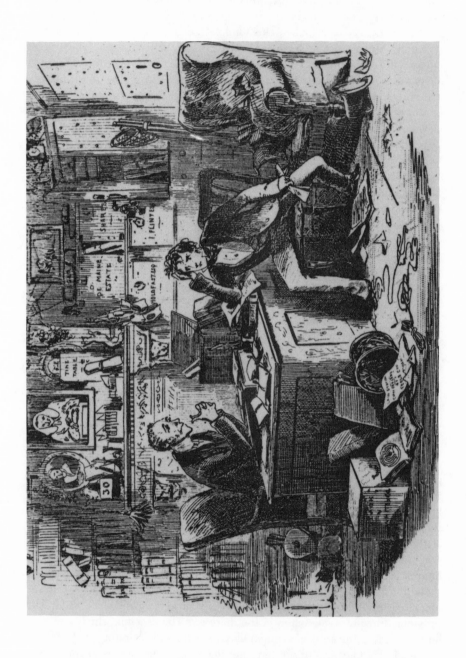

4. Attorney and Client—Fortitude and Impatience

The significant details are so numerous that in order to discuss them coherently it seems best to divide them into three broad categories:

1. *Emblematic representations of the law's confusion and delay.* These include a prominently displayed page of an open book showing a maze, a reference to Chancery and the Jarndyce and Jarndyce suit that echoes the text; a clock covered with cobwebs, suggesting the endless delay of the law and of Mr. Vholes's work for his client; a box of papers labeled "De Maine Estate," probably a pun on *demain;* and a skein of what is doubtless red tape, which stretches in a tangle on the floor and around the foot of the law's victim, Richard Carstone. The latter detail could also fit into a second category.

2. *The predatoriness of the law and its effects upon its victims.* Taking off from the textual detail of the cat and mousehole, Phiz includes a mortar and pestle (recalling Tom Jarndyce's remark, related by Krook, that being a Chancery suitor is like "being ground to bits in a slow mill"—ch. 5, p. 38); a snuffer and candle, suggesting Richard's rapid physical decline; a bellows, probably referring to the inflaming effect of Chancery, particularly as Weevle remarks to Guppy about Richard that " 'there's combustion going on there . . . not a case of Spontaneous, but . . . smouldering combustion' " (ch. 39, p. 391); and an ornamental pair of foxes reaching after grapes, a metaphor for the perpetual frustration of suitors. The paper at bottom center, reading "Law Stationer / Chancery Lane / Fools Cap," may refer to Richard's reduction to the state of a fool by Chancery. More specifically symbolizing Vholes's predation are a spider's web with a fly about to be caught in it, a net and fishing rods, a picture of a man fishing, and two lion heads on the fireplace. (Some of these emblems have already appeared elsewehere in Browne's work, most recently in "The Money Lender" in *Roland Cashel*, in which spider's web, net, and fishing tackle, as well as a fly trap and stuffed fish, are present.)

3. *Direct representation of the law.* Most prominent is the portrait of a judge with his spectacles off, whose eyes look quite blind; a time table, recalling the delays in Court; and several boxes of papers for various cases, whose names are clearly emblematic: "Black v. White," an ironic comment on the fact that Chancery cases are never clear-cut; "Holdfast, esq"; "I Flint, esq"; and "Sharpe," all alluding to the tenacity, greed, and heartlessness of Chancery suitors and, especially, attorneys.

Dickens and Browne evidently wished to overwhelm the reader with the sinister qualities of Chancery and Vholes, and the Hogarthian method was the simplest and most efficient way to accomplish this. Dickens in the text of chapter 38 sets an example for his illustrator, and it is pointless to object that Phiz has not captured *all* the qualities of Dickens' portrayal of Vholes in one etching.

The Vholes-Carstone illustration is not typical of the plates in the second half of the novel; of the last seventeen illustrations, ten are dark plates, and these are foreshadowed by two plates done with ordinary techniques in the first half. "The Lord Chancellor copies from memory" is linked to "Consecrated ground" (ch. 16 [illus. 5]) not only by its darkness but by the pointing hands of Krook and Jo, and the presence in the first of Esther and in the second of Lady Dedlock, each with her face mostly or fully hidden. Krook points to the letter "J" which he has just written, referring to Esther's connection with Jarndyce, while Jo points at the grave of Lady Dedlock's lover—in total ignorance, but the episode will involve him unwittingly in Tulkinghorn's pursuit of Lady Dedlock's secret. As J. Hillis Miller has remarked, Dickens clearly intended a connection between the pointing "Allegory" in Mr. Tulkinghorn's chambers—which will eventually point to his corpse when Lady Dedlock is the prime suspect for his murder—and Jo's pointing hand, for in the number plan he wrote, "Jo—*shadowing forth of Lady Dedlock at the churchyard.* / Pointing hand of allegory—consecrated ground / 'Is it Blessed?' "[20] "Allegory" is introduced in Part III, chapter 10, but its pointing hand is not mentioned until Part XIII, ch. 42, just after Hortense has threatened Mr. Tulkinghorn, although in its first appearance it is "staring down at his intrusion as if it meant to swoop upon him" (p. 92). This distant "shadowing forth" shows how consciously Dickens planned what might be called the emblematic structure of the novel; in this particular case, while he has certainly prepared the reader for "Allegory" playing a significant role, the connection between one "pointing" in chapter 16 and another in chapter 42 is perhaps too distant to be effective, particularly when the *visual* parallel is not completed until Part XV, chapter 48.

Esther and her mother see one another for the first time at a distance in the part following the graveyard episode, and here, in "The little church in the park" (ch. 18), Browne interprets the social role of the Dedlocks and its relation to the *Bleak House* world by means of several of his customary techniques. The overall scene recalls the Norfolk parish church, and the London church in which David is married in *David Copperfield;* not only is the cycle of life represented but so are various attitudes toward the hymn singing, from participation to boredom. The congregation is also divided between the lower gentry or middle class in the main pews, the servants from the manor in a pew behind the great one, the tenants standing in the aisle, and the party from Mr. Boythorn's cottage in his pew at some distance from the pulpit, while the Dedlocks seem to rule the entire scene from above in the great pew. But this dominance is undercut by a set of incidental details: in what may be a coincidental—but nonetheless effective—parallel to the third plate ("The Lord Chancellor copies from memory") in which, following the text, a pair of large, broken scales is shown, here an emblematically unbalanced pair of scales of justice is seen over the head of a life-size memorial effigy of a judge in robes and wig who bends over a law book; propped behind his robes a tome labeled "Vol. 30" hints at the law's interminability. This effigy is behind the Dedlocks' pew, implying a connection between the injustice of the Chancery world and the aristocratic "dandyism" of the Dedlock world.

But another possible reason to have this figure intrude on the space of

5. Consecrated Ground

the complacent and isolated Dedlocks is to imply that even as impervious in their magnificence as they seem, the Dedlocks will be judged, either in this life or the Hereafter. For such would seem to be the message of two inscriptions: "Easier for a camel" (above the Dedlocks' heads) indicates that their wealth may thwart chances for salvation, and "All shall be changed" (directly opposite them) suggests that the social arrangements visible in the congregation and assumed by Sir Leicester to be permanent will be altered. A memorial inscription, "Patient Grissle," above the Boythorn pew, makes one think of Esther, as the long-suffering woman who will eventually be righted, though here of course, it is not a husband but a mother who has caused her suffering; Browne may have had in mind only Esther's patient endurance, without thinking through all of the implications. Lady Dedlock herself is perhaps alluded to in the rather fuzzy but still legible carving on the pulpit of Eve and the Tree of the Knowledge of Good and Evil, recalling her temptation and fall in early life. Above the whole scene, however, is a shield with "Semper Virens," reminding one of the possibilities of forgiveness and eternal life. Taken together, the details strengthen the fundamental point of the scene: the first encounter, alive with possibilities of revelation and change, of Esther with her mother.

Esther's next encounter with her mother, in the illustrations, is in the second half of the novel, and although the etching is rendered in the ordinary mode it can be said to initiate the long series of dark plates. "Lady Dedlock in the Wood" (ch. 35) and "The Ghost's Walk" (ch. 36) are linked, occurring in the same number and forming a continuum in Esther's experience—the revelation of her mother's identity leading to her feeling of terror at the Ghost's Walk and at the idea that it is she "who was to bring calamity upon the stately house" (ch. 36, p. 362). The contrast of tone and mood between the two plates is notable. The first is structured by means of the tree under which Esther sits, which divides the space into three sections with one figure (Lady Dedlock, Esther, and Charley) in each. Phiz has been careful to dress Esther and her mother so that they appear very much alike, and Esther's face is hidden. It is here that the motif of the hidden face becomes most evident; this episode follows Esther's recovery from smallpox and in the illustrations her scarred face will remain hidden throughout. The text implies that Esther's illness is a kind of symbolic retribution for Lady Dedlock's crime of sexual waywardness, for Esther divests herself of her lifelong guilt feelings only after the illness and the encounter with her mother. Simultaneously, Lady Dedlock takes on a new and greater guilt, which can only be resolved through her death. From the point of this confrontation onward not only is Esther's face always hidden in the etchings, but her mother's is as well, silently implying a parallel between the two women, between Esther's scarring and Lady Dedlock's guilt. (Phiz apparently had no text to read, since an early but quite finished drawing [Elkins] shows Lady Dedlock walking toward her from the distance; Dickens probably provided inadequate directions and then realized upon seeing the drawing that it would have to be redone.)

Browne's reserving of the dark plate technique until the novel is more than halfway done proves to be an effective strategy, since it groups the dark plates together and restricts their special force (with one partial exception) to depicting the tragedy of Lady Dedlock. Like five others of the ten dark plates in this novel, "The Ghost's Walk" has no human figures (two others have only tiny and barely discernible ones); this is not typical of Browne's dark plates either for Dickens or for other novelists, and the effect here is to accentuate the novel's emphasis upon external, nonhuman or dehumanized forces as the dominant agents in man's life in society—Chancery, Parliament, Telescopic Philanthropy, Law, Disease. Without the special technique, "The Ghost's Walk" might not even be a very good illustration: lacking the varied dark tones that give the sky itself an ominous effect, the large proportion of empty space would unbalance the composition. The "grotesque lions" (ch. 36, p. 361) are, as details in a drawing, puerile, but the contrast of darkness with the white highlights saves them from being ridiculous.

The theme and tone of "The Ghost's Walk" are picked up in the next part, in "Sunset in the long Drawing-room at Chesney Wold" (ch. 40 [illus. 6]), which makes graphically more explicit the doom hanging over Lady Dedlock. At first glance the plate seems to have been executed by a totally different method than its companion in Part XIII, the Hogarthian confronta-

6. Sunset in the Long Drawing Room at Chesney Wold

tion of Richard Carstone and Mr. Vholes, for the dark plate technique gives it a powerful quality of depth, and the lack of human figures contrasts with the caricatural content and emblematic devices of the preceding plate. As John Harvey has pointed out, the shadow upon Lady Dedlock's portrait, stressed in the text (ch. 40, p. 398), is in the illustration so subtly combined with the other shadows that the viewer only gradually recognizes its presence and menace.[21] So strong are the effects of tone, perspective, composition, and the feeling that nonhuman forces are in control, that one is liable to overlook the fact that this illustration conveys its thematic emphases by means of methods as emblematic as those of its companion plate. Dickens provides in his text the central emblematic conception by dwelling upon the threatening shadow that encroaches upon the portrait of Lady Dedlock, and this in turn becomes the subject of the plate. But Phiz has added a central emblem, a large statue which gives the plate a focus distinct from the portrait and the shadow, and which complements them. It depicts a woman seated with a winged infant leaning upon her knee and looking up at her. In general terms this probably embodies the idea of motherly love, but its likely source in Thorwaldsen's sculpture of Venus and Cupid makes it possible to be more specific: in Thorwaldsen's piece, Venus is consoling Cupid for the bee sting he has just received, and the application at this stage of the novel would be not only to Esther's parentage, but to Lady Dedlock's failure to mother her, and to prevent her suffering as a young child.

The idea of nurture and protection is carried out further in the small ceramic of the Good Samaritan, while the ornamental doves represented as drinking from the bowl nearby may reflect further the theme of nonerotic love. (Thorwaldsen's group of Venus and Cupid also includes two doves, and I suspect that in his statue, and here, they are meant to de-eroticize the god and goddess of sensual love). The fan on the floor and the nosegay and shawl on the chair may indicate the recent presence of Lady Dedlock, but the guitar with its broken string must be emblematic, signifying loss as in *David Copperfield*. All of these emblems quietly introduce thematic emphases which would be maudlin if included in the text; since the drawing room is realistically done, and nothing in it seems out of keeping with the general style of decoration, only gradually do these emphases enter our consciousness. One other touch may be equally important: a bedroom is discernible at the very rear of the design. It is not clear whose room this is, but would it be too farfetched to associate it with the marriage bed and thus with the Dedlocks' disgrace? In the context of the second plate to the next monthly part it may take on an even more sinister meaning, as I shall suggest.[22]

"Tom all alone's" (ch. 46 [illus. 7]), perhaps the best known of all the dark plates, is what I have in mind. Although we lack Dickens' instructions, there is evidence pointing to its owing a good deal in conception to Hogarth's *Gin Lane*, probably by way of the novelist's own knowledge of that engraving. Comparing *Gin Lane* to Cruikshank's temperance works in the Ho-

7. Tom All-alone's

garthian tradition, Dickens had in 1848 suggested his relevance to his own time: the engraving emphasizes the causes of drunkenness and crime in the way it "forces on the attention of the spectator a most neglected, wretched neighborhood . . . an unwholesome, indecent, abject condition of life." Dickens quotes Lamb to the effect that "the very houses seem absolutely reeling," but that this as much implies "the prominent causes of intoxication among the neglected orders of society, as any of its effects." The church whose steeple is seen in the distance "is very prominent and handsome, but coldly surveys these things, in progress underneath the shadow of its tower . . . and is passive in the picture. We take all this to have a meaning, and to the best of our knowledge it has not grown obsolete in a century."[23] Some three years later (in a speech to the Metropolitan Sanitary Association), Dickens spoke of the certainty "that the air from Gin Lane will be carried, when the wind is Easterly, into May Fair."[24] Both the East Wind and the theme of the inevitable infection of all classes consequent upon the neglect of the lowest are of course central to *Bleak House*, which he was to begin a month later. And explicit mention of this theme turns up in the passage the plate is designed to illustrate: "There is not a drop of Tom's blood-but propagates infection and contagion somewhere" (ch. 46, p. 443).

When we look at Browne's version of "Tom" in this context, the connections with Hogarth seem inescapable. Here again, but even more prominently, we have a church tower passively overlooking a scene of degradation; here too, the buildings are in danger of collapsing and are held up by wooden supports. But whereas in Hogarth's picture human beings are central, in "Tom all alone's" they are absent; while Hogarth's composition gives a sense of chaos, Browne makes his composition as symmetrical as possible, so that the contrast between the visual repose afforded by the wooden supports in the middle of the picture and what we know to be their function is full of irony and tension. Most startling of all, Browne has framed the upper edge of the plate with a horizontal brace between two houses so that the very sky seems to be held up by this untrustworthy support, a brilliant way of underlining the relation between the condition of Tom-All-Alone's and the rest of society. In this regard the plate is reminiscent of the *Bleak House* cover, in which all of society is in danger of being brought down by the weight of Chancery. Through the arch at the rear we can see into the churchyard which, like *Gin Lane*, includes the pawnbroker's three balls, symbol of decline into poverty; presumably Esther's father has been buried in that filthy place. But what is most fascinating about this plate—and surely not accidental—is that the churchyard holds the same relative position in the composition as the bedroom in the "Sunset" plate. Hence a subtle connection is made between the liaison of Esther's parents, the Dedlock marriage bed, and the churchyard where Captain Hawdon lies and where Lady Dedlock will die.

Not only are these two plates linked, but connections are also made backwards to "Consecrated ground" and forwards to "The Morning," with the same churchyard visible through the gate at which the corpse of Lady Dedlock lies. But the earliest plate showing the churchyard also forms links with another dark plate, "A new meaning in the Roman" (ch. 48 [illus. 8]). I have already questioned the visual effectiveness of the connection between two such distant illustrations (one appearing in chapter 16 and the other in chapter 48) but the fact is that the *pointing* of Jo is more vividly brought out in the illustration than in the text. An additional difficulty in tracing the process of Dickens' thought about these parallels and his transmission of them to Browne is suggested by the evidence of a shift in Dickens' mental picture of the Roman "Allegory." Initially, the figure painted on the ceiling is described as "sprawling" (ch. 10, p. 92), and Browne's first version incongruously combines pointing with sprawling; evidently Dickens had Browne correct this excessively comic conception. The final version, with its imposing male figure pointing at the scene below, manages to make "Allegory" every bit as silly as the text suggests, by juxtaposing three figures who flee in terror with three or four jolly cherubs strewing flowers and blowing trumpets in the direction of the frightened figures. The dark plate technique is used tellingly, with a contrast between extremely dark shadows—the details nonetheless visible in them—and beams of sunlight coming in the window. As in other dark plates the only human figures are effigies. Phiz has also included the decanter of wine and a glass, to remind us of the buttoned-up Tulkinghorn's only real pleasure in life.

The immediate consequence of the murder, Lady Dedlock's increasing sense of guilt, as though she *had* committed that crime, and her preparation for flight, are depicted and summed up emblematically in "Shadow" (ch. 53), which is paired with another plate whose caption, "Light" (ch. 51), seems intended to suggest a link. Although Richard Carstone's decline in the toils of Chancery, the subject of "Light," and Lady Dedlock's impending flight do belong to separate strands of the plot, within Dickens' scheme they are in fact thematically related. Both individuals are seen as victims of their society's inhumane codes and institutions, yet both share some of the responsibility for their plight. The irony of the seemingly antithetical captions is that the plates are not really in contrast: "Light" refers only to Esther's sudden realization that Ada and Richard are married, and that Ada is devoting herself to him wholly in his decline; and the halo of light surrounding the couple sets off more starkly the hopelessness of Richard's condition. Visually, the illustration is linked to its companion through the figure of Esther, nearly central in the composition and with a hidden face, like Lady Dedlock in "Shadow." The latter caption refers back to the symbolic shadow encroaching upon her portrait, and here the shadows are closing in, so that only a portion of Lady Dedlock's figure remains in light.

The primary subject of "Shadow" is, ostensibly, Lady Dedlock's impression that she is sought for the murder of Tulkinghorn, for she is looking at the reward poster. But three emblematic details broaden the range of reference. Thorwaldsen's "Night," repeated from the stairway plate of *Dombey*, shows a

8. A New Meaning in the Roman

motherly angel carrying aloft an infant, recalling Lady Dedlock's failure to be a mother to Esther and her consequent guilt and self-torment. The "murderous statuary" of the text is specified by Phiz as a sculpture of what appears to be Abraham and Isaac at the point where Abraham is about to sacrifice his son but is stayed by the voice of the Angel of the Lord. Such a detail appears in the form of a print on the wall in *A Harlot's Progress*, III, where, Ronald Paulson suggests, it may allude to the contrast between God's and man's justice.[25] This contrast is certainly relevant here, and the possible allusion as well to Hogarth's fallen Moll is not entirely beside the point. But in addition, the idea of death being prevented by God relates to the fact that Lady Dedlock's child, whom she had thought dead, also has been spared. The third emblem is a clock above Lady Dedlock's head, in its particular position perhaps indicating that her time has run out; it is decorated below with an ominous mermaid, a detail which has some connection with the possible reference to Hogarth's "lost" woman. We may recall Thackeray's use of the mermaid as a simile for Becky Sharp—the creature's slimy tail submerged in the murky depths having to substitute for any detailed discussion of what Becky was actually doing in those disreputable days on the Continent after Rawdon had left her.[26] The implication for Lady Dedlock would be that her hidden, sexually sinful past is about to be revealed.[27]

The next step in Lady Dedlock's flight is represented by an extraordinary dark plate, "The lonely figure" (ch. 56). If ever Hablot Browne succeeded in expressing the essence of a text it is here, in his depiction of

> the waste, where the brick-kilns are burning with a pale blue flare; where the straw roofs of the wretched huts in which the bricks are made, are being scattered by the wind; where the clay and water are hard frozen, and the mill in which the gaunt blind horse goes round all day looks like an instrument of human torture;—traversing this deserted blighted spot, there is a lonely figure with the sad world to itself, pelted by the snow and driven by the wind, and cast out, it would seem, from all companionship. (p. 544)

The possibilities of the dark plate are evident, first of all, in the way the snowflakes have been done, through the stopping-out of tiny bits so that above the relatively even tone of the ruled lines they appear to be in front of the subject, between the viewer and the rest of the etching. Although the "pale blue flare" cannot be captured, Browne has given the kilns on the horizon hovering, ominous shapes, rather like Mexican pyramids. The image of the mill as a torture device is achieved by placing the shaft, with its straps for the horse, so that it points directly at the fleeing figure of Lady Dedlock. A detail not in the text, but which Browne is said to have made a special visit to a lime pit to get right, is the device for crushing lime, a contraption of huge spiked wheels, attached to a frame to be pulled by a horse.[28] It is placed at the top of a rise above Lady Dedlock and appears to threaten to descend and crush her. Even the three piles of bricks in the right foreground look like strange predatory animals, while the precarious board bridges across the pits suggest the danger of the path that the lonely figure is taking.

The first pair of dark plates within a single part, "The Night" (ch. 57) and "The Morning" (ch. 59), have captions which remind us of "Light" and "Shadow," but Browne apparently was confused about which was which, since on the paired proofs in the Dexter collection the penciled captions are reversed, and there is a note from Browne, "Which is 'Night' of these subjects?" Such confusion is understandable in view of the darkness of both subjects, and it suggests that Dickens did not always take Browne fully into his confidence by explaining the sequence of the plates and what they represent. Both are effectively in keeping with the dark tone of the novel. The narrative is indefinite about exactly where Bucket spots the brickmaker's wife disguised as Esther's mother, except that they first drive through a riverside neighborhood and then see the woman as they cross a bridge. The etching shows Westminster Abbey in the background, at an angle which suggests that this is where Millbank turns into Lambeth Bridge. The Abbey here has much the same connotations as does the parish church in "Tom all alone's," implying the church's isolation from human suffering.

"The Morning" is still darker in tone, and the more heavily bitten of the two steels is rather muddy, even in an exceptionally good impression. But the other steel is better: though startlingly dark, in a good impression the gravestones are possible to make out with a *putto* visible on one stone, a skull on another (as in "Consecrated ground"). Although these could not literally be the ones in the earlier illustration, an iconographic connection is made. This dark plate does center on a human figure, but it is still comparable to those which lack such figures because Lady Dedlock's corpse has been reduced almost to a thing by Browne's treatment of it as part of a pattern of light and shade—although her hand can be seen reaching through the bars of the graveyard gate, an important thematic emphasis. Browne has reached a stage in his own art where he seems to find it more and more fascinating to experiment with the possibilities of form, tone, pattern, and structure, and this could contribute to the deemphasis of human figures; yet although many of the dark plates for other novels demonstrate similar aesthetic concerns, they never again, within a single work, appear so devoid of recognizable human figures.

The four plates for the final, double number were executed as usual according to the novelist's directions; a letter survives which indicates that instructions for Part XVIII, and those for Part XIX–XX, six in all, were dispatched to Phiz from Boulogne within a few days of one another, which implies that Dickens had this group, at least, planned out in advance as a kind of sequence.[29] It is thus conceivable that the dark plate technique and the dehumanized subject matter were specified by him. Only one illustration in the double part pertains directly to any action in that part: "Magnanimous conduct of Mr. Guppy" (ch. 64), which is handled economically and with

somewhat more life than the other conventionally comic plates. "The Mausoleum at Chesney Wold" (ch. 46) corresponds to a passage which remarks that
although some of "her old friends, principally to be found among the peachy-
cheeked charmers with skeleton throats," said that "the ashes of the
Dedlocks . . . rose against the profanation of their company" by the presence of Lady Dedlock, in fact "the dead-and-gone Dedlocks . . . have never
been known to object." But the etching conveys nothing of this irony, being
an atmospheric dark plate of a rather static kind, which includes the trees
which "arch darkly overhead," but omits the owl "heard at night making the
woods ring" (ch. 46, p. 519). Its rather grim aspect does not fit very well with
the hopefulness of the novel's conclusion, although it may have been
Dicken's intention to have it represent reconciliation and peace. That Phiz
found the subject excessively sober is indicated by the working drawing
(Elkins), in the margin of which he has sketched three mocking devils, one
thumbing his nose with both hands, one laughing directly at the mausoleum,
and the third peeking around the border of the drawing with a smirk on his
face. How Dickens felt if he in fact saw this drawing we cannot know, but his
doubts about Browne, expressed at least as long before Mrs. Pipchin, would
not have been lessened by it.

The frontispiece and title page, although published originally with the
two plates just discussed, were planned with their ultimate position at the
opening of the bound edition in mind. The frontispiece shows the manor at
Chesney Wold in the distance, evidently at such time as "the waters are out
in Lincolnshire" (ch. 2, p. 6), for the foreground shows—with fine dark plate
technique—murky, marshy ground, while the trees are blown about in the
wind and the sky is full of dark clouds. The manor itself almost bears the
aspect of a haunted house; there is no specific indication that this haziness is
meant to convey an explicit idea like the fading of the nobility, but the effect
of the etching—for me, anyway—is one of ambiguous unpleasantness: loneli-
ness, sterility, the lack of human connection are all suggested. The charcoal
working drawing is itself quite different in tone from either steel, having
been done with free, broad lines, but it is equally effective in its spooky way.

As a complement to the manor, the small title page vignette shows the
opposite end of society—urban humanity in its lowest aspect. The subject is
taken from chapter 16 (pp. 156–58), the first description of Jo the crossing-
sweeper, and the comparison between the conditions of boy and dog in
which the narrator argues that the "brute" is in most respects "far above the
human" (p. 158). In the background, to add a touch of urban squalor, Phiz has
drawn tiny figures of two ragged women quarrelling, with a shabby man
watching idly. In the context of the novel, the contrast between these two
etchings emphasizes the indifference of the powerful classes toward the
powerless, but also conveys the feeling that the former, especially the nobility, are to be associated with death, the lower classes with life. The original
appearance of these plates with those of the Dedlock mausoleum (in the
double part) surely strengthens the point.

We may now frame some replies to Mrs. Leavis' general complaints about the *Bleak House* illustrations. True, Browne does not capture the sense of fog and mud so important in the text; but the dark plates create an atmosphere complementary to that of the text, especially in the literally dark and dehumanized plates depicting "Tom all alone's," "A new meaning in the Roman," "Shadow," "The lonely figure," "The Night," "The Morning," and the mausoleum and manor of Chesney Wold. In such illustrations, oppression, confusion, and the power of dehumanized institutions are evoked as effectively as in the symbolic fog of the text. Dickens truly has achieved new heights through the use of new techniques in *Bleak House*, but his reliance on "Hogarthian" devices has by no means vanished, and they actually appear in certain sections more heavily and emphatically than before. Thus Browne's use of emblematic devices is, again, complementary, and sometimes conveys meanings which might be maudlin or too glaring if included in the text itself. This complementary process operates one way in the Turveydrop and Chadband plates, which introduce a complexity of satiric allusion that would be difficult to achieve verbally; while it works another way in the drawing-room plate, which combines tonal subtlety with an emblematic statement of themes not made explicit in the text.

One need not attribute the apparent laxness of some of the more conventional plates to Browne's deterioration as an artist; rather, his interests seem to have shifted, so that much of the time the mere portrayal of characters does not engage his energy and he is more concerned with the arrangement of structures, light, and dark in seemingly abstract patterns. In the context of Victorian illustration as a whole, "The Morning," whatever its technical shortcomings, is a much more daring and experimental step than one expects from an illustrator whose role is usually thought of as subordinate to his author's, and subject to his author's will. The contemporary dismay at these etchings gives us a hint as to just how radical a departure it was, and Phiz's willingness to continue such experimentation into the last years of the decade may be evidence of the extent to which he desired to break through the limitations normally imposed on illustrators, as Dickens in his way was breaking through the limits of novelistic realism.[30]

Notes

1. Leavis, pp. 359–60.

2. Leavis, "Bleak House: A Chancery World," in *Dickens the Novelist*, p. 165.

3. Edgar Johnson, *Charles Dickens: His Tragedy and Triumph*, 2 vols. (New York: Simon and Schuster, 1952), 2: 750.

4. J. R. Tye, "Legal Caricature: Cruikshank Analogues to the *Bleak House* Cover," *Dickensian*, 69 (1973), 38–41.

5. Copied in this case by Doyle from Retzsch—"HB," *Political Sketches*, Series 2, No. 509, "Satan Playing at Chess With Man For His Soul," dated 29 September 1837.

6. H. P. Sucksmith, "Dickens at Work on *Bleak House:* A Critical Examination of His Memoranda and Number Plans," *Renaissance and Modern Studies*, 9 (1965), p. 67.

7. Again, the motif first turned up in John Doyle's *Political Sketches*, Series 2, No. 150, "A Will o' the Wisp," dated 22 August 1831. Cruikshank also created versions of the emblem but they post-date Browne's own use on the *Nicholas Nickleby* wrapper.

8. By Professor Irene Tayler, in conversation.

9. I know of no other use of this emblem by Browne, nor have I noted it in Cruikshank or his contemporaries. The animal is identifiable as a fox in this illustration (rather than the "wolf" at the door which Miss Flite speaks of) by its bushy tail.

10. I have not located with certainty the print Esther refers to, but it could be Doyle's "A Political Riddle," *Political Sketches*, Series 1, No. 21, dated 6 June 1829.

11. *Portrait of His Most Gracious Majesty George the Fourth*, dated 1821, engraved by G. Maile.

12. Sucksmith, "Dickens at Work on *Bleak House*," p. 69.

13. The drawing for "A Model of parental deportment" (Elkins) is much like the etching, but it is reversed and lacks the details on the screen; that for "Mr. Chadband 'improving' a tough subject" (Elkins), also used for transferring the design to the steel, is rather different from the etching: Chadband, instead of standing upright, is somewhat bent over, his right arm raised, but his left pointing at Jo, who faces the opposite way. The change in Chadband's position makes the parallel with Turveydrop much more evident. As usual, we have no way of knowing who originated the change, but since the drawing had been used for transferring it seems plausible that the original had already been approved by Dickens, and Phiz made the changes on his own. The drawing for this plate is reproduced in Kitton, *Dickens and His Illustrators*, fac. p. 92.

14. The pamphlet appears to have been immensely popular. It was perhaps the cleverest and best-illustrated satire of the Regent/King to have been published, and Browne might easily have seen a copy.

15. M. Dorothy George identifies Cruikshank's cut as an "adaptation" of Gillray's etching— see *BM Cat*, X (1952), p. 78.

16. Draper Hill, *Fashionable Contrasts: 100 Caricatures by James Gillray* (London: Phaidon, 1966), p. 163.

17. Trevor Blount, "Sir Leicester Dedlock and 'Deportment' Turveydrop: Some Aspects of Dickens's Use of Parallelism," *Nineteenth-Century Fiction*, 21 (1966), 149–65. Blount also stresses parallels between Turveydrop and Chadband.

18. Leavis, p. 360.

19. This drawing is in the Berg Collection of the New York Public Library, and is reproduced in Lola Szladits, ed., *Charles Dickens, 1812–1870: An Anthology* (New York: New York Public Library and Arno Press, 1970), p. 131.

20. Miller, Introduction to *Bleak House*, Penguin English Library edition (Harmondsworth: Penguin, 1971), pp. 16–17; Sucksmith, "Dickens at Work on *Bleak House*," p. 70.

21. Harvey, p. 155.

22. Two drawings survive: one, reversed and indented as usual (Elkins), contains all the details, though some are sketchy and the drawing as a whole—in charcoal—is a bit fuzzy; the other (Gimbel) is in pen and wash, not reversed, and almost certainly a preliminary drawing, since it contains neither guitar, nosegay, nor fan. Once again, I hypothesize that left-right orientation was important for Browne in this plate.

23. "Cruikshank's 'The Drunkard's Children' " (*Examiner*, 1848), *Collected Papers* (Nonesuch edition), 1:158.

24. Speech of 5 October 1851, in *The Speeches of Charles Dickens*, ed. K. J. Fielding (Oxford: Clarendon Press, 1960), p. 128.

25. Paulson, *Emblem and Expression*, p. 36.

192 Critical Essays on Charles Dickens's *Bleak House*

26. The relevant passage is in chapter 64 of *Vanity Fair*.

27. The similarity to the mermaid clock in *Sketches of Young Couples* (in the plate, "The old Couple") is not very strong—the latter clock has no threatening aspect, and is primarily a Cupid and Psyche design.

28. Kitton, *Dickens and His Illustrators*, p. 107.

29. E. Browne, pp. 292–93.

30. A contemporary magazine, *Diogenes*, published a parody entitled "A Browne Study," which included a supposed illustration of "Lady Dedlock Lamenting Her Happy Childhood." It suggested that the dark plates were nothing more than a way of avoiding proper draftsmanship— see *Dickensian*, 65 (1969), 144.

INDEX

Absolution, 111–12
Allegory and allegory, 54–55, 56, 83, 115,
    147, 148, 151, 152, 158, 161, 162, 178, 185
ambivalence, 107, 111
anonymity, 148, 149, 153, 154, 156; *see also*
    names
artistic creation, 87, 88–89, 94–95, 99n25
"Attorney and Client, fortitude and impa-
    tience" (Phiz), 175–77

Babel, 149–50
baptism, 107–8, 114, 115–16
"bar of England," 149–50
Barnaby Rudge, 27
battledore-and-shuttlecock, 165
Baumgarten, Murray, 2
Beckett, Gilbert à: *The Comic Blackstone*,
    165
Bible, 5–6, 99–118
black magic, 50
Blain, Virginia, 2
Bleak House: and the Bible, 5–6, 99–118; as
    classic, 64; and criticism, 1–12; as "docu-
    ment about the interpretation of docu-
    ments," 123–26; double narration in, 6–7,
    10, 11, 13–15, 38n3, 40–42, 65, 66, 81, 85,
    91–92, 97n9, 98n20–21, 103, 104, 124–25,
    138, 141–42; ending of, 43, 81, 117; illus-
    trations in, 3–5, 164–90; projected titles
    for, 23–24; psychoanalytic criticism of, 8–
    9; as social commentary, 7–8, 15, 21, 23–
    24, 25–29, 35–38, 39n11, 42, 46, 63; unity
    of, 15–16, 24, 42–43, 77, 92–93
Bleak House, 143, 156–57, 166
blight, 59–61, 81–82, 152; *see also* disease;
    fog; mud; slum; smoke
blindman's bluff, 165
blindness, 72, 79, 165–66
Bloom, Harold, 1, 2
Blos, Peter, 84

Book of Common Prayer, 99
boredom, 32–33, 65
Boythorn, 57–58
Browne, Hablôt Knight ("Phiz"), 3–5, 164–90
Bucket (Inspector), 9, 20, 85–92, 97n9, 154

caricature, 93
Carlyle, Thomas, 99, 100
cause and causal relations, 138–41
chance, 127, 132
Chancery, 19–32, 42, 46–47, 48–49, 51–52,
    64, 110, 125–26, 127–29, 135, 138, 139,
    140, 150–51, 165–66, 175–77
chaos, 127, 138, 141
Chartist agitation, 28
Chesney Wold, 70, 81–82
chess, 165
Chesterton, G. K., 2
circles, 127–42
Collins, Philip, 1, 6, 91
Confession of Sins, 111
confusion, 134, 139–40, 141; *see also* cause;
    chance; chaos; circles; connection-
    disconnection
connection-disconnection, 9–11, 13–38, 71,
    73, 75, 77, 79, 80, 85–86, 89–90, 92–93,
    109, 119n14, 134–35, 137, 141, 143; *see
    also* circles; disintegration; disorder; names
"Consecrated ground" (Phiz), 177–78, 179,
    184–85
contagion. *See* disease
content vs. structure, 94
Coolidge, Archibald: *Charles Dickens as Se-
    rial Novelist*, 3
Corinthians (I), 67
corruption, 20, 34, 36, 63; *see also* disease;
    evil; parasitism
Creation, 125
Crews, Frederick, 84